GO-BPO-002

Between Two Worlds

Between Two Worlds

George Tyrrell's Relationship to
the Thought of Matthew Arnold

Nicholas Sagovsky
Vice-Principal
Edinburgh Theological College

Cambridge University Press

Cambridge
London   New York   New Rochelle
Melbourne   Sydney

Published by the Press Syndicate of the University of Cambridge
The Pitt Building, Trumpington Street, Cambridge CB2 1RP
32 East 57th Street, New York, NY 10022, USA
296 Beaconsfield Parade, Middle Park, Melbourne 3206, Australia

© Cambridge University Press 1983

First published 1983

Printed in Great Britain by the University Press, Cambridge

Library of Congress catalogue card number: 82–22102

British Library Cataloguing in Publication Data
Sagovsky, Nicholas
Between two worlds.
1. Tyrrell, George   2. Arnold, Matthew
3. Authors, English – 19th century – Biography
4. Jesuits – England – Biography
5. Catholics – England – Biography
I. Title
282'.092'4   BX4705.T9
ISBN 0 521 24754 3

BX
4705
.T9
S23
1983

UP

The Burning Bush

When Moses, musing in the desert, found
The thorn bush spiking up from the hot ground,
And saw the branches, on a sudden, bear
The crackling yellow barberries of fire,

He searched his learning and imagination
For any logical, neat explanation,
And turned to go, but turned again and stayed,
And faced the fire and knew it for his God.

I too have seen the briar alight like coal,
The love that burns, the flesh that's ever whole,
And many times have turned and left it there,
Saying: 'It's prophecy – but metaphor.'

But stinging tongues like John the Baptist shout:
'That this is metaphor is no way out.
It's dogma too, or you make God a liar;
The bush is still a bush, and fire is fire.'

Norman Nicholson

(Reprinted by permission of Faber and Faber Ltd from *Five Rivers* by Norman Nicholson)

Contents

Acknowledgments

The writing of this book has represented my induction into a generous community of those who undertake and those who aid research. I cannot acknowledge all debts to those who wrote, encouraged and suggested. However, amongst others, I would like to thank the staff of the University Library, Cambridge; the staff of the Manuscripts Room at the British Library; Mme Callu and the staff of the Manuscripts Room at the Bibliothèque Nationale, Paris; Mr Smart, Mrs Gascoigne and the staff of the University Library, St Andrews; Father Osmund Lewry of Blackfriars, Oxford; Dom Mark Pontifex of Downside Abbey; Father Francis Edwards S.J., archivist at Farm Street; Dr A. W. Adams; Mme A. Louis-David; Mrs K. Pirenne; Father André Venard and Professor Marc Venard, all of whom helped me with manuscript material. Drs J. Coulson, E. Duffy, É. Goichot, E. Leonard, J. M. Livingston, A. R. Vidler and M. J. Weaver all helped me with criticism, information and encouragement. I am most grateful to the trustees of the Harold Buxton Trust and the Bethune-Baker Fund, and to the Master and Fellows of St Edmund's House, Cambridge, for financial assistance; to my sister, Lin Dennis, and to Jo Wallace-Hadrill, for accurate typing. My greatest debt of gratitude is to Professor Nicholas Lash, for the extreme care that he took in supervising the thesis that was the first draft of this book. He has taught me so much more than I can adequately express about 'doing theology on Dover Beach', not least that it is fun. Finally, I must thank my wife, Ruth, who has cheefully given me every support over five years of research, and my son, Alexander, who waited patiently 'between two worlds' until, two hours after the last section of the book had gone to the typist, he decided to be born.

Abbreviations

AL1	*The Autobiography of George Tyrrell* (London, 1912)
AL2	M. D. Petre, *The Life of George Tyrrell from 1884 to 1909* (London, 1912)
BM	British Museum (i.e. British Library)
BN	Bibliothèque Nationale, Paris
CA	M. Arnold, *Culture and Anarchy* (1869)
CCR	G. Tyrrell, *Christianity at the Crossroads* (London, 1909)
CF	G. Tyrrell, *The Church and the Future* (reprinted, London, 1910)
CM	A. R. Waller (attributed to Waller, in fact by Tyrrell), *The Civilizing of the Matafanus: An Essay in Religious Development* (London, 1902)
EC1	M. Arnold, *Essays in Criticism*, first series (1865)
EC2	M. Arnold, *Essays in Criticism*, second series (1888)
EFI	M. D. Petre (ed.), *Essays on Faith and Immortality* (London, 1914)
ER	G. Tyrrell, *External Religion: Its Use and Abuse* (London, 1899)
FM1, 2	G. Tyrrell, *The Faith of the Millions: A Selection of Past Essays*, first and second series (London, 1901)
GB	M. Arnold, *God and the Bible* (1875)
HS	G. Tyrrell, *Hard Sayings: A Selection of Meditations and Studies* (London, 1898)
LC	G. Tyrrell, *Lex Credendi: A Sequel to Lex Orandi* (London, 1906)
LD	M. Arnold, *Literature and Dogma* (1873)
LE	M. Arnold, *Last Essays on Church and Religion* (1877)
Letters I, II	G. W. E. Russell (ed.), *Letters of Matthew Arnold* (2 vols., London, 1895)
LO	G. Tyrrell, *Lex Orandi; or, Prayer and Creed* (London, 1903)
MAL	G. Tyrrell, *A Much-Abused Letter* (London, 1906)
ME	M. Arnold, *Mixed Essays* (1879)
Med.	G. Tyrrell, *Medievalism: A Reply to Cardinal Mercier* (London, 1908)

NV	G. Tyrrell, *Nova et Vetera: Informal Meditations for Times of Spiritual Dryness* (London, 1897)
OW	G. Tyrrell, *Oil and Wine*, reissue with a new preface (London, 1907)
PMLA	*Publications of the Modern Language Association of America*
PQ	*Philological Quarterly*
RES	*Review of English Studies*
RFL	E. Engels (pseudonym for G. Tyrrell), *Religion as a Factor of Life* (Exeter, 1902)
S	R. H. Super (ed.), *The Complete Prose Works of Matthew Arnold* (11 vols., Michigan, 1960–77)
SAUL	St Andrews University Library
SL	M. D. Petre (ed.), *George Tyrrell's Letters* (London, 1920)
SPP	M. Arnold, *St Paul and Protestantism* (1870)
TSC	G. Tyrrell, *Through Scylla and Charybdis; or, The Old Theology and the New* (London, 1907)

Note on references

Most references to major primary printed sources are given in the text. For Tyrrell, bibliographical details of books can be found with the abbreviations. I have not listed all other references to Tyrrell's works in the bibliography, as the relevant references are given in the notes at the end of each chapter, and the general selection is inevitably eclectic. Thomas Loome's bibliography (*The Heythrop Journal*, 10 (1969), 280–314; 11 (1970), 161–9; *Liberal Catholicism, Reform Catholicism, Modernism* (Mainz, 1979), pp. 218–27), and that of David Schultenover, *George Tyrrell* (Shepherdstown, USA, 1981), pp. 434–62, can be confidently used for further information. The whereabouts of letters can be discovered from the list of unpublished sources in the bibliography. Where I have used printed sources for letters, these are given in the text or notes. For Arnold's prose I have used the Michigan edition of *The Complete Prose Works of Matthew Arnold*, edited by R. H. Super. This is referred to by an 'S', followed by the volume number, an indication of Arnold's original title where appropriate, and the page number. For his poetry I have used *The Poems of Matthew Arnold*, edited by Kenneth Allott, second edition, edited by Miriam Allott, in the Longman Annotated English Poets series (London, 1979).

1

Tyrrell and Arnold
'between two worlds'

On 7 September 1851, with his new wife Fanny Lucy, Matthew Arnold climbed through a freezing mist high in the Alps to visit the ancient monastery of the Grande Chartreuse. A stranger, a married man, a Protestant, for one brief night he entered the religious world of the Middle Ages, retiring at half-past seven and rising at eleven to join the monks for midnight mass. Here, in the chill and clinging damp, he watched cowled figures with white faces chant the service by the light of flickering tapers as they had done for almost eight hundred years. Here the monks maintained a belief that had once been that of all Christendom. The son of Dr Arnold was captivated.

Matthew Arnold's own, largely eroded, Christianity had been formed in the demanding atmosphere of Rugby chapel, where the preaching of his father concentrated on moral integrity and maintained towards the imaginative fullness of medieval Roman Catholicism a sharp critical detachment. He had surrendered his belief in the resurrection and atonement some years before,[1] feeling that neither the devotion of the Carthusians, nor that of his father was possible 'for both were faiths, and both are gone'.[2] Since there was no help on the mountaintop he could only return with his wife from the Grande Chartreuse to the 'darkling plain', and there continue his search for a faith which combined continuity with the past and openness to the future. He was left

> Wandering between two worlds, one dead,
> The other powerless to be born.[3]

Nearly thirty years later, George Tyrrell did not find the same impossibility about Roman Catholicism. He had been brought up in the austere evangelicalism of fashionable Dublin, educated at a school modelled on Dr Arnold's Rugby, and he had found his faith in an Anglican church where the most moderate ceremonial (there were not even candles on the altar) and high church teaching had provoked a riot. It was there, at All Saints, Grangegorman, that he met Robert Dolling, later a notorious and impenitent ritualist and outstanding

1

Anglo-Catholic priest in Portsmouth. Dolling guided Tyrrell's reading for about two years, leading him towards his own Anglo-Catholicism, and when it became clear that Tyrrell was fatally disenchanted with the Anglicanism of Dublin, he invited him to help at a mission to postmen in London, where he could sample the worship of St Alban's, Holborn, a *real* ritualist church that would never have existed in the polarised atmosphere of Ireland. For Tyrrell, who was then eighteen, this was a chance to break with his childhood and commit himself to the catholic faith for which he yearned. However, on his first Sunday at St Alban's, Palm Sunday 1879, the whole liturgy struck him as an insincere charade. He was seized with a fit of loathing and fled in confusion. Outside, while he paced up and down waiting for Dolling, the largely Irish congregation of the nearest Roman Catholic church, St Etheldreda's, Ely Place, was assembling for mass. He was irresistibly drawn to the crypt church. Here he found none of the immaculate splendour of St Alban's, but, 'Oh the sense of reality! here was the old business, being carried on by the old firm, in the old ways; here was continuity, that took one back to the catacombs' (AL1 p. 153). At this stage the Roman Catholic Church offered both the continuity with the past and the dogmatic certainty which he needed. It never occurred to him that he would later become one of the most notorious critics of the Church, that he would be first suspended and then excommunicated, and that for the last years of his life he would sadly describe himself as a Catholic *in spe*, in hope, for he had now discovered that the Church he thought he had joined, the Church of Augustine, Aquinas, à Kempis and Ignatius Loyola, a Church of flexible spirit which encouraged both holiness and intellectual honesty, had been locked into a dogmatic fortress where unquestioning obedience was the beginning and the end of virtue.

George Tyrrell is known today as one of the leading Roman Catholic Modernists – that heterogeneous group of thinkers and writers condemned in 1907 by the Encyclical '*Pascendi*'. Their concerns were various: Biblical criticism, apologetics, philosophy, science, history, but what they had in common was a desire to relate traditional Christianity to the needs and aspirations of the day. Tyrrell defined a Modernist as 'a churchman, of any sort, who believes in the possibility of a synthesis between the essential truth of his religion and the essential truth of modernity' (CCR p. 5). He believed that there was nothing to lose and everything to gain by learning from the philosophy of Kant and Bergson, the Biblical criticism of German Liberal Protestantism, the work of historians like Harnack; by facing contemporary questions about evolution, socialism and the impossibility of miracles. Most of those with authority in the Church did not share his openness. They were disturbed and threatened by the questioning mood and the scientific progress of the nineteenth century. In 1864 Pius IX had solemnly pronounced it an error to believe that 'the Roman Pontiff can and should reconcile and adapt himself to progress, liberalism, and the modern civilisation'.[4] Forty years later, men like Tyrrell, Loisy and Buonaiuti were seen as doubters of the faith, insubordinate to its duly appointed guardians, and ultimately as heretics. Modernism was denounced by Rome as 'the synthesis of all heresies'.[5] Those who, like Tyrrell, felt that they were being pressurised to renege on intellectual honesty, were left 'between two worlds': the old world of unbending orthodoxy and the new world of incipient secularism. This was the Modernists' tragedy.

It was sixty years before the wind truly changed. At the Second Vatican Council, from 1962 to 1965, the Church belatedly reviewed its self-understanding, its notion of revelation, its attitude to the secular world, to other Christian traditions and other religions; and in doing so it drew upon the researches of those who had learnt from the Fathers, the early scholastics, from Protestant scholars and from Catholics who had in many cases been suspected, silenced or condemned. In the years that followed the Council there was a new willingness to rethink fundamental questions: about authority in the Church, the historical origins of Christianity, questions of Christology, ecclesiology and the relation of the Church to the contemporary world. It is because these questions cannot be balked, or prematurely settled by an illegitimate dogmatism, and because the Church handled them so disastrously at the turn of the century, and might do so again, that the Modernist crisis rightly continues to attract a great deal of attention. It is possible to look back and see in the events of, say, fifteen years a microcosm of the encounter between a Church stuck in its 'medievalism' and a world that cannot be anything but 'modern'. For those who see the issues that were sharply, intemperately raised as unresolved or perennial tensions in the life of the Church the study of the Modernist tragedy is particularly compelling. As yet, it remains impossible to grasp it in its entirety, because the Vatican archives remain closed beyond 1903, but in the meantime specific studies, like this of Tyrrell and Arnold, will continue to illuminate the aims and limitations of individual figures. For a just assessment of their achievements we have to wait.

It is not my intention to tell the story of the Modernist Movement again here.[6] The aim of this book is much more modest. It is to contribute towards the understanding of one man who was neither theologian nor philosopher, nor even the great spiritual writer he might have been, but who had a superb intuition for the questions that needed to be faced and who burnt himself out in twelve years of frenetic and isolated activity as he struggled for answers. My aim is to look at Tyrrell in a new light, suggested by the comment of his close friend Henri Bremond. Bremond surmised that a third of Tyrrell was in Matthew Arnold, especially Arnold's *Literature and Dogma*. This idea is particularly suggestive, because it turns attention away from those continental writers with whom Tyrrell is often associated – Laberthonnière, Loisy (Bremond acknowledged his particular debt to these two), Blondel, Bergson, A. Sabatier, von Hügel – towards a man of whom he was outspokenly critical, who was English, non-Catholic, flagrantly liberal and not even a professional Biblical critic. However, if Bremond is right, we ought to see Tyrrell's Modernism in a different light. We need to recognise the importance of the *English literary tradition* for Tyrrell's profoundly Catholic theology, and also to look at Matthew Arnold afresh, as a serious theological thinker. George Tyrrell was one writer who took to heart Arnold's fundamental point about the fatal confusion in the minds of theologians between scientific and poetic language. I hope this study will bring out the extent to which Tyrrell was prepared to draw on Liberal Protestant methods, filtered by the English literary mind, in the forlorn cause of a renewed Catholicism.

For many, it is not Tyrrell the thinker that attracts so much as Tyrrell the man. He never claimed to have an original or scholarly mind, but he had extraordinarily quick wits, and he was haunted by the questions of intellectuals who, often enough, were referred to him for help. Like his mentor Newman, he had a profoundly sceptical streak about the limits of human knowledge, but, unlike Newman, he tended to be credulous of 'experts'. There is an unevenness, but not an incoherence, about his work. The coherence, will, I hope, emerge in this study. It is largely the fruit of Tyrrell's boundless empathy. With so little conviction of his own worth, he entered passionately into the needs and sufferings of others. He was much too flawed to be a saint, but he was a doughty fighter for liberty and truth. There is a kind of tragic intensity about his life.

The story has been well told by Maude Petre.[7] What she had to work with was an autobiography written to convince her of Tyrrell's worthless character, and her own close knowledge of him in the last nine years of his life. She loved him, but the love was not reciprocated. She was his most faithful ally, and as a Modernist in her own right knew what it was to be excommunicated and to outlive all the survivors of the *débacle* that 'Pascendi' represented. It would be a mistake to take the *Autobiography* at face value (it is partly modelled on Augustine's *Confessions*), and a mistake to accept Maude Petre's reading of Tyrrell's life as in any sense objective.

Tyrrell was born in Dublin on 6 February 1861, to a family of what has been called the 'professionocracy'. His father, a well-known Protestant Tory journalist, who moved among doctors, lawyers and clergymen in the better parts of town, died shortly before George was born, leaving his wife to care for William, aged nine and already deformed by a serious accident in the nursery, Louisa, aged one, and the new baby. There was very little money. Tyrrell's early years were dominated by financial insecurity, the struggle to keep the family together, the powerful Calvinism of a widowed aunt, who lived with them, and Willy's academic brilliance. In reaction, he himself cultivated indolence (school magazines bear out his academic mediocrity) and while Willy became an atheist, George began to attend church on his own. When George was fifteen, Willy died after a brilliant career at Trinity College, Dublin. Two months later George joined 'The Guild' of All Saints, Grangegorman. In the next two years he failed to win a sizarship at Trinity College, he came under the influence of Robert Dolling, began to experiment with Catholicism, and, at the end of March 1879, he left Ireland forever.

Once he arrived in London, it took Tyrrell only six weeks to become a Roman Catholic. He received instruction from Father Christie of the Jesuit community at Farm Street, who had been a fellow of Oriel with Newman. Tyrrell was amazed to find that his tentative enquiries about becoming a Jesuit were not rebuffed because he had neglected his Greek. However, as a new convert, it was deemed wise that he spent a year teaching in Jesuit schools, first in Cyprus, where he lived happily with Father Harry Schomberg Kerr, and then in Malta, which was a thorough disappointment. On his return, in 1880, he began a two-year noviceship at Manresa House, Roehampton, with an unsympathetic novice-master who stretched the highly-strung novices to breaking-point. Gerard Manley Hopkins, who was living in the same house as a tertian in his last year of training, wrote, 'Fr Morris's novices bear his impress and are staid: we used to roar with laughter if anything happened, his never do.'[8]

The next ten years Tyrrell regarded as largely wasted because they were spent in teaching him the theology of the Catholic Church as it had crystallised in the rigid scholastic mould. For three years he was at Stonyhurst learning philosophy. Here he found that the rigorism of Father Morris was openly criticised, and he now came under the unsettling influence of Thomas Rigby, who by-passed the accredited commentators on Aquinas to teach 'Aquinas his own interpreter'. This Tyrrell loved, and he entered enthusiastically into debate with Bernard Boedder, the second-year teacher, who was committed to a Suarezian interpretation of Aquinas. In this year his mother died and Tyrrell barely passed his exams. At the end of 1885 he returned to Malta as a teacher.

Three years later, he was sent to study theology at St Beuno's in North

Wales, where, a decade before, Gerard Manley Hopkins wrote much of his best-known poetry. Here he endured four more years of scholasticism, and he began to write for the amusement of his fellow-students. On 20 September 1891 he was ordained and a year later he left for his tertianship, a further year in which he returned to the regime of a novice at Manresa. Just as he had done shortly after joining the Society, he made the thirty-day retreat, using Ignatius' *Spiritual Exercises*. By the end of the year he had spent thirteen years preparing to begin. After a short time in Oxford, during which he wrote an important review of *W. G. Ward and the Oxford Movement*, Wilfrid Ward's account of his father's early years, he was moved to parish work in St Helen's. Here he spent the happiest year of his life. He was doing the kind of work which had attracted him in Dolling and drawn him to the Jesuits: preaching, teaching, ministering to the poor. When he was recalled to teach ethics at St Mary's Hall, Stonyhurst, he was distraught.

In the next two years Tyrrell began to exercise his intellectual power as he had never done before. Like his teacher Rigby, he drew material direct from Aquinas, in the spirit, as he thought, of Leo XIII's Encyclical *Aeterni Patris*, which had commended a return to the 'golden wisdom' of St Thomas. He and his friend William Roche, another former pupil of Rigby, were in constant conflict with Boedder, who was still on the staff. For Tyrrell, Aquinas was a systematic thinker of genius who should be studied as Dante is studied, not for information, but for his method and his spirit. For Boedder, Aquinas, interpreted by Suarez, had given to the Church a systematic statement of unchanging Catholic truth. He told Tyrrell that some of his views, taken to their logical conclusion, would lead to agnosticism. There were public rows, and Tyrrell, like Rigby and Roche before him, was removed. He had shown his promise and his prickliness. He was not in disgrace, but he was deprived of contact with students. Now he became a staff writer on *The Month*, living with the Jesuits in Mayfair.

These were years of regular literary production, new friendships, preaching and pastoral counselling. Tyrrell clearly identified himself with those Catholics who wanted to pursue a more open and liberal policy towards scientific thought and towards Anglicanism. His important essay 'A Change of Tactics' (*The Month*, 86 (1896), 215–17) was written just before he moved to Farm Street. The Protestant controversy, he argued, had absorbed Catholic energy and distorted Catholic self-understanding for long enough. Now it was time to show the Catholic faith in all its beauty and cohesion to an unbelieving world. This was the keynote for the next four years. In 1897, his first book, *Nova et Vetera*, a series of 'informal meditations for times of spiritual dryness' was published and immediately welcomed for its freshness of approach. One of those who responded warmly was Baron Friedrich von Hügel, who wrote to thank Tyrrell for the book and to invite him to luncheon.

So began one of the most important friendships of Tyrrell's life. Von Hügel was forty-five, a self-taught scholar of profound learning and wide culture. He had known W. G. Ward and Newman; he was friendly with scholars, historians and critics like Duchesne, Loisy, Laberthonnière and Semeria; he maintained a vast correspondence in French, German and Italian. In the following winter Tyrrell helped his daughter Gertrude through a spiritual crisis, and from then on von Hügel, who became a much respected mentor for the lonely Jesuit, involuntarily brought Tyrrell nearer to the abyss. He introduced him to the work of the French philosopher Blondel, and his exponent Laberthonnière; he discussed with him his critical work on the hexateuch; he asked for his advice when he was writing about the psychology of St Catherine of Genoa. New horizons opened for Tyrrell with each long letter from the Baron.[9]

In the next year, 1898, Tyrrell began a regular correspondence with Henri Bremond,[10] a French Jesuit who had trained in Wales and was well-versed in the tradition of English literature. Bremond was in trouble with his vocation, and questioned Tyrrell closely about his reasons for remaining a Jesuit. Even less than Tyrrell was he a theologian or Biblical critic, although he was a friend of Loisy and Blondel, but he was an outstanding man of letters who later became a member of the French Academy. Bremond was Tyrrell's most intimate friend. Tyrrell's letters to him are the frankest and most outspoken that we have. Whilst at Farm Street, Tyrrell became friendly with Maude Petre,[11] who was at that time English superior of an order for women, the *Filles de Marie*. A woman of outstanding courage, who had studied theology in Rome, she was a prolific writer, and close friend, not only of Tyrrell, but also of von Hügel and Bremond. At this time Tyrrell also corresponded with Wilfrid Ward,[12] whose loyalty to Newman he found congenial. Ward introduced him to the Synthetic Society, where he came into contact with the foremost philosophers of religion in his day – men like Arthur Balfour, Henry Sidgwick and Charles Gore.

In this year Tyrrell's second book, *Hard Sayings*, a less successful sequel to *Nova et Vetera*, appeared, and in 1899 he departed from devotion with a little book called *External Religion*, which originated in a number of conferences on the Church given to undergraduates at Oxford. In this the influence of Newman and Blondel was manifest; von Hügel sent a long letter with an appreciative critique. During these years Tyrrell was regularly writing reviews and articles for *The Month*, all, within the terms of the day, of a markedly liberal or progressive type. In December 1899 he published an article entitled

Between Two Worlds

'A Perverted Devotion'[13] in which he criticised the over-zealous and over-literal preaching of Hell by two Redemptorists and called for 'a certain temperate agnosticism, which is one of the essential prerequisites of intelligent faith'. The article was condemned in Rome and Tyrrell had to publish a retraction. From now on he was told he could write only for *The Month* and he found himself quietly dropped from giving retreats. He was clearly under suspicion, and it was convenient both for Tyrrell and his superiors when he opted for a life of retirement in Richmond, North Yorkshire.

Such retirement only gave Tyrrell the chance for more reading, writing and thinking. At the end of 1900, the English Catholic hierarchy published a Joint-Pastoral Letter on 'The Church and Liberal Catholicism', based upon a two-tier ecclesiology of the *ecclesia docens* and the *ecclesia discens*. Tyrrell called it 'reaction on the rampage' and set about a campaign of vigorous attack by anonymous and pseudonymous writing. He produced a virtually complete article against the Joint-Pastoral, which was published in *The Nineteenth Century* over the name of Lord Halifax. Utterly alienated from the ultramontane ecclesiology officially endorsed by the hierarchy, for six months he campaigned at white heat.

He was at the same time concerned to establish his own orthodoxy and sort out his relations with his superiors. In 1901 he produced *The Faith of the Millions*, two volumes of essays selected from those he had contributed to *The Month*. He told a correspondent:

Till about the date of my first essay I had, not a firm faith, but a firm hope in the sufficiency of the philosophy of St Thomas, studied in a critical and liberal spirit. The series represents roughly the crumbling away of that hope and the not very hopeful search for a substitute. (AL2 p. 164)

In the years from 1899 to 1902 Tyrrell's views underwent a rapid change. He passed from a moderate liberalism to a radical reappraisal of the whole of Catholic dogma. No longer did he believe in revelation as the communication of propositions; more and more he stressed 'revelation as experience'. From 1902, he clearly saw in the teaching of the Church the attempt of man to express the experience of God's immanent spirit in whatever language or imagery might be to hand. Later, he apparently moved in a more conservative direction as he began to lay more stress upon the normative importance of the apostolic 'form of sound words' in the New Testament, but the fundamental shift in his view of the nature of dogma was not reversed.

These were years in which Tyrrell produced a stream of important books: *The Civilizing of the Matafanus*, a Christological allegory in the style of Swift, published in 1902 under the name of A. R. Waller; *Religion as a Factor of Life*, a short essay in religious philosophy much indebted to Blondel and Bergson, also published in 1902 under the name of a fictitious Dr Ernest Engels; *Oil and Wine*, Tyrrell's last full-length devotional book; *The Church and the Future*, attributed to a fictitious Hilaire Bourdon in 1903; *Lex Orandi*, a reworked version of *Religion as a Factor of Life*, published in the same year, and the slim *Letter to a University Professor*, later republished as *A Much-Abused Letter*. Tyrrell had learnt German and was working hard to absorb the material sent him by von Hügel: books by Eucken, Troeltsch, Sohm and Schweitzer. In these years he was increasingly influenced by Liberal Protestants like A. Sabatier, Harnack and Arnold. With dismay, he watched Loisy struggle against the condemnation of *L'Évangile et L'Église*. The doubts about his own vocation and faith increased continually. In 1902, he passed a terrible Christmas when, as he told Bremond, he 'could have damned all the critics into hell, if they had but left me such a receptacle'. As far as the Society of Jesus was concerned, he was almost finished.

By 1905 Tyrrell was seeking a way to leave the Jesuits. If he was to remain a priest, it was necessary to find a bishop to accept him, but he was rejected by Westminster and Dublin. Matters came to a head when the *Corriere della Sera* published some poorly translated extracts from Tyrrell's *Letter to a University Professor*. Tyrrell acknowledged authorship, refused to retract what had been published, and was dismissed from the Society. He left Richmond on 1 January 1906.

Tyrrell's position was now very difficult. As a priest, he was suspended, and he could not recover his right to celebrate mass without the help of a friendly bishop. Archbishop Mercier of Malines was ready to receive him, but Cardinal Ferrata, Prefect of the Sacred Congregation of Bishops and Regulars, laid down the condition that Tyrrell was to 'pledge himself formally neither to publish anything on religious questions nor to hold epistolary correspondence without the previous approbation of a competent person appointed by the Archbishop' (AL2 p. 300). Tyrrell chose to be infuriated by the thought that his private correspondence was to be censored, but he also shrank from the yoke of the censor on his published works. He repudiated the condition. *Lex Credendi*, a sequel to *Lex Orandi*, had now been published, and so, too, had the offending *Much-Abused Letter*.

1906 was a year of unsettlement and unhappiness, much of Tyrrell's time being spent in France with Bremond. In February, Tyrrell and Bremond went to Freiburg im Breisgau; later they were in Brittany and Provence. A month was spent in revising Baron von Hügel's massive study of *The Mystical Element of Religion*. When in England, Tyrrell stayed in Clapham to be near his friends, Norah Shelley and her mother. He wrote incessantly, many of the essays from this period being collected in *Through Scylla and Charybdis*, one of his most important volumes, mostly concerned with questions of revelation and the development of dogma. This was published in 1907, the very year in which Modernism was comprehensively condemned, first by the decree '*Lamentabili*' in July and then by the Encyclical '*Pascendi*' of 8 September. On 25 September, Tyrrell replied to '*Pascendi*' in the *Giornale d'Italia*, on 30 September and 1 October in *The Times*. These acts of reckless self-destruction sealed his ecclesiastical fate. On 23 October he heard that he had been forbidden the sacraments.

Now began the last phase of Tyrrell's life: a year and three-quarters in which he moved between Storrington, where Maude Petre provided a home for him, and Clapham, where he stayed with the Shelleys, though he also revisited the Continent. Increasingly, he suffered from migraine and kidney disease, but he continued to work desperately. Much time in the first months of 1908 was spent in further revision of von Hügel's *Mystical Element*. In this year also *Medievalism* appeared as a riposte to Cardinal Mercier who had written against Tyrrell in his Lenten Pastoral. For his last months Tyrrell was working on *Christianity at the Crossroads*, a vigorous reassertion of the place of apocalyptic in Christianity, much influenced by Weiss and Schweitzer, and virtually ready for publication when Tyrrell died on 15 July 1909. He had been tempted to return to the 'church of his baptism', tempted to become an Old Catholic, but in the event he waited, unrepentant, on the doorstep of his own communion, where he felt he truly belonged. He received absolution but he retracted nothing. For this reason, when he was buried, prayers were led by his friend Bremond, but there was no funeral mass and his body was laid in the Anglican graveyard.

At the end of his life, Tyrrell wrote to Arthur Boutwood, 'My own work – which I regard as done – has been to raise a question which I have failed to answer' (SL p. 119). That question – in effect, the whole question of Christianity in the modern world – is with us no less today. We owe Tyrrell his due because he explored it with utter disregard for the cost to himself. He may well have been crude in many of his statements, and hasty in his conclusions, but his whole life was devoted to proclaiming that there *was* a question which had to be answered and to proclaiming his faith that an answer would be found.

Tyrrell's important work was done in the decade between 1899 and 1909. Matthew Arnold's most significant works on religion appeared between 1867 and 1877, when he was already known as one of the foremost poets of his age. From 1857 to 1867 he had been Professor of Poetry at Oxford, lecturing three times a year in the midst of a busy schedule as a school inspector. *Essays in Criticism* appeared in 1865, *Culture and Anarchy* in 1869 and *St Paul and Protestantism* in 1870. It is important to see the continuity between Arnold's work as a critic of poetry, of society and of religion. He did not approach religious questions as an academic theologian. He had a wide experience of the workings of religion in society; he knew the imaginative literature of the classical world, of Germany and France. However much he appears a theological iconoclast, his right to comment cannot be questioned. It should also be remembered that he saw what he was doing as 'an attempt conservative, and an attempt religious' (S VII (GB) p. 398). He wrote in *defence* of the Bible when he felt that theologians were denying the people access to its riches.

The immediate occasion for Arnold's best-known religious work was the attitude of Lord Salisbury, Chancellor of Oxford University, when Arnold visited the University to receive an honorary Doctorate of Civil Law in June 1870. He wrote to his mother that Salisbury was 'a dangerous man...chiefly from his want of any true sense and experience of literature and its beneficent function. Religion he knows, and physical science he knows, but the immense work between the two, which is for literature to accomplish, he knows nothing of' (*Letters* II p. 35). Salisbury was a dogmatist. Arnold set out to attack the understanding of dogma fostered by the theologians. He wanted to rescue religion from those who made it a matter of spurious technicality. He wanted to recover the sense of Christianity as an expression of 'imaginative reason', to show what kind of enterprise it was. This is why he could seem both radical and conservative at the same time. He was a true revolutionary, who in 1873 produced *Literature and Dogma*, in 1875 a reply to his critics, *God and the Bible*, and in 1877 four *Last Essays on Church and Religion*. In the last decade of his life, content that he had made his protest with absolute clarity, he returned to literary matters and politics, in particular the Irish question. This was the period in which he twice made lecture tours in America. He died in April 1888.

In the pages that follow my chief concern is Tyrrell. I hope that, chapter by chapter, what emerges is a coherent account of his theology, set within the general framework of a literary and imaginative tradition.[14] Inevitably, the account of someone studying Tyrrell's debt to Aquinas, Newman or Ignatius Loyola would be different. I believe that the method I have adopted shows certain facets of his work that are indispensable for understanding it as a whole, but this is in no way a complete or definitive account. Underneath that, I hope there emerges a coherent, though less original, account of Matthew Arnold's critique of religion which establishes some of its limitations as they show themselves to the theologian. There are further subsidiary themes: the limitations of Liberal Protestantism, the close relation between religion and literature, the importance of imagination, the nature of symbols, and the richness of the English tradition that stemmed from Coleridge, fertilising the works of Newman, Maurice, Arnold, Tyrrell, T. S. Eliot, and others. Within this tradition, I believe it is possible to see how well-tried language can be used in the contemporary world without depriving the words and the symbols of cognitive significance. In these writers there is a literary tact of immense importance for the health of modern religion. It is not just the notion of tradition, but the experience of participating in a common tradition, that can bring together separated worlds, whether those of the Middle Ages and modernity, science and religion, or Protestantism and Catholicism. Unfortunately, those who see this all too often face blindness and hostility from both sides as they wander painfully in between.

2

The history of an opinion

The development of George Tyrrell's thought can readily be traced in terms of the intellectual debts that he owed. As a student and a young professor of ethics he was a passionate exponent of Aquinas, not because he believed that Aquinas had provided the definitive philosophical and theological expression of the Catholic faith, but because he offered a systematic presentation of Christianity, unrivalled in its cohesion, grandeur and incisiveness. Tyrrell believed in Aquinas 'studied critically as *a* system; but not delivered dogmatically as *the* final system' (AL2 p. 46). Looking back, he acknowledged that Aquinas first started him on 'the inevitable, impossible, and yet not all-fruitless quest of a complete and harmonious system of thought' (AL1 p. 248). Even at the end of his life he pounced on a copy of the *Summa*, taking it from Maude Petre because he considered that 'he had the best right to it' (AL2 p. 46).

From an early stage, however, Tyrrell recognised that there were many questions with which Aquinas could not help and, often enough, he turned to Newman for answers. It was Newman who showed him how Christian doctrine had developed, and who provided a dynamic account of religious knowledge which rang true to his experience. When assessing his debt to Newman, Tyrrell acknowledged that the *Grammar of Assent* 'did effect a profound revolution in my way of thinking...just when I had begun to feel the limits of scholasticism rather painfully' (AL2 p. 209). In time he became impatient with Newman for he felt that he never really followed the historical path far enough: he did not go behind the Scriptural record to the historical roots of the Christian tradition in the experience of Jesus and the apostles. As with Aquinas, it was 'the spirit, temper and method'[1] of Newman that Tyrrell really wanted to emulate.

A third major influence was von Hügel, who introduced Tyrrell to the work of his contemporaries on the Continent, encouraging his nascent interest in Biblical criticism, new forms of religious philosophy and even Liberal Protantism. For a decade Tyrrell struggled to inform himself in areas that he felt the Church had neglected for too long, but where certain thinkers like Loisy, Blondel, Bergson, Weiss and Schweitzer had essential truths to teach. This was no gentle introduction to new and exciting ideas, but a crash course that involved the reconstruction of Tyrrell's faith from the foundations. Meanwhile, von Hügel, under whose tutelage Tyrrell felt he had grown 'from a boy to a man'[2] urged him on, but continued, as Tyrrell did not, devoutly to visit the Blessed Sacrament.

These are some of the obvious, and much-discussed, intellectual debts, but there are other, less obvious, debts that are important to an understanding of Tyrrell. He was profoundly influenced by Ignatius Loyola, in whom he saw an original genius, ill served, like Aquinas, by later commentators and interpreters. What Ignatius had to offer particularly was an alertness to Scripture, together with confidence in the reason of the heart and the place of feeling in the Christian life.[3] Again, it was the 'elasticity of the spirit' of Ignatius (AL2 p. 72) which attracted Tyrrell. As he loved Ignatius (but loathed what he called 'Jesuitism'), so he loved Augustine for his *Confessions*, he was deeply indebted to the spirituality of the *Imitation of Christ*, and he rejoiced in his discovery of Julian of Norwich.

Tyrrell's remarkable ability to express traditional truths in fresh and living language was undoubtedly fostered by his wide reading in nineteenth-century English literature, that hidden source with which we are here particularly concerned. Questions of doubt and faith form the backdrop against which all of Tyrrell's most admired writers in this tradition worked: Coleridge and Newman; Jowett and Matthew Arnold; George Eliot, Tennyson and Browning. Each of them felt this tension within themselves, and however varied their attitudes towards Catholic Christianity, expressed it in their writing. Tyrrell did no less. He had read these writers since he was a schoolboy, and continued to read them more for pleasure than for information. When he, in turn, wrote, he drew on wide reading in a rich literary tradition of doubt and faith. Many of his readers understood and appreciated this; some Catholics were more cautious. Von Hügel once wrote to Bremond admiring, but distancing himself from, the way Tyrrell expressed himself: 'It will never be *our* way of putting things, that he will spontaneously understand.'[4]

This debt to English non-Catholic writers, many of whom were theologically liberal, or even agnostic, was one that Bremond *did* understand because he was widely read in the tradition himself, having begun to devour English literature avidly when a student at Mold. In December 1898, he told Blondel of his plans to write on Stanley and Jowett.[5] In an article on Sidney Smith he identified Newman, George Eliot, Ruskin, Pusey, Matthew Arnold, Stanley, and others as 'masters of contemporary English thought'.[6] In 1901

14

he was thinking of writing a series of portraits of thinkers, writers and men of action who embodied the religious life of contemporary England. He wanted to write on Jowett, Gordon, Martineau and Matthew Arnold.[7] There was growing in his mind a master-plan for a history of liberalism in nineteenth-century England. For him, this was

Un magnifique drame, et plein de leçons. Voilà une série d'hommes, très chrétiens, amenés par leurs études à douter du christianisme, et cependant ne voulant pas l'abandonner, tâchant d'en conserver le plus possible.[8]

This was exactly how he saw Tyrrell,[9] as he indicated to Loisy in a famous letter of 1913.

Loisy had been puzzled to read a book by Edmond Vermeil, which seemed to imply that he himself, Newman and Tyrrell were all indebted to the Catholic school of Tübingen, and in particular to Möhler's *Symbolik*.[10] Knowing this not to be true of himself, he wrote to ask the opinion of von Hügel and Bremond about any debt that Newman or Tyrrell might have owed to these German thinkers of the 1830s. Von Hügel dismissed the idea out of hand, and Bremond wrote back,

Vous savez que le meilleur Newman vient de Butler. Pour Tyrrell, vous l'avez façonné, ainsi que Laberthonnière; et les grands libéraux anglais ont fait le reste. Je regrette que Miss Petre n'ait pas plus insisté sur les influences subies: Mat. Arnold, *Literature and Dogma*, – un tiers de Tyrrell est là-dedans, – Jowett etc.[11]

Loisy quoted the remark in his *Mémoires* and, since then, scholars have requoted Bremond's opinion with surprising frequency, though it has never been closely examined. Certainly, it was more than a throwaway remark in a letter. Loisy had asked about a specific influence on Tyrrell and Bremond answered by pointing him in a quite new direction: not just to one individual, but to Loisy himself as a Biblical critic, Laberthonnière as a religious philosopher and exponent of the obscure Blondel, and to the tradition of English liberalism. He had in mind remarks like the following, in a letter he received from Tyrrell late in 1899:

All you say of the genuine goodness and implicit godliness of Eliot, Jowett and Co. is painfully true. They denied, not the true God or the faith, but the idolatrous form in which they conceived it; so that there was more faith and reverence in their denial, than in the reckless confession of many a Christian.[12]

We shall discuss what Tyrrell had to say of Matthew Arnold in the next chapter. For the moment, it is clear that when Bremond identified Tyrrell's debt to Arnold and the liberal tradition, he spoke as an informed observer who knew these writers well and had discussed them with Tyrrell. Bremond put his finger on an aspect of Tyrrell's intellectual make-up that almost no-one else, and certainly not Miss Petre, had identified. To many of Tyrrell's friendly critics, such an attribution would have been too damning; to Bremond it was an accolade.

Within Tyrrell's lifetime, only Percy Gardner, a friend of von Hügel's, but not well known to Tyrrell, made the link with Matthew Arnold. When he reviewed *Through Scylla and Charybdis* in *The Hibbert Journal* he spoke of 'the drift of liberal religious thought in the direction of Arnold' and added, 'Mr. Tyrrell almost throughout his book is preaching from Arnoldian texts, though with some reservations.'[13] He later repeated this opinion in *Modernism in the English Church*.[14] Gardner was always an advocate of Arnold's religious criticism, and considered his account of Paul's theology in *St Paul and Protestantism* the best short account that he knew.[15]

The classic, albeit brief, discussion of Bremond's opinion is that in A. R. Vidler's *The Modernist Movement in the Roman Church*.[16] He claims that Bremond's 'statement about *Literature and Dogma* may at first sight appear to be extravagant...If, however, one reads *Literature and Dogma* in close conjunction with Tyrrell's writings, the justice of Bremond's estimate is confirmed.' This is the exact list of parallels that Vidler finds:

An antipathy to metaphysics and rationalism and to making theology a matter of abstruse reasoning and philosophical speculation; the sense that religion is primarily concerned with life and conduct and experience; the inadequate, analogous and non-scientific character of religious affirmations; the falseness of the common antithesis between natural and revealed religion; the abandonment of the attempt to prove the truth of Christianity by the argument from prophecies or miracles; and an intense personal devotion to Our Lord: all this is in *Literature and Dogma*, and all this is in Tyrrell.

In a footnote Vidler lists a number of explicit references to Arnold which 'are, however, critical, and do not express any consciousness of indebtedness on Tyrrell's part'. However, he remains agnostic on the extent of Tyrrell's debt to Arnold and the other 'grands libéraux anglais', but he does acknowledge that Tyrrell was 'keenly affected by English Liberal Protestantism. Affected we say, rather than influenced, for in any case Tyrrell's differences from *Literature and Dogma* are no less significant than his affinities thereto.' Vidler is explicit about the differences:

The aim of his writings is to show that the criterion of experience justifies no Arnold's vague liberalism, but a full and rich Catholicism...He shows too that dogma is necessary because of the need of thinking about religion...and that dogma is useful since it assists or ought to assist the development of religion...He ...shows that the Christ to whom criticism points is by no means the Christ of Arnold.

By and large, subsequent scholars do little more than echo Vidler.

For example, although James Laubacher notes certain new references to Arnold in a footnote to his excellent study,[17] he follows Vidler in saying both that 'these references really criticise Arnold' and that 'there is a resemblance between many of Tyrrell's sayings and those of Arnold'. John Ratté overstates: 'Henri Bremond told Loisy that at least a third of Tyrrell's ideas came from Matthew Arnold',[18] and he claims that 'A friend of Tyrrell's youth said the influence of Arnold was great.'[19] If this is inaccurate, as it seems to be, it is unfortunate to see David DeLaura quoting Ratté as his authority for the opinion that 'Arnold was a major influence on the chief Roman Catholic "Modernist" in England of that period, George Tyrrell'.[20] Bernard Reardon notes that Vidler considers Bremond's estimate sound, though his own opinion is that Bremond exaggerates.[21] Mme David also notes Bremond's comment and herself later adds, 'Matthew Arnold comptait beaucoup pour Tyrrell.'[22]

There is a helpful discussion of the relation between Tyrrell and Arnold in a note by Thomas Loome.[23] He quotes Bremond's remark and observes that Arnold's influence 'touched less the question of revelation than that of theology and dogma'. He suggests that *Literature and Dogma* could well have been subtitled 'The Limits of Theology' but notes that Tyrrell actually wrote on ' *The Rights and Limits* of Theology'. Loome asserts that Arnold and Tyrrell were at one in trying to protect religion against Victorian scepticism, following in the wake of 'science', in their despair of the traditional defences of Christianity, and in their estimate of the language of Scripture as 'prophetic' or 'poetic' rather than scientific. He concludes that 'though there is much in common between Arnold and Tyrrell, the former's influence should not be exaggerated – nor Bremond's passing remark to Loisy be given undue weight'.

William Robbins comes to the problem with a certain freshness because he is concerned to understand Arnold rather than Tyrrell.[24] He finds Tyrrell an interesting example of how far the genuinely religious temperament can 'go with Arnold, and where it must draw the line'. Robbins notes two ways in which Tyrrell would have found Arnold inadequate. In the first place, Arnold found the higher or moral self "natural" to man; Tyrrell goes further and finds the supernatural, the super-rational, "natural" to man.'[25] Secondly, Arnold's God was a deity that could not satisfy the need to love. Robbins notes that Tyrrell found something 'frigidly Anglican and respectable in Matthew Arnold's "righteousness" as the characteristic of the Divinity' (SL, 199). This criticism Robbins accepts. He agrees that Arnold 'has in the main addressed himself to the reason rather than to the emotions'.

Gabriel Daly considers Bremond's remark an exaggeration, though 'difficult to verify or falsify, since Tyrrell rarely quotes sources or explicitly acknowledges intellectual parentage'.[26] Nevertheless, Daly acknowledges that 'there is more than a grain of truth in it'. In discussing Tyrrell's ambivalent attitude to Liberal Protestantism, he notes that Tyrrell is attracted by the Liberal Protestant stress on the ethical dimension of religion, but emphatic that religion can never be reduced to ethics. Where Arnold spoke of religion as 'morality touched by emotion', Tyrrell would substitute 'mysticism' for 'emotion' and would widen the notion of 'morality' to include thought and experience as well as conduct.[27]

John Coulson finds a strong continuity between Arnold and Tyrrell in his study of *Religion and Imagination*. He quotes Arnold's remark that the 'real superiority' of the Catholic Church 'is in its charm for the imagination – its poetry', which arises from 'its age-long growth...unconscious, popular, profoundly rooted, all-enveloping'.[28] He finds Arnold and Tyrrell caught between Scylla and Charybdis, 'that is between the two worlds of rational explanation and traditional Christian metaphors and symbols'. In trying to give an account of their faith, both are thrown back onto the continuity of religious experience in an imaginative tradition. It is this patent similarity of approach, and a common appreciation of the Catholic tradition as one of profound imaginative resources that for Coulson establishes the justice of Bremond's remark.

David Schultenover is another who considers Bremond's remark an exaggeration, but he follows Vidler closely.[29] Arnold is for him one of the 'lesser lights'; Loisy, Blondel, Eucken and Bergson were all 'greater lights' who contributed more to his philosophy of religion. In terms of pure intellectual indebtedness this is undoubtedly true, but Arnold's was a different, a subtler kind of influence, something of which Bremond was well aware. Tyrrell never took Arnold for his tutor, as he did Loisy and, for a time, Blondel. It was more as though he and Arnold had been to the same school or college. Without studying at any university, Tyrrell owed a great debt to the ethos of Oxford. He was an heir to that tradition of which Coleridge was the fountainhead and Newman the outstanding Catholic thinker and also the pre-eminent stylist. Just as Arnold learnt from Coleridge and Newman, Tyrrell learnt from Arnold. They were members of the same literary and theological 'culture', which expressed itself as much in poetry as in prose. This means that we cannot explore Tyrrell's debt to Matthew Arnold solely in terms of explicit borrowing, or in isolation from the influence of a figure as commanding as that of Coleridge or Newman. When he wrote to Loisy, Bremond might well have chosen to mention the influence of Newman on Tyrrell, but he did not, because he knew that when Newman and Arnold disagreed, Tyrrell's radicalism usually led him to side with Arnold, at least until he saw where that would lead. But Tyrrell was restless. At the end the day, neither Loisy, nor Laberthonnière, nor the English liberals satisfied him. They may have helped to fashion his thought, but his final position was very much his own, and that, too, was changing.

3

'Definite evidence'

Vidler, as we have seen, assembled certain pointers to show that Tyrrell was influenced by Arnold, but he also wrote, 'In the absence of more definite evidence we may hesitate to put forward any certain conclusion as to the extent to which he was directly influenced by Arnold and the other "grands libéraux anglais".'[1] Actually, there is a good deal more definite evidence than Vidler saw and in this chapter we shall examine those places where Tyrrell refers to or draws upon Matthew Arnold. However, before doing that it is important to enter certain caveats.

In the first place, as a cultured man who moved in an atmosphere of literary and theological discourse, Tyrrell picked up all kinds of ideas and phrases from books that he never actually read. Furthermore, Arnold deliberately coined phrases like 'Power that makes for righteousness', 'Philistines', 'Sweetness and Light' and so on, intending that they should become part of the common linguistic currency. Tyrrell was in many ways a theological journalist and his use of such phrases by no means implies attentive reading of Arnold. On the evidence to be set out here, we can confidently say that Tyrrell, an avid reader increasingly interested in liberal expression, did read Arnold, but we should recognise that, like many of us, he always tended to be influenced by the last book he read, and a sudden spate of references to Arnold, or phrases from Arnold, does not necessarily signify permanent or even lasting indebtedness. Even if there were such influence, so unacceptable would the name of Arnold be to the vast majority of Tyrrell's Catholic readership, that he could not openly acknowledge the debt, and the references in private correspondence would be much more revealing. What could be said there could not be broadcast in the books and reviews of a member of the Farm Street *scriptorium*. It is not surprising that almost all the public references are critical.

The Arnoldian echoes in Tyrrell's work begin in September and October 1898, with a review of Andrew Lang's *The Making of Religion* (*The Month* 92, pp. 225–40, 347–63) in which Tyrrell picks up Arnold's phrase 'The Power that makes for righteousness' and uses it to his own ends. The review is in effect an extended discussion of contemporary anthropology, supporting Lang in opposition to Tylor's influential theory that the conceptions of God and the soul arose in the primitive mind from the experience of dreaming. For Lang belief in a world of the spirit more probably arose from experience of those phenomena that we can call 'para-normal' (telepathy, clairvoyance, etc.). Tyrrell records Tylor's belief that primitive man's gods are non-ethical and 'do not make for righteousness' and returns to the phrase when he talks of the investigator who is misled by his hypothesis and therefore does not see any evidence there may actually be for primitive belief in a 'personal Power that makes for Righteousness' (pp. 226, 351).[2]

Tyrrell's letters to Bremond throw a little more light on this period. From the beginning of the correspondence, in July 1898, he discusses English 'liberal' writers: Mrs Humphry Ward, Jowett (read 'with great pleasure, though not with entire sympathy'),[3] and Arnold. At this time Bremond, who was planning to write on Stanley and Jowett, must have been asking about material on Arnold as well. On 11 January 1899 Tyrrell writes that he has looked for a volume of Matthew Arnold's letters, and says that he will check what is available in the way of biography next time he visits the British Museum.[4]

In the Lent Term of 1899, Tyrrell gave a number of conferences on the Church to the Catholic undergraduates of Oxford which he later published as *External Religion*. In a passing reference, he showed how he had made Arnold's 'Power that makes for righteousness' his own. His general theme is the relation between the external form of the Catholic religion and personal devotion. At one point, when he refers to conscience, he calls it 'this indwelling Will of God, this Power within making for justice' (ER p. 32). He argues that such a Power is present in all men but that in many cases it is too weak to command attention. Hence the need for an incarnation of this Power in Christ. Tyrrell's concern to link 'internal' and 'external' religion via the person of Christ ('the voice of conscience and of Christ and of the Church is to our ears all one' (ER p. 149)) makes him suspicious of a phrase as apparently impersonal as 'the Power that makes for righteousness', but he finds it convenient, because it spans the immanent activity of the Christian God, and the individual's subjective experience of this activity. This is how Tyrrell will use Arnold's phrase in the future.

In July 1899, Bremond was under considerable pressure as he was about to make his final vows and he was trying to resolve his doubts about the Jesuits. Tyrrell wrote him an important letter[5] in which he used specifically Arnoldian phraseology to set out the basis of his faith:

As for my faith, so far as it must necessarily be rooted in some kind of experience and not merely in propositions and principles accepted on hearsay, it rests upon the evidence of a Power in myself and in all men 'making for righteousness' in spite of all our downward tendencies.

On the basis of this experience, it is possible to recognise the nature and status of Christ:

My Christianism is based on the concrete and intuitive recognition of the full manifestation of that said Power in the man Christ as known to us historically – so full, that I can trust Him and take Him as a teacher sent by God.

The thought comes from Newman and W. G. Ward, who found in conscience 'the echo of God's voice' and saw the Church as 'the exponent of conscience' – points noted by Tyrrell six years earlier in his review of *W. G. Ward and the Oxford Movement* (*The Month*, 79 (1893), 562). At this time, however, he preferred to express the same ideas in an Arnoldian way. Only when it comes to his Roman Catholicism has Tyrrell no words from Arnold, but an inarticulate statement of undimmed faith:

I could hardly tell, though I know them, all the concrete impressions that make me feel that the Roman Church is the only authorised representative of Christ on earth; and that whatever truth is revealed is to be found in her general teaching like gold in the matrix.

Since we have not Bremond's letters to Tyrrell we can only surmise how he responded, but, given his interest in nineteenth-century English liberal theology, we may safely assume that he was very much in sympathy.

At this time Tyrrell was writing a number of prefaces to *Lives of the Saints* published by Duckworth. The last that he wrote, for a life of St Francis de Sales,[6] begins with a discussion of the position of primitive Christianity, when confronted by an alien culture:

As Matthew Arnold would say, it was the Hebraistic and not the Hellenistic side of human perfection that most needed emphasis and protection in those days; it was the sense of the sovereign rights of God and conscience; the duty of struggling and fighting for truth and right that had to be secured, rather than any kind of ethical nicety or delicate finish of character. Strength was the first consideration, sweetness might come after as its efflorescence. (p. v)

Immediately, he plunges into a discussion of the problems of pagan and Christian culture, reminiscent of Arnold's essay 'Pagan and Medieval Religious Sentiment' in *Essays in Criticism*, and still more of *Culture and Anarchy*, with its epigraph 'Estote ergo vos perfecti!' and first chapter on 'Sweetness and Light'. We may compare Tyrrell on St Francis de Sales and 'the even and harmonious development of every faculty of his soul' (p. vii) with Arnold's 'perfection' as 'a harmonious expansion of *all* the powers which make the beauty and worth of human nature' (S V (CA) p. 94). When Tyrrell writes

'Take us as we are, with our limited energy and limited light', one cannot miss the debt to Arnold's *Culture and Anarchy*. For example, at the beginning of his chapter on Hebraism and Hellenism, Arnold says: 'We show, as a nation, laudable energy and persistence in walking according to the best light we have, but are not quite careful enough, perhaps, to see that our light be not darkness' (p. 163). When Tyrrell writes that 'narrowness as such is ever detrimental to character, nor can the neglect or perversion of any single faculty be without prejudice to the rest', he is repeating Arnold's attack on bigotry in 'Porro Unum est Necessarium'. Tyrrell acknowledges the fact of uneven development in all of us and then outlines as remedy a social ideal closely akin to Arnold's 'culture':

The very effect of wholesome society on the individual ought to be and is in some sense to correct eccentricity, and without destroying individuality to secure a more even and all-round development of character. (p. ix)

In Arnold's terms, St Francis de Sales was a man of 'culture':

Of [the] identification of sanctity in its fulness with the harmonious development of the entire human soul, St Francis was at once a remarkable example and an admirable exponent; or, to revert again to Matthew Arnold's idea, in him the interests of Hebraism and Hellenism were reconciled in a way that had seemed impossible in ruder times. (p. x)[7]

There is one final half-echo to be noted. Tyrrell writes of 'the development of the imaginative no less than of the rational side of his mind' (p. x); for Arnold the fusion of these two powers is 'the main element of the modern spirit's life', exemplified supremely in the Greek poetry of the fifth century B.C. (S III (EC1) pp. 230–1). Tyrrell and Arnold would be agreed that St Francis de Sales exemplifies the finest product of human expression, the 'imaginative reason'. So explicit is the borrowing that it seems reasonable to suppose that Tyrrell wrote this preface with *Culture and Anarchy* and, perhaps, *Essays in Criticism*, on or near his desk.

Tyrrell's important essay on 'The Relation of Theology to Devotion' was first published in *The Month* for November 1899. In it, he distinguished sharply between religious language, which tends to be concrete, imaginative, and with regard to God, flagrantly anthropomorphic, and philosophical or theological language, which is more abstract, analytical and apparently 'scientific'. Both have their part to play in religious life, and it is as dangerous to scorn the first for its rudeness as to credit the second with a spurious adequacy. With regard to this second danger, Tyrrell quotes approvingly from Andrew Seth:

Our statements about the 'Absolute'...are actually nearer the truth when they give up the pretence of literal exactitude, and speak in terms (say) of morality and religion...Such language recognises itself in general (or at least, it certainly should recognise itself) as possessing only symbolical truth – as being, in fact, 'thrown out', as Matthew Arnold used to say, at a vast reality.

(*The Month*, 94, p. 466; FM1 p. 238)

At this point, where Tyrrell is insisting on the inadequacy of even philosophical language for speech about God, he finds himself at one with Arnold, but Arnold remains for him an iconoclast who went too far, because he found no cognitive value whatsoever in any of the traditional language about God. Although moving in the same direction, Tyrrell is far more confident of the power of religious language to speak about God by analogy and symbol. He is quick to dissociate himself from Arnold's more radical conclusions.

In 'The Mind of the Church' (*The Month*, 96 (1900), 125–42, 233–40; FM1 pp. 158–204), written the following year, Tyrrell pillories the reductionism of Arnold and Renan, quoting with approval R. H. Hutton's judgment that Arnold uses Bible language 'to express the dwarfed convictions and withered hopes of modern rationalists who love to repeat the great words of the Bible after they have given up the strong meaning of them as fanatical and superstitious'.[8] Tyrrell's own comment is this:

According to Matthew Arnold, who in this is a type of the extreme latitudinarian, the kernel of Christianity freed from the husk, consists in a few platitudes of the higher ethics which have been involved in a vast complexus of historical and dogmatic propositions, partly through the unclearness of those minds which created the system, partly in order to bring home to the emotional and imaginative faculties of the multitudes those living truths which in their abstract baldness would appeal only to the philosophical elite. (FM1 pp. 194–5)

It would have been impertinent to say the least for Tyrrell to have joined in the polemic without first-hand knowledge of *Literature and Dogma*. In view of his rapidly changing views, and the specific references to Arnold that were to occur in *The Civilizing of the Matafanus*, it is worth noting how Tyrrell ends the paragraph:

The longer the latitudinarian reflects on Christianity, the less it means for him; the longer the Church reflects on it, the more it means for her...In the one case it is like the attempt to describe the institutions of savages in terms of modern European civilisation; in the other, it is an endeavour to translate high civilisation into the language of savagery.

The contrast is pursued at the end of a review of Basil Champneys' biography of Coventry Patmore, written perhaps four months later. Here Tyrrell concludes by contrasting the ways in which Arnold and Patmore looked to the Catholicism of the future:

What [Arnold] hoped for was, roughly speaking, the preservation of the ancient and beautiful husk after the kernel had been withered up and discarded; what Patmore looked forward to was the expansion of the kernel bursting one involucre after another, and ever clamouring for fairer and more adequate covering.   (*The Month*, 96 (1900), 573; FM2 p. 60)

Tyrrell agreed with Arnold on the inadequacy of any form of religious language to its object. He joined in Arnold's protest against the 'cocksure' use of religious terms, as though finite men could comprehend the infinite realities of which they spoke, other than by feeble analogy and inadequate symbol. Yet, despite all inadequacy, Tyrrell still believed in the cognitive value of such pictorial language in a way that Arnold did not. For Tyrrell, at least in his public writings, Arnold remained the extreme latitudinarian reductionist.

It is with *The Civilizing of the Matafanus*, written by early 1901, that Tyrrell's attitude towards Arnold is clearly shown to be more ambivalent. The Matafanus are a fictitious primitive tribe who, after initial resistance, are attracted to the values of 'civilisation' by Alpuca, one of their own members, who has absorbed the knowledge, ideas and values of 'civilisation' under hypnosis. Of course, in their primitive state, the Matafanus cannot possibly understand what he is trying to tell them, and he is forced to resort to crude symbolism in order to communicate at all. Alpuca is, predictably, murdered, and, after his death, the record of his teaching is taken far too literally by the 'orthodox', who fail to perceive its symbolic nature because they have no conception of the 'civilisation' about which he was trying to speak. Tyrrell's elegant little tale is really about the nature of religious language. It is an attack on the literal-mindedness of the Catholic Church.[9]

Arnold appears twice, both as latitudinarian rationalist (p. 24) and as a 'prophet of the new civilisation' (p. 35). In the first guise, Tyrrell regards him as fair game:

The glorious onward march of science had long ere this established the sufficiency of '*absolute morality*', of Christianity without Christ, of divinity without God, of a moral government without a moral governor. In fact the religion of that date was the '*Reformed Catholicism*' foretold by Matthew Arnold – catholic because it was held by all alike, but for no other resemblance to the obsolete religion that used to go by that name.   (p. 24)

This is, of course, grossly unfair to Arnold, who never preached 'Christianity without Christ' though he may have preached 'divinity without God'. Arnold was quite explicit that his intention was to *defend* the Bible and when he wrote, 'A Catholic Church transformed is, I believe, the Church of the future' (S VIII (LE) p. 110), he was commenting on the imaginative deficiency of a faith reduced simply to ethics. The fact that Tyrrell picked up the 'catholic' strand in Arnold's thinking – which is not in *Literature and Dogma*, an essay that contains little comment on the social form of Christianity – shows that he was aware of Arnold's wider religious writings, even if superficially so. In fact, Tyrrell's subsequent work shows that he was already moving to a position not so far from Arnold's 'Reformed Catholicism'.[10]

Arnold is again pilloried a little later in the tract, when a second attempt is made to civilise the savages, the first having collapsed. No longer do the 'apostles of culture' denounce 'everything, at once, that fell short of the home standards of right in military, social, moral and material arrangements' (p. 29) but they appear 'solely with the love of "sweetness and light" and "culture" as inculcated by...Matthew Arnold' (p. 35). This is the approach that is ultimately successful. It is striking that the inspirer of both phases of missionary endeavour, the unsuccessful and the successful, is one and the same, Matthew Arnold. Any apparent inconsistency is indicative of Tyrrell's engagement with various aspects of Arnold's thought at this time. Arnold's sense of 'culture' is something he found sorely lacking in the Catholic Church, which remained, with its dogmatic literalism, in the state of the unenlightened Matafanus.[11] Speaking of the record of Alpuca, Tyrrell makes a quite Arnoldian criticism about the abuse of religious language:

The most tempting fallacy in its interpretation was that of a sort of 'realism', ascribing the forms of language and thought to the reality represented; ascribing the qualities of the paint and canvas to the original of the portrait.   (p. 62)

Yet the way he applies this differs from Arnold. Following his remarks in 'The Mind of the Church' against the latitudinarian reduction of Christianity, which is an organic whole, to a few ethical maxims, he concludes:

It was not that the language was too full and big for the idea; but rather it was because the idea and reality so immeasurably transcended the language and poor symbolism through which it was hinted and glanced at, that all these struggles, and blunders, and misunderstandings were the inevitable price of advance.
(p. 70)

Tyrrell is not arguing that the Church should abandon traditional language, but that it should learn how to use it. Arnold would agree, at least with respect to the language of the Bible, but behind their apparent unanimity there remains an important difference in understanding of revelation. Tyrrell at this stage held that the Church grew into fuller understanding of an original revelation which was in part conceptual; for Arnold the revelation was perennial, ethical, and even within the Biblical record, let alone the developed teaching of the Church, it was obscured by a gothic edifice of dogmatic complexity.

26

At this time Tyrrell maintained his public attack on Arnold if he mentioned him at all. In *Religion as a Factor of Life*, published pseudonymously in 1902, he distinguishes between his own view of religion as a 'sentiment' and the 'sentimentalism' of Matthew Arnold. He implies that for Arnold 'the use of religion is the awakening of certain aesthetic emotions akin to those evoked by music or poetry, and as fruitless of any after-result' (p. 4). This is a travesty of Arnold's position, which was actually reasonably close to Tyrrell's own in that he continually stressed the link between religion and conduct. However, for Tyrrell, a vivid awareness of the 'personality' of God transforms ethical practice into religion (what Arnold would call 'morality touched with emotion'):

As soon as the equivalent 'personality' of God is appreciated, our actions put on a new aspect in reference to Him, as accordant or discordant with His Will. This is their religious as superadded to their merely ethical aspect.   (p. 16)

The difference between Tyrrell and Arnold is clear: Tyrrell is by far the more confident of the analogical truth of attributing personality to God. For Arnold this is merely a heuristic device to galvanise our wills. He is agnostic about any analogical value in such a concept. Both, however, find the heart of religion in the human realm of feeling, and explore the relation of feeling to conduct. Tyrrell's position *includes* Arnold's and therefore at times seems indistinguishable:

No one pretends that our conceptions of God, as an object, are adequate or more than analogous and symbolic; yet they possess an equivalent or practical truth in the measure that they guide our conduct more or less surely in the right direction.   (p. 6)

Tyrrell still protests that he is not a rationalist like Arnold:

In saying, as we may, that all revelation is directed to love, and to the life of religion, we are in strict opposition to those who say that it is directed solely to conduct.   (p. 33)

This he made abundantly clear in 'Religion and Ethics', which appeared in February 1903 (*The Month*, 101 (1903), 130–45). Here he attacked 'the confusion of the territory of ethics with that of religion' (p. 131). Ethics is to religion what grammar is to speech: it 'regulates and rationalizes it, and thereby mutliplies its utility' (*ibid.*). The message of Christ cannot be reduced to a special method of teaching ethics, for it cannot 'by any extravagance of rationalizing be thinned down to aught less than the love of God and man' (p. 130). Tyrrell's specific attack on Arnold's definition of religion as 'morality tinged with emotion' is directed at the weakness of his concept of 'emotion'.

Arnold

tells us nothing of the object or nature of this emotion, and seems to regard it as a mere decoration of morality, a glow of enthusiasm in the cause of morality. He does not explain it as that affection or love which binds a man to God and to his fellows, and which is the very substance of the life of religion; and of which morality is the due though absolutely separable decoration. Still less does he remember that such an affection gets its whole shape and character from some unformulated view of the spiritual order which, if formulated, would be called dogma. Using his own style, we might rather define religion as: 'Divine love, making for righteousness or morality'. (p. 141)

In switching phrases, Tyrrell gives the priority not to morality, nor to Arnold's impersonal 'Power', but to that Divine love, which, in the phrase of his beloved Dante, 'moves the sun in heaven and all the stars'.[12]

In *The Church and The Future* which was privately circulated in 1903, Tyrrell continued to differentiate himself from an Arnoldian position. He was now engaged with the Biblical and historical critics, who had by their work undercut the traditional view of Biblical inerrancy and the dogmatic development of the Catholic Church. It is clear that Tyrrell had been deeply shaken by his reading:

The *consensus* of current criticism of even the more moderate sort makes the Bible an insufficient basis for the scientific establishment of a single indisputable miracle or of a single clear fulfilment of prophecy. (p. 20)

This sounds like Arnold, who roundly asserted that 'Miracles do not happen' (S VI (LD) p. 146) but Tyrrell was not crudely dismissive as Arnold had been:

The cocksure Philistine denial of the possibility of miracles has gone out of intellectual fashion together with the grosser forms of materialistic philosophy. (*Ibid.*)

Thus, Tyrrell's own rejection of miracle is more discriminating:

As an effect without a cause; as against nature in the widest sense; as a divine *déraison* and contempt of law and order, of course a miracle is impossible. It must always have a cause and be in the order of nature, even though, like the visit of a comet whose year is a million of our years, it be an occurrence unique in the brief day of human history. (pp. 20–1)

For Tyrrell there is a divine logic behind all things, whether we perceive them as miraculous or not. The patent part of that logic is that known to science; the partially understood is expressed in analogical language. Tyrrell still abhors 'sentimentalism' which asserts that 'religion is so entirely of the heart and affections that dogmatic beliefs are as indifferent as ritual and symbolism' (p. 47). Both 'intellectualism', which confounds faith with theological ortho-doxy, and 'sentimentalism', which confounds faith with feeling, come from the same cause: a failure to distinguish between 'the true, mysterious and often utterly unattainable and inexpressible explanation of an instinct or sentiment, and its more or less probable, relative, and inadequate intellectual expression or symbol' (p. 46). The structure of 'two worlds' which lies behind Tyrrell's expression here is the starting point for *Lex Orandi*. Tyrrell never entirely ceased to hold on to it, however immanentist the drift of his thought.

Lex Orandi is often depicted, because of Tyrrell's use of pragmatic argument,[13] as the book in which he draws closest to Arnold. We should be careful of jumping to conclusions: the book begins with an exposition of 'the sacramental principle' and the 'two worlds' in which it operates, all of which Arnold would have found far too tidy. The convergence comes because both Tyrrell and Arnold are in full reaction against rationalistic theology and both are concerned to ground religion in human moral experience. For Tyrrell, however, the object of religion is transcendent; behind his pragmatism is the philosophy of the will-world:

The 'religionising' of conduct is not religion, but only one of its principal conditions and consequences. It is in the field of conduct that we work the work of God, and thus bring our wills into communion with His; but this will-communion is the end, of which conduct is but the occasion or means; and not conversely. (LO pp. 47–8)

For Arnold, however,

The paramount virtue of religion is, that it has *lighted up* morality; that it has supplied the emotion and inspiration needful for carrying the sage along the narrow way perfectly, for carrying the ordinary man along it at all.
(S III (EC1) p. 134)

Tyrrell and Arnold draw together to speak of *feeling* as the primary human level with which we have to deal. They also speak of the corporate nature of human expression, and the importance of standing within a tradition. Where Arnold writes,

Criticism, real criticism...obeys an instinct prompting it to try to know the best that is known and thought in the world. (S III (EC1) p. 268)

Tyrrell has:

Not till we have learnt and appropriated from society the best that is known and attained, have we a right to venture a step beyond and include all this in some further attainment of our own. (LO p. 36)

By this means he justifies adherence to the tradition of Christian expression that is maintained in the Catholic Church. If asked why the symbols and images of Catholic worship are 'the best', the proof is pragmatic. For instance, he writes of 'the fatherhood of God',

From the proved practical fruitfulness of the belief, from its evident correspondence to the laws of spiritual life 'always, everywhere, in every one' just
in the measure that it is realised and followed out in action, we infer its
fundamental truth as representing analogously and in terms of appearances the
world of invisible reality. (LO p. 113)

This of course, Arnold would not grant. We might say that for Arnold religion
collapses into ethics, whereas Tyrrell expands ethics to religion:

As soon as men come to realise that God is necessarily a righteous God and that
righteousness is another name for the will of God – for what God wills – the
interests of religion and ethics are identified. Prior to this realisation the instinctive
love of goodness is not explicitly understood as an instinctive desire of friendship
and will-union with God. (LO p. 194)

However close they seem to be, Tyrrell and Arnold stand on opposite sides
of an important divide.

Yet Tyrrell obviously appreciated how close he was growing to Arnold.
In two private letters he adopts a very different tone, speaking warmly of
Arnold and even identifying himself with him. In December 1904, he wrote
to Dora Williams, sister of 'Willy' Williams:

No, although Protestant, I am also very Catholic in the non-sectarian sense, which
is more or less the Matthew-Arnoldian, but not at all the Wilfrid-Wardian sense.
That, however, is a big question which I have dealt with in a little work which
he has never seen and is now extinct. (SL p. 239)

The 'little work' is *The Church and the Future*, which would have offended
Wilfrid Ward by the new view of revelation that Tyrrell was putting forward,
stressing the Spirit as that which has been *and continues to be* revealed. It is
interesting to see that, despite his clear repudiation of 'cocksure Philistine'
over-simplification in the text of *The Church and the Future*, Tyrrell could in
retrospect identify himself with Arnold – even if only to make the contrast
with Ward; once more Tyrrell was making use of Arnold's Catholic
sympathies.

The breach with Ward had by this time become irreparable, because of
Tyrrell's behaviour over 'Semper Eadem', an ironic review of Wilfrid Ward's
Problems and Persons.[14] Tyrrell had intended to develop his own views in a
second article but this only saw the light of day in *Through Scylla and Charybdis*.
In this ('Semper Eadem (II)') he tried to show that Newman's theory of
development as stated in the last of the 'University Sermons' was incom-
patible with the application of the theory in the *Essay on Development*, because
he had shifted his concept of the 'deposit of faith', which in the first was an
'idea in the mind of the faithful' that might be transmitted in fallible and
shifting human language and in the second was a 'form of sound words' that

could not be altered.[15] Tyrrell saw the first as, in principle, a liberal position and the second as in principle conservative 'in default of a distinction which Ward does not see, but which is the whole theme of M. Arnold's *Literature and Dogma*'.[16] This was the distinction – between the scientific and the poetic use of language – which allowed Tyrrell to find some stability in his view of revelation. Until 1899 he had accepted that revelation implied the supernatural communication of propositional truth, but he abandoned this position as he recognised the extent to which the language of the Bible, and of theology, is perforce poetic or symbolic. From 1899 on, he stressed the immanence of the divine spirit within the struggling spirit of man, the experience of which man strives to express as best he can. This brought him close to Matthew Arnold's understanding of religious language as 'thrown out at a vast reality'. Such a position did not satisfy Tyrrell's more conservative instincts for it left the Biblical record much degraded as only one attempt to express God's continuing or 'natural' revelation. He continued to argue for revelation as 'experience' rather than instruction and for the 'prophetic' or 'poetic' nature of the language in which such experience is described, but he now laid decided stress on the apostolic 'form of sound words' as the classic account of the experience of Christ and the Early Church, to be taken as a whole, but taken for what it is, a symbolic or imaginative record. In the introduction to *Through Scylla and Charybdis*, written in 1907, he made it plain this was the position he now adopted.[17]

At about the time Tyrrell made the final adjustment to his concept of revelation, in late 1905, 'Willy' Williams wrote two articles in *Demain*[18] in which he quoted Arnold extensively. Tyrrell wrote to Bremond:

I confess I don't see why Williams' articles made such a trouble. We all know that Matthew Arnold is a Doctor of the Church.[19]

These are the warmest words that Tyrrell ever wrote about Arnold – though it is as well to remember that Tyrrell's real love was reserved for the saints and not the doctors of the Church.

Tyrrell was always a borrower of thoughts and expressions, as he himself acknowledged and many writers have stressed. One clear instance of such semi-conscious borrowing occurs in *Lex Credendi*. Arnold included in *St Paul and Protestantism* some haunting lines:

> Below the surface-stream, shallow and light,
> Of what we *say* we feel – below the stream,
> As light, of what we *think* we feel – there flows
> With noiseless current strong, obscure and deep,
> The central stream of what we feel indeed.
>
> (S VI (SPP) p. 51)

31

In a letter to von Hügel, written on 20 February 1901, Tyrrell dismissed a tendency of thought as 'a surface-stream'; in *Lex Orandi* (p. 48) he talked of 'our surface life'; and then in the Preface to *Lex Credendi* he wrote:

It is not by what a man says he believes (or disbelieves), or by what he explicitly and consciously thinks he believes, but by the Faith implicit in his spontaneous life and action and in the whole orientation of his feeling and will that the deep, subconscious convictions of his heart find true utterance.   (LC p. xiii)

There are the three strata: saying, thinking, feeling; the echo is unmistakable.

On the other hand, *Lex Credendi* contains the most explicit of Tyrrell's attacks on Arnold, who is singled out as representative of the error of 'practicality':

Conduct, he insists with somewhat wearisome iteration, occupies exactly three-quarters of life; art and science each one-eighth. Three-quarters of conduct, *plus* one-eighth of art, *plus* one-eighth of science, equals life. Right conduct is righteousness. Instead of God we are given a 'Not-Ourselves that makes for righteousness'. This 'Not-Ourselves' is, then, concerned about three-quarters of our spirit-life, about conduct. It is indifferent to the remaining quarter, – to science and art; it does not make for truth or for the beautiful.

Now this is to divide the spirit with a hatchet.   (LC p. 39)

As a swashbuckling summary of *Literature and Dogma* this is not unfair. What upsets Tyrrell about Arnold is his failure to see the 'organic and indissoluble' connexion between conduct, science and art:

Instead of 'the Not-Ourselves that makes for righteousness' (i.e. for right conduct), let us rather say 'that makes for truth – truth in conduct, truth in thought, truth in feeling' – that is, for the truth of the whole spirit-life of man, for its progressive correspondence to the life of the Eternal Spirit. By the time we have made this amendment, we have got back from Matthew Arnold's divinity to that of the Fourth Gospel.   (p. 40)

In one sense, Tyrrell is equating religion and ethics even more boldly than Arnold:

Conduct is not three-quarters, but the whole of life...Conduct, thought, and feeling are each the whole of life, – three dimensions of the same thing; there is no 'human act', no movement of the spirit-life, into which they do not all enter.[20]   (p. 40)

The key is that he finds Arnold's presentation two-dimensional: the whole transcendental will- or spirit-world disappears to nothing; he is 'blind to the mystical depth of Righteousness and of Divine Love, to their latent implication of a world of supernatural reality beyond the little sphere of our clear vision'. This is mere 'surface seeing'; for Tyrrell,'it is through the conduct-dimension that we are to get at the other two, and so to grasp the *whole*'.[21]

Throughout this period, Tyrrell's engagement with Arnold is highly confused, for he is in fact trying to work out a *via media* between Arnold's liberalism and the conservatism with which he had eventually come to identify Newman. In the introduction to Bremond's *Mystery of Newman*[22] he repeats a claim that Newman, in the *Essay on Development*, 'neither says nor wishes to say anything that he has not found in the Fathers'. For Tyrrell such a position was, in the face of Biblical and historical criticism, simply untenable, but if forced to choose between Newman and Arnold, he would in many ways incline to Newman, who goes some distance with Arnold, but by no means all the way. Newman

may have insisted more explicitly than other theologians on what is universally allowed as to the inexact and analogous character of inspired utterance, whose form is literary and imaginative rather than scientific; he may have felt more distinctly the fallacy of making such loose utterances the premises of deductive arguments; he may have recognised more fully that while and because the 'Deposit of Faith' is the subject-matter of dogmatic theology it can in no sense be itself a theology or a constitutive part of that theology; but he would have cordially anathematised those conclusions which the author of *Literature and Dogma* endeavours to draw from such admissions, and which seem to punish the aggressions of theology by a wholesale denial of its rights.   (p. xiv)

As Loome notes,[23] Tyrrell wrote on '*The Rights* and Limits of Theology'. He stands uneasily between Newman and Arnold. With Newman, he believes in, and looks for, an appropriate understanding of religious dogma, but he felt that Arnold had faced questions about religious language from which Newman simply retreated. In a review of *The New Theology* by R. J. Campbell (*The Hibbert Journal*, 5 (1907), 917–21), having noted that religion was suffering from the 'entanglement of revelation with theology' (p. 918), one of his most prominent and persistent themes, he went on, 'That particular ailment will not be remedied by exchanging Philo and Aristotle for Kant and Hegel, but by facing the problem raised, though surely not solved, by Matthew Arnold's *Literature and Dogma*.' Tyrrell is prepared to grant Arnold the honour of having spotted what is probably *the* critical question for religion in his time – that of the nature of religious language – but he still wants to defend both the Church and the God of Newman. As Vidler wrote,

He accepts Arnold's methods, his presuppositions even, and applies them not only to the Bible, but to the whole stream of religious experience in general and Catholic experience in particular, and claims that they issue in a justification not merely of 'morality touched with emotion', but of the whole complex of Catholicism.[24]

In dealing with religious experience, Arnold gave Tyrrell a phrase that he, like many of his contemporaries, used again and again. Tyrrell wrote to

Charles Devas in 1904 of 'the Power which works in nature and in the soul of man';[25] in *Lex Orandi* of the 'Power that makes for righteousness' (p. xxxi), a passage repeated in *Lex Credendi* (p. 251); and in the *Much-Abused Letter* (pp. 71, 76) he refers to 'that Force which we feel within ourselves impelling us upward and onward towards the Ideal, towards the Better and Best; a force which we may obey or resist, but in obedience to which alone we can find rest and peace'. This is pure Arnold, but Tyrrell characteristically adds: 'To think of it as less than personal, as otherwise than spiritual, is not practically possible.' (p. 72) For Tyrrell experience of the 'Power that makes for Righteousness' was no less than experience of God:

God makes Himself directly and immediately felt through His effects and workings in the religious experience of every one as a 'Power which makes for Righteousness'. (TSC p. 315)

In an extended critique, Hakluyt Egerton challenged the legitimacy of Tyrrell's position,[26] asserting that Tyrrell went beyond the evidence in attributing his moral experience to 'God'; for why should there be any personal cause or origin for our moral experience? He drew from Tyrrell an unequivocal, if at times tortuous, statement of his position in 'Revelation as Experience' (*The Heythrop Journal*, 12 (1971), 117–149), a paper read at King's College, London, shortly before he died:

Is the Power that makes for Righteousness [Egerton] would ask, the same Power that creates the world and moves every creature to its proper kind of perfection, even as it moves man towards his moral and spiritual perfection? I should certainly say Yes; while agreeing with Mr. Egerton that this identity is not given directly in our moral experience, but is only a legitimate theistic interpretation of that experience. (p. 143)

Yet Tyrrell goes on to assert that for him this personal interpretation of the origin and nature of the 'Power' remains inescapable: 'A Power that makes for Righteousness is no blind brute force; it is a spiritual will drawing our wills into union and personal relationship with itself.' Immediately we are reminded of the philosophy of the will-world expounded in *Religion as a Factor of Life* and *Lex Orandi*, and of the conviction in Tyrrell that the voice of conscience is the voice of God:

If experience gives us a Power that makes for Righteousness it gives us God...not in a statement but in the moral and religious impulse that proceeds from him (p. 144)

For Tyrrell, when he thought of God, Matthew Arnold's 'righteousness' was not enough. He found it 'a bloodless sort of attribute; and so comprehensible even when qualified by "eternal" as to starve the mystical sense' (SL p. 199)

As with God, so with Jesus, who was more than 'righteous or sweetly reasonable'. Tyrrell's God 'includes but transcends' Matthew Arnold's God of righteousness.

The discussion is pursued in *Christianity at the Crossroads*, where Tyrrell is particularly concerned with the apocalyptic imagery of the Gospels: inward experience does not give us any privileged way of conceiving God – that is to say, some divinely imbued image, symbol or idea. The many religions of the world bear witness to the variety of symbolism by which experience of God has been expressed. The images used are, however, subject to the pragmatic test of man's 'felt harmony or discord with the transcendent' (p. 111). Since, as Tyrrell would maintain, the finest imagery, in religious terms the most *serviceable* imagery, for the origin and nature of the mysterious 'Power that makes for Righteousness' (p. 108) is *personal* (an estimate confirmed by the recognition of that same Power in the life of the Christ who talks of his 'Heavenly Father', and in the life of the Church that prays to 'Our Father'), no less-than-personal way of talking of this Power will be adequate.

Tyrrell does not argue for the transcendent: he points to it in experience, and, as we have seen, believes that we can talk intelligently, albeit obliquely, about it. In his discussion of the 'Power that makes for Righteousness' he has hardly got his eye on Arnold's use of the phrase at all. He just took the phrase as a good phrase which served his turn better than 'conscience', for it made the link between the religious experience of the individual and that immanent force which Tyrrell identified with the will of God. In two letters, written towards the end of his life, however, it is clear that he continued to respect Arnold's thought on particular points. The first was written in 1906,[27] and concerned Church government:

Not that I am insensible to M. Arnold's plea for Erastianism. It means a reintroduction of the lay mind and voice into Church affairs, albeit in a crooked and undesirable way...Still, lay influence need not be State influence and ought to be purely religious.

Only deep disgust with the government of the Church could have elicited Tyrrell's sympathy for the views of the Arnolds, father and son. This is a desperate remedy for the exclusion of the laity from the dominant ecclesiology of the day.

At the end of his life, Tyrrell could sometimes lose all patience with the philosophical analyses of Blondel and Laberthonnière, although he clung to the fact that,

The infinite complexity of a human act, expressive of the whole personality of the doer, is past all analysis. It is there, and we like it or leave it; its motive power is as mysterious as the charm of music.[28]

In this mood, Tyrrell could fall back on Arnold as an ally against the legion of intellectualists he had fought for so long:

What M. Arnold says of poetical criticism is applicable no less to ethical. We cannot really define or explain what it is that makes a good lyric, or makes one better than another. We make our anthology of lyrics that are admitted by all to be first-class, and we use it as a standard of judgment. So neither can we tell what it is that commends a certain character or action as heroic and ideal, or why it rebukes and inspires us...You will say: This makes morality a matter of taste, and leaves no objective criterion. I answer that good taste, whether in art or conduct, is something quite objective, and that human nature is an excellent, permanent and independent criterion.

We are back at that fundamental level of agreement between Tyrrell and Arnold: the level of experience and of the limits of analysis; when it comes to philosophy and metaphysics both are easily exasperated. As soon as they turn to the level of reflection, of intellectual construction upon the basis of fundamental experience, of the rights of theology, Tyrrell never ceases to find Arnold a crude iconoclast.

Nevertheless, much of Tyrrell's work was directed to the breaking of images: of God, of Christ, of the Church, of the Christian virtues. Those images, built up in the service of an intellectualised scholasticism, and cracked beyond repair under the pressure of scientific Biblical and historical study, must be smashed, yet if the hammer be swung too fiercely (as Arnold swung it) nothing of ultimate value would be left. At the end of his life, Tyrrell feared that this is what he had done. He wrote to von Hügel:

I feel that my past work has been dominated by the Liberal-Protestant Christ and doubt whether I am not bankrupt...If we cannot save huge chunks of transcendentalism, Christianity must go. Civilisation can do (and has done) all that the purely immanental Christ of Matthew Arnold is credited with.[29]

In this judgment, picking up a theme particularly congenial to von Hügel, Tyrrell was unnecessarily, if typically, hard on himself. The remark has been taken and used against him,[30] and it certainly shows how aware Tyrrell was to the end of his life of the liberal Charybdis. Throughout his work his intention to use immanentist apologetic tools in the service of supernatural, transcendental religion was plain. In the succeeding chapters we shall see more closely to what extent he succeeded.

This chapter has been an introductory survey, bringing together Tyrrell's clear references to Arnold, and affording some preliminary idea of the debt he might have owed to him. It has not been possible to outline the religious philosophy of either man in such a small compass, and so the effect of comparison must at this point be somewhat two-dimensional. However, from the evidence so far collected we may draw two preliminary conclusions:

1. Tyrrell was attracted to Arnold because he felt that Arnold understood the nature of religious language as orthodox theologians did not. This was, at root, what they had in common.

2. Tyrrell was *always* fearful of Arnoldian reductionism. For him Arnold frequently appeared as an iconoclast, from whom, in his public writing, he wished to be differentiated. Often enough, he would be tempted to say, '*Non tali auxilio*'.

Tyrrell's attitude to Arnold was thus ambivalent. We shall consider in more detail specific areas of agreement or disagreement, but this preliminary survey has already shown the extent to which he was engaged with Arnold in all the fundamental areas of his theology: in epistemology, ecclesiology, Christology and the doctrine of God. Despite all disagreement Tyrrell always respected Arnold as a critic who understood imaginative language, including the language of religion. He is a 'Doctor of the Church'.

4

Fundamental convergence: epistemology and metaphysics

The first essay in *Through Scylla and Charbydis* is a lengthy apologia for catholicism, which concludes in the following rather ambiguous way. Tyrrell writes:

The Fathers have long since discovered an image of the Church in Eve, drawn from the side of Adam to be a helpmeet for him, albeit a costing one in many ways. In some respects the Hindu legend of the same event is even more illustrative. It tells us that when the Creator had taxed a million contradictory elements of the universe for contributions which he blended into a new creature and presented to man, the man came to him in eight days and said: 'My Lord, the creature you gave me poisons my existence. She chatters without rest, she takes all my time, she laments for nothing at all, and is always ill.'

And Twashtri received the woman again.

But eight days later the man came again to the god and said:—

'My lord, my life is very solitary since I returned this creature.'

And Twashtri returned the woman to him.

Three days only passed, and Twashtri saw the man coming to him again.

'My lord', said he, 'I do not understand exactly how, but I am sure the woman causes me more annoyance than pleasure. I beg of you to relieve me of her.'

But Twashtri cried: 'Go your way and do your best.'

And the man cried: 'I cannot live with her!'

'Neither can you live without her', replied Twashtri.

And the man was sorrowful, murmuring: 'Woe is me! I can neither live with nor without her!'   (pp. 83–4)

So Tyrrell concludes his account of the Church with words that echo the words that Arnold wrote in the Preface to *God and the Bible*:

At the present moment two things about the Christian religion must surely be clear to anybody with eyes in his head. One is, that men cannot do without it, the other, that they cannot do with it as it is.   (S VII (GB) p. 378)

These words have been taken as a 'motto' that epitomised Arnold's basic attitude,[1] and the same could obviously be said about the story from Tyrrell. The two shared a fundamental disquiet, and in this chapter we shall be looking at those similarities which make it possible to think of the two men as fellow-travellers, to speak of Arnold as 'the founder of English Modernism'[2] or of Tyrrell as 'preaching from Arnoldian texts'.[3] An obvious starting point is this sense that they shared of being born into an impossible inheritance, with the burden of mediation between a religious synthesis that could no longer be sustained and one that had yet to be found. Alfred Fawkes applied to Tyrrell the words of Arnold when he depicted him as

> Standing between two worlds – one dead,
> The other powerless to be born.[4]

The perception of urgent and rapid transition, of development and change as of the essence of the contemporary world; of immobility and insensitivity within the Church, and therefore of tragic and culpable loss, was something that united both men. From vastly differing backgrounds, they shared, as we shall see, a common vision, a common frustration, and, to some extent a common strategy.

We have already observed, in a preliminary way, that there is some similarity of approach between Arnold and Tyrrell and that, however disparaging Tyrrell may have been publicly, he privately acknowledged his debt to Arnold, and allowed that in *Literature and Dogma* Arnold had put his finger on perhaps the most urgent religious question of the day. Now we seek to go deeper. We shall look at six points in the general area of epistemology and metaphysics where there is a definite parallel between Arnold and Tyrrell. We are not now seeking to determine the extent of Tyrrell's *dependence* on Arnold, but to establish a general similarity of approach, a convergence at the most fundamental level.

It was within ethical commitment, within engaged action, that Arnold looked for the ability 'to see life steadily and see it whole'.[5] If Christianity is true, it will be found to be true in *life*. The first priority is to ground religion on the firm basis of experience, 'For whatever is to stand must rest upon something which is verifiable, not unverifiable' (S VI (LD) p. 149). In this, Arnold is at one with Tyrrell: *both Arnold and Tyrrell reacted against intellectualist and rationalist apologetic and stressed the experiential verification of Christianity.* They rejected logical proof as a paradigm for all verification and thought much more in terms of experiment and induction.[6] For both of them this meant a radical break with the prevailing theology of their day, especially the conventional arguments for the existence of God. Arnold dismissed metaphysics as a 'dismal science' (S VII (GB) p. 173) and complained of the traditional metaphysical arguments for the existence of God that they 'have convinced no one, they have given rest to no one, they have given joy to no one'

(S VII (GB) p. 199). Tyrrell would have agreed wholeheartedly. In 1908 he wrote to Houtin, the French Modernist,

Je suis sûr que c'est une faute d'essayer de prouver l'existence de Dieu. Ce que j'essaie de prouver, c'est que tout homme, honnête ou malhonnête, croit en Dieu, au moins dans sa subconscience, par le seul fait qu'il croit en la vérité et dans le droit, qu'il ne croit pas dans la fausseté et dans le mal.[7]

Shortly before he died, he reiterated his commitment to a metaphysic 'that is not *a priori* but is suggested and verified by experience at every step' (SL p. 143).

Arnold explicitly attacks 'the assumption with which all the churches and sects set out, that there is "a Great Personal First Cause, the moral and intelligent Governor of the universe", and that from him the Bible derives its authority'. The assumption 'cannot be verified' (S VI (LD) pp. 149–50). 'Here, then, is the problem: to find for the Bible, for Christianity, for our religion, a basis in something which can be verified, instead of in something which has to be assumed' (p. 150). This is to find the basis of Christianity in *fact*:

What essentially characterises a religious teacher, and gives him his permanent worth and vitality, is, after all, just the scientific value of his teaching, its correspondence with important facts and the light it throws on them... The licence of affirmation about God and his proceedings, in which the religious world indulge, is more and more met by the demand for verification.

(S VI (SPP) pp. 8–9)

Arnold argued in *Literature and Dogma*:

that righteousness is salvation verifiably, and that the secret of Jesus is righteousness verifiably; and that the true faith which the Bible inculcates is the faith that this is so.[8] (S VII (GB) p. 230)

He wanted to base the Christian religion on empirically verifiable facts and asserted that the appropriate facts are *there* to be discovered in the world.

Unfortunately for Arnold, you cannot bark your shins on moral facts as unequivocally as you can upon the stone that Dr Johnson kicked to prove that it was *there*, even though Arnold at first claimed that you could. Charles Secrétan, reviewing *Literature and Dogma*,[9] had criticised Arnold on precisely this point:

The Power making for righteousness, the Secret of Jesus, are not really experimental notions which any man can verify. The contrary is true. The Secret and the Power are objects of *faith* only. Experience offers every day abundant contradictions to the reality of the Power. (S VII (GB) p. 230)

In the face of this criticism Arnold's original position simply crumbles. He no longer talks in terms of the purest empiricism, and begins to grope for a more sophisticated notion of verification. Though he has expelled all theological hypotheses by the front door, he is forced to leave the back door ajar.

Replying to Secrétan in *God and the Bible*, Arnold first suggests that the truths under discussion 'are the matter of an immense experience which is still going forward'. Now this is to shift their verification into an uncertain future, which is precisely to make it a matter of *faith* in Secrétan's sense. Then Arnold says, 'It is easy to dispute them, to find things which seem to go against them; yet, on the whole, they prove themselves, and prevail more and more.' That is to say, each time clear counter-instances are produced (which Arnold admits to be easy) the conception of 'the whole' must be adduced, so that the counter-instances are rendered insignificant. Again, this is to invoke 'faith' in Secrétan's sense. Finally, Arnold says of 'these truths',

If any man is so entirely without affinity for them, so subjugated by the conviction that facts are clean against them, as to be unable to entertain the idea of their being in human nature and in experience, for him *Literature and Dogma* was not written. (p. 231)

This exclusive attitude does not conceal Arnold's inconsistency: when 'the facts' are for him they are 'facts', when they are against him they are merely a 'conviction', and if a person cannot see the 'facts' all is not lost: he can approach them by first 'entertaining an idea'. Such sophistication of Arnold's original empiricist approach leaves the argument of *Literature and Dogma* in ruins. One could almost turn Arnold's own remark against him and say, his religion 'has materialised itself in the fact, in the supposed fact...and now the fact is failing it' (S IX (EC2) p. 161).[10]

When dealing with the important subject of miracles in *Literature and Dogma*, Arnold had shown his awareness of subtler modes of argument, but he was clearly impatient of them. In the Preface to the popular edition Arnold concludes by stating bluntly, '*miracles do not happen*' (S VI (LD) p. 146).[11] In *Literature and Dogma* he wrote of 'a great many persons' who have 'made up their minds that what is popularly called *miracle* never does really happen' (p. 244) and he observed that 'it is what we call the *Time-Spirit* which is sapping the proof from miracles' (p. 246). In *God and the Bible* Arnold went into the subject in greater depth, only to admit that,

The case against the Christian miracles is that we have an induction, not complete, indeed, but enough more and more to satisfy the mind, and to satisfy it in an ever-increasing number of men, that miracles are untrustworthy. (p. 165)

Now this is an important hint, for an induction of this type is not the same as the experimental verification of a hypothesis. It involves the kind of imaginative reasoning and the kind of conviction that Newman discusses in the *Grammar of Assent* (a book to which Arnold never refers). In his work as literary critic Arnold appealed constantly, not to the methods of natural science, but to 'culture', 'taste', and 'judgment'. Arnold the literary critic and observer of human nature makes a far shrewder – and overtly non-scientific – judgment when he says on the same page,

Poor human nature loves the pretentious forms of exact knowledge, though with the real condition of our thoughts they often ill correspond. (S VII (GB) p. 165)

At root, Arnold was arguing that the knowledge Christianity offers is available to anyone who will make the experiment of living the Christian life. This is perfectly defensible if scientific and moral knowledge are not confused. Unfortunately, Arnold does confuse them, and so weakens his case.

Tyrrell is no less committed than Arnold to the experiential verification of Christianity, but he is a little less confused as to what it means. He writes in *Lex Orandi*:

Religion is not a dream, but an enacted, self-expression of the spiritual world – a parable uttered, however haltingly, in the language of fact. It is...a construction that has been forced upon us and verified by our experience, step by step, and part by part.   (LO pp. 168–9)

In comparing this with Arnold one notices immediately the juxtaposition of 'construction' and 'verification'. Tyrrell is much more ready to acknowledge the place of imagination in the forming of hypotheses than Arnold, though he is no less committed to the experimental and pragmatic testing of the religious hypothesis. Tyrrell was sharply critical of the sort of bone-headed positivism that

assumes too readily that 'direct perception etc.' is the only road to fact. Every moral man *believes* that truth and right will prevail at last; that honesty is *also* the best policy somehow or other; that goodness will ultimately spell happiness. These are as much predictions of *fact* as those of the astronomer; but they are got at in a more scientific way as the implications of conscience or of our moral sense. The results are as vague and inexact as the method; still they are very sure.[12]

This is a more careful statement of the same position as that of Arnold. A little later Tyrrell adds, 'And does he think to get to any fact, even the commonest without faith and intuition; and by purely scientific procedure?'[13] We can see at once that Tyrrell's 'participatory' epistemology, which has ample room both for the fashioning and the finding of truth, is to be differentiated from Arnold's shaky empiricism. The characteristic delicacy of Newman's epistemology was not lost on Tyrrell.[14] Tyrrell understood this aspect of Newman's work where Arnold, despite his enduring respect for the epitome of the Oxford sentiment, did not.[15]

Tyrrell's hermeneutical approach can be seen in his careful handling of the question of miracles. Unlike his historically trained friends Thurston and von Hügel, he rarely discusses what may or may not have happened in any particular case (though he was deeply influenced by the sceptical bias of the Biblical criticism he read). He is not interested in 'explaining away', or in 'explaining' at all, because he does not believe miracles should be used to prove anything. The ultimate 'proof' of, say, the divinity of Christ is his compelling moral integrity and attractiveness. As he wrote in a review of 1897, 'We need less than formerly to be dazzled with the wonderful, and more to be drawn to the lovable' (*The Month*, 90 (1897), 603; FM1 p. 258). This became his settled position. In *Lex Orandi*, he told Ward, he tried to give an account of Christianity 'after the miraculous has been excluded'.[16] The idea of miracle 'as a conquest of the power of nature by a Higher Power' (CCR p. 139) was simply an irrelevance. Claims to miracles were likely to be impossible to substantiate (CF p. 20). Even if they were substantiated they 'proved' nothing. The point of Christianity was not the coercion of the intellect, but the cooperation of the human will with the Will of God.

It may be that in this comparison we are being excessively harsh on Arnold, whose books are partially intended to meet scientifically-minded observers on their own ground, and to show that theologians do not belong there. When he is arguing '*ad hominem*' against those who say that there is no 'scientific' basis for Christianity, he appeals strongly to observation of the world, to positive data. However, he proves himself an indifferent scientist by overstating the amount of positive data on which he can safely draw. Tyrrell, on the other hand, works very differently. As a student of Newman and Blondel, he proceeds to a large extent by introspection, and offers a hermeneutical account of actual believing. This divergence of focus is important. In his religious writings Arnold assumes the critical grounding of contemporary scientific practice and looks for the 'scientific' basis of religion; Tyrrell tends to assume the critical grounding of moral or religious praxis, and from that basis to comment on the supposed certainty of 'science'.[17] In both cases they appeal to the test of 'experience'.

This brings us to a second point of virtual identity: *both Arnold and Tyrrell again and again stress the primacy of the ethical, of 'conscience' and 'conduct' in Christianity.* Arnold can be dealt with swiftly. In *Literature and Dogma* he is quite dogmatic about the relation of science and religion,

And so, when we are asked, what is the object of religion? – let us reply: *Conduct*. And when we are asked further, what is conduct? – let us answer: *Three-fourths of life*.   (p. 175)

By 'conduct' Arnold simply means practice, what we *do* –

Eating, drinking, ease, pleasure, money, the intercourse of the sexes, the giving
free swing to one's temper and instincts, – these are the matters with which
conduct is concerned.   (p. 173)

As we have seen, he goes on to assert that good conduct, or 'righteousness'
leads to happiness, this being a matter of experimentally verifiable 'fact'.
Arnold is rather less rumbustious when he talks of 'conscience'. Here he
acknowledges a debt to Butler (S VIII (LE) pp. 31–2), and he makes
'conscience' the lynch-pin of his account of the teaching of Paul, who 'starts
with the thought of a conscience void of offence towards God and man, and
builds upon that thought his whole system' (S VI (SPP) p. 29). What is
fascinating is to see Arnold at an earlier stage applying the term to intellectual
matters. He can say, 'A Frenchman has, to a considerable degree, what one
may call a conscience in intellectual matters' (S III (EC1) p. 236). He prefers
to talk of this as 'sensitiveness of intelligence', but he obviously thinks that
what we might call 'good taste' (he is writing about 'The Literary Influence
of Academies') acts in the same way as moral 'conscience': an apparently
instinctive perception of right and wrong. Arnold's intellectual ideal is thus
linked with 'conduct' through the medium of 'conscience'. In this sense
'conscience' is not three-quarters but the whole of life.

This is something with which Tyrrell would have gladly concurred. The
voice of conscience was always for him the voice of God. Here we have the
most consistent element in his theology: the fundamental *unity* of his work
is most apparent if one thinks of it as a theology of conscience.[18] Tyrrell
himself wrote in 1908,

I own that, for me, religion stands or falls with the divine character of conscience.
If I have learnt this from Newman I have verified it by my own experience and
reflection; and it is a conviction that grows stronger every day.   (SL p. 228)

Later he says, 'It is in my own conscience that I know God immediately' (SL
p. 230).

This emphasis on conscience is evident in Tyrrell's earliest published work.
The first part of his review of Wilfrid Ward's *W. G. Ward and the Oxford
Movement* (*The Month*, 79 (1893), 560–8) concentrated on this point. Having
quoted W. G. Ward, who constantly stressed that in conscience one hears 'the
echo of God's voice' (p. 562), he made his own summary:

Conscience, therefore, according to Ward and Newman, is the faculty whereby
we discern the things of God; and the condition of its exercise is obedience to
its behests, in other words, purity of heart.   (p. 565)

Tyrrell himself develops even this account of conscience when he speaks, in *External Religion*, of 'the Christ that lives in the conscience of every man who comes into this world' (ER p. 57). This was the abiding basis of his anthropology and his Christology, and we shall return to this point. Here it is sufficient to note the primacy that he gave to the ethical over the intellectual. As he wrote in his *Autobiography*, 'When there is an antimony between the conclusions of ethics and logic, it is plain that one must stand by ethics' (AL1 p. 158). If the theoretical grounding of Christianity appeared to collapse, this was only secondary anyway, and this did not mean that God need be lost:

I am clear that no man can be in sympathy with the mind of God – can love right *as* right, truth *as* truth; can hate evil *as* evil – and not be implicitly, but most really, contrite in the full theological sense, though he never have heard of God. (AL1 pp. 160–1)

Religion as a Factor of Life was Tyrrell's attempt to ground this view of religion: that it is first of all a will-attitude and only after that a doctrine. The unity of will between Creator and creature is the end to which conduct is the primary means. In stating his metaphysical view, Tyrrell differentiates himself sharply from Arnold. He talks of 'the life of religion as distinct from the life of ethical conduct' (p. 32). He distinguishes where Arnold saw no fundamental distinction: 'The "religionising" of conduct is not religion, but only one of its principal fruits' (pp. 32–3). Conduct is placed within the Augustinian metaphysic of the Will and Charity; the heart of religion lies in the cultivation of love, the unity of the human will and the Divine Will. This is the activity in which ethics and logic and aesthetics are united. For Tyrrell, it is simply not enough to see conscience as a kind of spiritual litmus-paper by which we tell right deeds from wrong. It is to be understood in the context of the *relationship* of the Divine Will to individual human wills. It is seen as the self-awareness of human activity, realised as truly human in action directed towards the Will of God and correspondingly aware of diminishment in action counter to the Will of God. We can see why he continually differentiates himself from the 'sentimentalism' of Matthew Arnold, who speaks of religion as '*morality touched by emotion*' (p. 4; S VI (LD) p. 176).

Nevertheless, the actual process of living the religious life or living the moral life may be very similar for both men. All his life Tyrrell used images of blindness, of groping and stumbling, to describe how men come to discern and picture God. Both the early allegories, 'The Contents of a Pre-Adamite Skull' (*The Month*, 67 (1889), 56–73) and 'Among the Korahites' (*The Month*, 72 (1891), 81–93) turn on the question of the knowledge of God. In the first the narrator encounters a people of hypersensitivity to God; in the second the savants, who, like all the Korahites, are blind, reject out of hand the

45

possibility of sight. Somewhere in between these two extremes of awareness and blindness comes the narrator, spiritually groping and stumbling his way to the light. It is not surprising to find that the epigraph to *The Civilizing of the Matafanus* was Plato's myth of the cave. The important point to note is that for Tyrrell this unsteady progress, by trial and error, guided by conscience and experience, has positive cognitive value,[19] whereas for Arnold it does not. For Tyrrell, as belief is expressed pictorially, and those expressions which foster will-union with God survive whilst those that do not drop away, knowledge *of God* accumulates. For Arnold all that accumulates is knowledge of *those actions* which are or are not in tune with the 'Power that makes for righteousness'. This is a fundamental difference.

We now come to a third point of comparison between Tyrrell and Arnold: *both perceive an immanent, teleological force at work in the world.* We shall return to this question in chapter 7 where we must look at the unsteady coalition of immanence and transcendence in Tyrrell's theology, but we may note here, in a preliminary way, that immanentism is a fundamental and consistent part of his thinking. With splendid asperity he attributes his discovery of the impugned 'method of immanence' not to his reading of Kant, but to Ignatius of Loyola (Med. p. 110). Nevertheless this is purely tactical and the roots of his attachment to immanentism must be traced back to the same fundamental impulse that led him to such a powerful stress on conscience. God is found in man:

Doubtless God speaks in history, but it is a polysyllabic word of which we miss the ends and therewith the meaning; and unless He is to be found within each soul He is practically unfindable.[20]

This to Bremond, when Tyrrell was at a particularly low ebb because of the Biblical criticism he was reading. Increasingly, Tyrrell used the phrase 'Power that Makes for Righteousness' to describe God as perceived by men. Such a minimal expression was entirely compatible with much stress on an immanent spirit, but whether Tyrrell's frequent reference to 'the spirit' (on occasions given a capital letter) remained within the bounds of orthodoxy is highly questionable.[21] Sometimes the spirit is recognisably the Spirit of God, sometimes it is the *Zeitgeist*. For example, after '*Pascendi*', Tyrrell wrote to Kitty Clutton:

Anyhow the substantials of Catholicism and of religion can take care of themselves. It is ill gibing at Conscience and the Holy Ghost. Who falls on that stone shall be broken[22]

where the spirit is clearly that of God. In his letters, though, he often refers to ideas, or criticism of life as though they were immanent forces. In

November 1900, he wrote to thank Bremond for an article he had written:

I wondered if, as you wrote, you were struck with, or intended, the remarkable parallelism between 'la théorie des énergies latentes de la patrie française' and the theory of the latent energies and ideas of Catholicism...I am no optimist, God knows, but I do believe, not, as with faith, but *as with science*, in the irrepressible energy of such latent ideas; in their power of casting aside every worthless or violently imposed accretion, and of working themselves out to their legitimate finality as infallibly as the roots of a tree make for the water through and round every obstacle. (SL pp. 3–4)

This was also one of the themes of Tyrrell's correspondence with Loisy:

Eppur si muove. Facts are stronger than Cardinals; nor will the whole Curia be able to prevent the tide of history coming in and sweeping down all barriers that are of sand instead of rock[23]

and again:

As to what a new Pope may mean we cannot remotely conjecture; still the laws of life and mental growth are eventually irresistible.[24]

Arnold's perception of immanent, teleological activity *always* tends towards the impersonal, as his indebtedness to Spinoza would lead one to expect. Where Tyrrell will talk about 'spirit' Arnold prefers to talk about '*Geist*', often about '*Zeit-Geist*',[25] about 'the progress of humanity towards perfection' (S V (CA) p. 222) or 'truth and the natural progress of things' (S VI (SPP) p. 92). He tends to hypostatise the '*Zeit-Geist*', to present it as an irresistible force with it own momentum, and even its own purposes. This, of course, serves his polemical intent when he wishes to castigate what he sees as religious and cultural atavism. Thus, he writes of, 'one irresistible force, which is gradually making its way everywhere, removing old conditions and imposing new, altering long-fixed habits, undermining venerable institutions, even modifying national character: *the modern spirit*' (S II p. 29). With characteristic ironic reference he writes, 'The Spirit of Time is a personage for whose operations I have myself the greatest respect; whatever he does is, in my opinion, of the bravest effect' (S VIII (LE) p. 69). This links with his belief that the emergence of a more adequate Biblical criticism is ultimately inevitable: 'The adequate criticism of the Bible is extremely difficult, and slowly does the "*Zeit-Geist*" unveil it' (S VI (LD) p. 348), but it will come, and the old, inadequate criticism will be superseded. In this Arnold and Tyrrell are at one, but for Arnold the dialectical criticism of the '*Zeit-Geist*' is also important. He writes of the Pope as, 'in his idea, the very Time-Spirit taking flesh, the incarnate "*Zeit-Geist*"' (S VI (LD) p. 162). He is this 'in his idea'; the historical Pope both is and is not such a figure. This sort of dialectical criticism defends Arnold from the charge of historical positivism, for it is clear 'perfection' or the goal of history is more than the emergence of what emerges. Arnold can call for resistance to the 'Zeit-Geist' in the name of 'perfection'. For instance, there is the early letter to Clough in which he talks about 'Sellar and the rest of that clique',

Yes I said to myself something tells me I can, if need be, at least dispense with them all, even with him: better that, than be sucked for an hour even into the Time Stream in which they and he plunge and bellow.[26]

Edward Alexander has summarised Arnold's conflicting attitudes to the 'Zeit-Geist': 'The wish to submit to the historical process in the guise of nature or the *Zeitgeist* was contradicted by the will to resist it in behalf of human perfection.'[27]

The question that must be asked of Arnold is again that of critical grounding; from where does he derive his criteria? On what basis is the discernment of the immanent force to be validated, or is the whole concept actually reducible to a tautology? What kind of purchase is given to any critique of the immanent *Zeitgeist*? These are the sorts of questions which cause philosophers to lose patience with Arnold; but then Arnold never had any patience with philosophers. With Tyrrell, however, it is easier to discern the intended contours as specifically Christian. In trying to reconcile an immanentist philosophy with a critical interpretation of the Christian tradition he was both more energetic intellectually and more circumspect. He had a better sense of the *form* of what must be preserved from his Catholicism. It was always within the immanent that Tyrrell looked for the transcendent; the critical grounding of transcendence must ultimately be found in the mystery of human experience.

We come now to a fourth point of comparison between Arnold and Tyrrell: *the acceptance of a rigid distinction between 'science' and 'religion'*. They both, to some extent, placed themselves within the Kantian tradition to which Liberal Protestants like Ritschl were deeply indebted. Kant's fundamental distinction between 'pure' and 'practical' reason, between the empirical realm and the realm of the will, affected the whole religious development of the nineteenth century. Although both Arnold and Tyrrell looked for terms that would transcend this distinction – hence the immanentist strain in the thought of both – they accepted it in a provisional sense because they placed the freedom of 'science' from the illegitimate hegemony of religion above any premature reconciliation of their competing claims. Let them stay apart until it could be said in what sense they might validly come together. In a second sense, then, Arnold and Tyrrell, like so many of their contemporaries, found themselves 'wandering between two worlds'.

F. Dudley[28] points out that Arnold uses the word 'science' in two senses 'sometimes consciously distinguished and sometimes unconsciously confused'. In the first sense, which is always approved, he uses it to designate thorough, objective knowledge of 'things as they really are'. This could apply to any or all of the fields of knowledge. So, in 1865, he writes to his sister of ' *Science*, in the widest sense of the word, meaning a true knowledge of things as the basis of our operations' (*Letters* I p. 246), and asserts that 'the bent of our time is towards science, towards knowing things as they are' (S III (EC1) p. 298). However, this becomes confused with the second sense, which is that of 'natural' or 'physical' science, the sort of science with which literature is contrasted in 'Literature and Science', the Rede Lecture of 1882. Again it is clear that he has this much more limited sense in mind, when he writes in 'Maurice de Guérin',

The interpretations of science do not give us this intimate sense of objects as the interpretations of poetry give it; they appeal to a limited faculty, and not to the whole man. (S III (EC1) p. 13)

When he talks of what is 'scientific' he says he means 'what is admittedly certain and verifiable' (S VI (LD) p. 190). Dudley rightly says that Arnold knows 'no real grasp of hypothesis and deduction, of the exploratory purposiveness of experimentation, of the tentativeness of scientific truth'.[29] But then how many of his contemporaries did? There is for Arnold a sort of 'higher' and 'lower' science:[30] the lower can be the means to the higher – where it will be one with the excellences of poetry, religion, culture in general. As Arnold wrote to Huxley,

The dictum about knowing 'the best that has been known and said in the world' was meant to include knowing what has been said in science and art as well as letters...I never doubted that the formula included science.[31]

On another occasion it is 'the name of God' which offers hope for the reconciliation of the warring factors. It is a point 'in which the religious and the scientific sense may meet, as the least inadequate name for that universal order which the intellect feels after as a law and the heart feels after as a benefit' (S VI (SPP) p. 9). In fact, there is only hope of reconciliation when religion and science are kept in place.

Arnold discusses the religious life as distinguished from the intellectual or scientific, in his essay 'Dr Stanley's Lectures on the Jewish Church' (S III (EC1) p. 65–82). His comments are deliberately distanced because he speaks not *in propria persona* but in the *persona* of 'literary criticism', which guise he uses to avoid questions of an ultimate nature. 'Literary criticism' simply observes that for some rarified spirits like Parmenides, Spinoza or Hegel, all life is subject matter for *thought*, but the majority 'seek the aid of religion' to achieve the life to which they aspire (p. 65). Their religious life 'resides not in an incessant movement of ideas, but in a feeling which attaches itself to certain fixed objects' (p. 67). Arnold is very clear that in 'the religious life' the priority is always with the realm of feeling, and intellectual ideas come second. The parallel with *Lex Orandi* is evident when the needs of the religious life are adduced as the criterion by which doctrine may be evaluated:

Only, if your doctrine is evidently not adapted to the needs of the religious life, – if as you present it, it tends to confound that life rather than to strengthen it, literary criticism has the right to check you; for it at once perceives that your doctrine as you present it, is false.   (p. 7?)

Just as with Tyrrell, Arnold argues that 'there is truth of science and truth of religion' (p. 74). What is true in the realm of science may actually be *false* if presented in crude contradiction to religious truth. Arnold argues, exactly as Tyrrell was later to do, that when Galileo declared that '"*the earth moves*"...speaking as a philosopher in the sphere of pure thought' (i.e. as scientist) he perceived and spoke the truth.

But if Galileo himself, quitting the sphere of mathematics, coming into the sphere of religion, had placed this thesis of his in juxtaposition with the Book of Joshua had applied it so as to impair the value of the Book of Joshua for the religious life of Christendom...his '*the earth moves*' in spite of its absolute truth, would have become a falsehood.[32]   (pp. 67–?)

Arnold attacks Colenso because he behaves as Galileo did not behave, *thrusting* mathematical or scientific thought into the religious sphere with supreme insensitivity. In this situation Arnold sees himself – as literary critic – called upon to protect values of permanent importance for the life of man. Religious life is one aspect of the life of man, in fact the deepest level of his life, but for all its depth it needs both protection and development in dialectical engagement with the ideas put forward by intellectuals. When the theologians fail to adopt this role one sees the contemporary *trahison des clercs*. Like Tyrrell Arnold does not offer positive criteria for the fostering of this process, but negative criteria for discerning when it has patently gone wrong. Where Arnold differs from Tyrrell is in resolutely prescinding from metaphysical discussion about the foundation of the religious life, and so he leaves the way open for religion to be assimilated to morality on the one hand, and poetry on the other.

  Tyrrell's approach to science is broadly similar to Arnold's.[33] He is even more sharply aware of the present conflict between science and religion as two forms of positive knowledge, and opposed to any premature synthesis between the two. Nevertheless he holds to the idea of their ultimate unity, and although it was, if anything, even more important for him than it was for Arnold to insist on the rights of science against the 'license of affirmation' taken by the Church, he never failed to look towards the ultimate synthesis of the two. The ideal of synthesis had been with him since he first studied Aquinas. However, the vision of a renewed Thomism failed him. He found the scholastic categories too crude, too materialistic to express the dynamic complexity of life. For a time he looked to Newman, who offered in his writings on reason and faith a far subtler account of the way in which these jarring elements of the human soul may be reconciled in the community of faith, but Newman, too, was found wanting because Tyrrell saw in his conception of the *deposit* the possibility of an illegitimate domination of faith – transmuted into dogmatic science – over free enquiry.[34] The two were to be kept almost entirely distinct in all Tyrrell's works from the Richmond period on.[35]

The only hope that Tyrrell could then see lay in distinguishing sharply between faith or revelation, and reason, science or theology, as 'generically different orders of Truth and Knowledge' (TSC p. 86). This is a division fundamental to all his later work. It is not an ultimate division, but for the time being, in the present critical climate, it is important to see that revelation and theology cannot be held together epistemologically. Tyrrell accepts the temporary eclipse of the unity of truth and knowledge, for only by working with the bifurcation that prevails in contemporary culture can he engage with contemporary understanding.

Tyrrell sought to define the rights and limits of faith, and the rights and limits of science, or theology. When he wrote specifically on the latter topic he seemed to make concessions so radical that the basis of faith was destroyed. It was clear that he conceded absolutely the right of science, including Biblical criticism, to free enquiry, since he maintained that the assertions of faith were made at a different level.[36] Here and now, there was no meeting place for religion and science – even though there would be a new synthesis in the future. In speaking for the freedom of science Tyrrell undoubtedly weakened his case by a somewhat naive acceptance of what Biblical science was offering in his day. He abandoned an early reticence towards 'the fluctuating character of science and criticism' (*The Month*, 79 (1893), 563) and spoke of 'the indubitable data of history or science or philosophy' (LO p. 207), not at this stage recognising the extent to which any historical or scientific or philosophical account is itself a synthesis of changing data and therefore subject to revision. In *Christianity at the Crossroads* Tyrrell wrote with greater maturity, 'Religion cannot be the criterion of scientific truth, nor science of religious truth. Each must be criticised by its own principles' (p. xv). He insists upon the right of the scientist to apply logic where logic is appropriate and wherever it may lead. Hence his support of Loisy and the methods of Loisy.[37] The problem for Tyrrell is that the rigid distinction between reason and faith, religion and science appears to clash with the sacramental dimension of his thought.

Here we have an important difference between Arnold and Tyrrell. The sacramental dimension is something that Arnold barely has, and it is characteristic of Tyrrell. Tyrrell is always working with the distinction 'supernatural/natural', but he stresses the immanence of the supernatural in the natural. What he sees as having happened is a conflict between the two – a conflict which in the end is certain to be resolved because the two are complementary. So, he wrote in his *Autobiography*, 'If the supernatural is real at all, it must include the natural, as the greater does the less' (AL1 p. 167); 'include' but not destroy. Ultimately there can be no purely 'natural' science. If one thinks of the supernatural and the natural as separate and competing elements of life – as the naturalist does, often because of bad theology on the part of Church teachers – one misconceives the relationship entirely. The supernatural fulfils, completes and complements the natural. This is the central theme of the *Faith of the Millions*: 'the immanence of the supernatural in the natural – the inextricable permeation of the latter by the former' (FM1 p. xx). It contains an implicit challenge to Arnold:

The natural and the supernatural are not sundered, nor are they violently yoked together; but the lower ministers to the higher and the higher perfects, crowns, and elevates the lower.   (FM1 p. 12)

This is perfectly exemplified in the Incarnation, in which one sees the humility of God and the fulfilment of man. However difficult he found it to justify such language theoretically, it was to this way of speaking, to the *sacramental* view of 'two worlds', that Tyrrell always wanted to return.

Tyrrell was prepared to accept, for the time being, and under pressure of the *Zeitgeist*, 'two orders of assent' – that of reason and that of faith – because he felt the ultimate unity of knowledge to be assured. *Because* he looked on the world as God's sacrament he believed, with von Hügel, that free, scientific enquiry would actually bring men to God. This sacramental view of the world is a recurrent thought in the devotional books:

Nature, then, is the garment of God; and by the light of natural reason, and the impulse of the natural heart, man can draw near from behind, and touch with trembling hope the fringe of His vesture, and be healed of his infirmities.
                                                                 (NV pp. 127–8)

It is *through* our response to the creature (even as scientists) that we respond to the Creator:

To the discerning, every purification and elevation of the natural taste, every new appreciation of hitherto unappreciated excellence, is a step upwards, a new remove from the wisdom that is from beneath, towards the wisdom which is from above... (pp. 169–70)

So, *Lex Orandi*, five years later, begins with a chapter entitled 'The Sacramental Principle' and 'The Two Worlds'. He writes,

We seen then, that in virtue of our twofold nature we live in two worlds – one bodily, the other spiritual; one the shadow and the sacrament; the other, the substance and the signified reality. (p. 10)

He accepts an epistemological dualism, but he also wants to hold these 'two worlds' together in a dynamic unity:

Between the inward and the outward, between the world of reality and the world of appearances, the relation is not merely one of symbolic correspondence. The distinction that is demanded by the dualism of our mind does not exclude, but implies and presupposes, a causal and dynamic unity of the two. (p. 165)

He always maintains that the religious and the scientific are two complementary, if asymmetrical, ways by which to apprehend one transcendent reality mediated in the life and action of this world.

This brings us to a fifth point of comparison between Arnold and Tyrrell: for both, *the distinction between religion and science involves a clear bifurcation in the use of language*. In Arnold's case the division is between language that is 'fluid, passing, and literary' and language that is 'rigid, fixed, and scientific' (S VI (LD) p. 152). Tyrrell, most characteristically, talks of 'the language of prophecy' and the 'language of exact thought' (e.g. LC p. xv). This bears out and extends the thesis of Abrams who believes that in the early Victorian period 'all discourse was explicitly or tacitly thrown into the two exhaustive modes of imaginative and rational, expressive and assertive'.[38]

Arnold's fundamental quarrel with the theologians is that they have misunderstood the nature of Biblical language:

What is called orthodox theology is, in fact, an immense misunderstanding of the Bible, due to the junction of a talent for abstruse reasoning with much literary inexperience. (S VI (LD) p. 279)

Anyone with a certain amount of 'culture', that is to say 'some experience of how men have thought and expressed themselves, and some flexibility of spirit' (S VI (LD) p. 152), would be in no doubt of the essentially literary nature of Biblical language, but he feels that literary sensitivity is in eclipse, especially among theologians,

It is curious how the feeling of the chief people in the religious world...seems to be just now against letters, which they slight as the vague and inexact instrument of shallow essayists and magazine writers; and in favour of dogma, of a scientific and exact presentment of religious things, instead of a literary presentment of them.[39]   (S VI (LD) p. 165)

This dualism extends throughout Arnold's writings.

The first clear hint of the application of this to religion comes in *Culture and Anarchy*, where Arnold writes,

Who, I say, that has watched Puritanism, – the force which so strongly Hebraises, which so takes St. Paul's writings as something absolute and final, containing the one thing needful, – handle such terms as *grace, faith, election, righteousness*, but must feel, not only that these terms have for the mind of Puritanism a sense false and misleading, but also that this sense is the most monstrous and grotesque caricature of the sense of St. Paul, and that his true meaning is by these worshippers of his words altogether lost?   (S V p. 182)

This is the seed from which *St Paul and Protestantism* develops,[40] and then the indictment of mishandling language is further sharpened in *Literature and Dogma*, 'Terms, in short, which with St. Paul are *literary* terms, theologians have employed as if they were *scientific* terms' (S VI p. 170).[41] In the same passage Arnold defines what he means by 'literary' and 'scientific' terms. Literary terms are those used

in a fluid and passing way, as men use terms in common discourse or in eloquence and poetry, to describe approximately, but only approximately, what they have present before their mind, but do not profess that their mind does or can grasp exactly or adequately.   (*Ibid.*)

He thinks of the word 'God' as

a term of poetry and eloquence, a term *thrown out*, so to speak, at a not fully grasped object of the speaker's consciousness, a *literary* term, in short; and mankind mean different things by it as their consciousness differs.   (p. 171)

Now the scientific term is one with a meaning 'definite and fully grasped' (p. 170): one which stands for 'a perfectly definite and ascertained idea, from which we might, without more ado, extract propositions and draw inferences' (*Ibid.*). This suggests that the determining factor is one of clarity, which in Arnold means an 'obvious' or demonstrable relation to reality. If one can establish 'the common substratum of idea' on which a range of uses rests, one finds 'the real sense of the word', and can use it 'scientifically' (p. 171).[42]

The point is that the literary – the inexact and expressive – comes first, to be followed by the precise and referential scientific language. Where we cannot define with precision we should recognise the status of the language that we use. This is why dogmatic theology is 'utter blunder' (p. 384) and those pictorial and apocalyptic ideas that Arnold calls '*Aberglaube*' are not and cannot be science (p. 212). The Creeds are described as 'the science of Christianity' (pp. 340 ff). That is to say they are misconceived as science. The point of religion is not to convey ideas of the Beyond with scientific precision, but to galvanise our efforts after morality in this life.

Only gradually did Tyrrell come to a position where he would have been in sympathy with Arnold's trenchant words. Bit by bit, he loosened his hold on analogy: the analogy by which we speak of God is more and more general and opaque. J. Goetz[43] shows how Tyrrell began from a strictly neo-scholastic orthodox position based on the *analogia entis*, yet Tyrrell was well aware that 'the Catholic theologian had always said that human language is inadequate to the statement of the divine'.[44] So he wrote in 'Coventry Patmore' of 'the infinite inadequacy of even the noblest conceivable finite symbolism to bring God down to our level' (*The Month*, 96 (1900), 572). He was still confident, when he wrote those words, of the power of analogy to speak of God and to 'keep the Church in balance between the Scylla of anthropomorphism and the Charybdis of agnosticism'.[45] Over the next three years, however, he lost the confidence that the Church could say wherein the analogy lay. The awareness of mystery overwhelmed the confidence in analogy.

Tyrrell's fidelity to the term 'analogy' is explained by his scholastic background, but we have seen that he left his Thomism behind:

I no longer accept as adequate, or as more than ingeniously illustrative, the simple categories of form and matter, purpose, pattern, by which scholasticism seeks a mechanical explanation of things spiritual and celestial, in the terms of the works of men's hands. (AL1 p. 248)

He came to perceive more and more the dynamic function of words. In his Newmanite phase he wrote that 'the language of Scripture and traditional dogma is not scientific and abstract, but natural and concrete' (FM1 p. 111). In the same year he also wrote, 'It is important to remember the abstract character of certain theological conclusions, and the superiority of the concrete language of revelation as a guide to truth' (FM1 p. 243). He later spoke not so much of 'concrete' language but of 'prophetic' or 'poetic' language, less of analogy and more of symbolism. The nature of religious language is a major theme of *Through Scylla and Charybdis*. Tyrrell wrote in the introduction:

Were it possible to show that underneath the obvious sense of revelational and dogmatic utterances there lay a deeper sense, a truth of an entirely different order; were it possible, in the light of the comparative study of religions and of an immensely deepened psychological insight, to give a more real and undeniable value to the notion of 'prophetic truth' than I can claim to have done, then it seems to me we might perhaps be able to reconcile perfect fidelity to the ancient principles of Catholic tradition with an equal fidelity to the fullest exigencies of scientific truth and moral truthfulness.[46] (p. 10)

This was an idea that had been growing in his mind for some time. In 1905 he wrote to the Abbé Venard, giving the outline of a chapter he would have added to *Lex Orandi* if he could have got it past the censors. The subject of the letter is 'prophetic truth':

'Prophetic' truth is analogous with poetic, artistic, dramatic truth in that the religious and moral values of its utterances, like the aesthetic values of artistic utterances, are to a certain extent independent of the fact-values or historical values.[47]

The key lies in the modifying 'to a certain extent'. Tyrrell is suggesting that there is a kind of spiritual discernment of the form or flow of history practised by the prophet, and, although his utterances always stand to be corrected by historical science, yet they may be 'true' in another sense. He writes of the prophet's judgment: 'Even if historically wrong it may be *truer* than history; truer to the inward reality, to the intimate meaning of things, to what is in process of becoming.'[48] Like Arnold's view of the moral order, such a position is non-falsifiable, but suggestive – though Tyrrell wants to maintain that it is ultimately falsifiable, again like Arnold. The point here is Tyrrell's fidelity to the notion of two sorts of truth. About the same time as the letter to Venard, Tyrrell wrote 'The Rights and Limits of Theology'. Again the notion of two sorts of truth is made clear. He writes of:

this notion of prophetic truth whose object, unlike that of science or history, is the ideal rather than the actual; the future, or else the eternal, rather than the past or present; what ought to be and is in process of becoming, rather than what is. The character of what, by way of contrast, we may call fact-truth is coherence or consistence with that systematic reconstruction of the world which is slowly built up by the labour of the understanding.   (TSC p. 231)

Tyrrell did not want to tie down the concept of 'prophetic' truth to language, and deliberately spoke of 'utterances', but, faced with language, it is important to determine what sort of language is being used and not to confuse the prophetic with the scientific. Yet the two are linked in much the same way for Tyrrell as for Arnold:

All language is poetical in its origin. It tries to express the whole inner state – not merely the truth, but the emotions and feelings in which the truth is embedded; for the so-called 'faculties' – mind, will, feeling – have not yet been marked off from one another by abstract thought. It is only later that the utility of exact ideas and corresponding verbal signs leads to prosaic precision, and turns what once were living metaphors into sober measurements.[49]   (TSC p. 32)

For Tyrrell, the genetic priority of poetic or prophetic language links with his view of immanent spirit:

Prophetic truth (and artistic truth in some way) is reached, not by reason working on sensible experience, but by the sympathy of man's spirit with the Divine spirit immanent in man's spirit; it is a divination guided by a spiritual sentiment. As God is the root and immanent cause of all that is and is going to be, or is in process of becoming, this sympathetic divination of prophecy reaches the truth of what *is* in the divine or eternal order of reality; and the truth of what *ought to be* but *is* not, or is only in process of becoming, in the order of finite reality.[50]

Because of the 'sympathy of man's spirit with the divine spirit', faced with prophetic utterance, he can say, 'this is *true*, but I do not yet understand this truth'. In fact, with religious mysteries this will always be the case. Nevertheless, we do try to understand, and to explain our understanding theologically. In doing so, we have to be aware of what we are doing with language:

Language, like outward sensation, is at best suggestive – a few points, a few lines which the responsive mind fills in from the storehouse of memory, and so more than half creates the object of its apprehension.   (LC p. 86)

With this statement of participatory epistemology, clearly echoing Wordsworth,[51] Tyrrell shows his superiority to Arnold in understanding the function of language. This is the base from which he calls the hypotheses of physical science 'fictions founded in fact' (CCR p. 174). All language shares this insufficiency, but there remains an absolute distinction between scientific and literary usage. As with Arnold, dogmatic theologians are accused of muddling the two:

The view of the nature, range and temper of Christ's teaching, which is assumed by the 'official' theory of the Church's doctrinal vice-gerency, is a mistaken one; inasmuch as that teaching was directly prophetic and only by remote implication theological.   (CF p. 50)

Or again,

For centuries [Christianity] has in many cases treated the prophetic and inspired language of Revelation as possessing exact philosophical or scientific value, and has thus deduced prosaic conclusions from quasi-poetical premises. (MAL p. 33)

This is just what Arnold says. Tyrrell simply goes deeper.

There is one final point of comparison between Arnold and Tyrrell. *Both attempted, in different ways, to express the essence of Christianity, to discern the spirit from the letter; in the terms of Liberal Protestantism, to distinguish the kernel and the husk.*

Arnold is never shy of trying to capture the essence of anything, and he does not see the philosophical problems involved in the attempt. With Protestantism, with poetry, with America, or culture, he plunges in; and, of course, he does this with Christianity. Here he finds the essence to be:

something not very far, at any rate, from this: *Grace and peace by the annulment of our ordinary self through the mildness and sweet reasonableness of Jesus Christ.*[52]

(S VI (SPP) p. 121)

The central point about Jesus is that,

he restored the intuition of God through transforming the idea of righteousness; and...to do this, he brought a *method*, and he brought a *secret*.

(S VI (LD) p. 286)

The 'method' comes down to the application of conscience to conduct, and the secret to dying to oneself; not even the fatherhood of God, but the supremacy of conscience and the means to apply this in the world. With this ethical interpretation of the Gospel and the neglect of eschatology, Tyrrell joined battle unforgettably in *Christianity at the Crossroads*.

Tyrrell had, however, already been speaking against Matthew Arnold's stark reductionism for some years. In 1900, he called Arnold, 'a type of the extreme latitudinarian', for whom 'the kernel of Christianity freed from the husk, consists in a few platitudes of the higher ethics which have been involved in a vast complexus of historical and dogmatic propositions' (FM1 p. 194). It was not the strategy of which Tyrrell disapproved, even at that stage. He positively recommended it for desperate cases; and he used it himself. He wrote in 'A Perverted Devotion':

If, in behalf of those who possess the faith, the attempt to sever tares from wheat may often be dangerous, for those who are seeking the faith, which they have lost or which they never had, the severance is all-important. As a rule, it is not the truth that is doubted or rejected, but the setting in which the truth is embedded, the husk which encases the kernel and makes it all-repulsive and unappetising.

(EFI p. 170)

This is exactly his approach in *A Much Abused-Letter*, which he described as 'a strong and dangerous remedy prepared to meet a comparatively small number of desperate cases' (p. 19). If it came to the issue, Tyrrell was prepared to drop science if he could keep faith. His distinction corresponded to his epistemological divide:

Heretics, who, as a rule, have been more interested in the mind-truth than the will-truth, have assailed the former on the score of mental difficulties; they have quarrelled with the husk and threatened to throw away the kernel along with it.

(RFL p. 63)

If the flesh, in the form of the science of this world, would not minister to the spirit, but opposed and destroyed it, which was the situation as Tyrrell saw it, then away with the flesh and live by the spirit! This is his advice to the 'Professor of Anthropology' who set out to defend Catholicism but found it in its contemporary form indefensible. A consistent theme of Tyrrell's work is the desire to discern and live by the spirit.[53] He used it as his central hermeneutic principle: 'It is not by the *Summa Theologica* that we are to measure St. Thomas but by the broad synthetic progressive spirit of which it is the fruit' (*The Monthly Register*, 1 (1902) 264–5). The same applies to Newman:

Yet he is no true disciple of Newman's, nor can he deeply appreciate or understand him, who does not recognise and study his limitations; who does not care far more for his spirit, temper and method than for the matter with which he dealt or for the results which he reached. (p. 264)

He sums up his critical position at the end of the same article:

What is valuable in the man is just what is distinctive, not what is common; and what is distinctive is not this position or that, but the method and movement by which they were reached. To sift these elements therefore from one another...belongs to the study of his limitations...Only through such a critical process of limitation can we sunder the abiding spirit from its perishable embodiment. (p. 265)

In a statement such as this, written in 1902, we can see exactly how close Tyrrell was to the approach of Arnold, and yet why he would eventually draw away from it. Arnold's critical approach was to isolate what he found to be 'distinctive' about Jesus, his 'method' and his 'secret', and commend these, whilst airily dismissing his eschatological teaching as '*Aberglaube*'. Once Tyrrell had digested Weiss and Schweitzer, with their stress on eschatology as the key to understanding the ministry and teaching of Jesus, he saw clearly that it could not be cut away as nineteenth-century liberals, and he himself, had tended to do. One could only discern the 'spirit' of Jesus by paying closer attention to the historical material than Arnold had been prepared to do. If one were to think in terms of kernel and husk, no longer could any of the apostolic 'form of sound words' be dismissed as husk: here was *the kernel*, for the words *in their totality* bore witness to the experience of revelation. The husk which protected the kernel, but was utterly dispensable, was theology. This is not quite how Tyrrell put it, but it is the position he had reached in *Christianity at the Crossroads*.

This chapter has dealt with the fundamental epistemological and metaphysical judgments made by Arnold and Tyrrell. It has not been our intention to determine the exact extent to which Tyrrell does or does not depend on Arnold, or take similar positions to Arnold on fundamental issues, for both are often contradictory and confusing writers. The aim has been more limited: to show enough points of convergence in this area that the comparison between Arnold and Tyrrell be taken seriously. We have not yet done with comparison at this fundamental level for there is more to be said about the whole corporate life of action, feeling and intellect, which for Tyrrell is expressed primarily in the Church, and for Arnold in 'culture' or 'civilisation', though not, in either case, exclusively, for Tyrrell is concerned to link catholicism and culture, and Arnold is concerned for the future of catholicism.

5

The life of the spirit: ecclesiology and culture

In his *Autobiography*, Tyrrell, always attributing to himself the most paradoxical motives, describes how he was drawn by the externals of Catholicism, 'the very fringe and extreme outskirts of Christianity' (p. 102). He presents this as a boyish attraction to ritual and mystery which only developed into a serious quest for God, when he recognised his need 'to find a basis for a system that hung mid-air save for the scaffolding of mixed motives which made me cling to it blindly, in spite of a deep-down sense of instability' (p. 112). If he was to be a Catholic, he had to believe sincerely in God. Such conviction was hard-won, but in time it became the lynch-pin of his faith. As a mature man he listed his deepest convictions in precisely the reverse order from that in which he had come to them: 'my dominant interest and strongest conviction is Theism; and dependently on this Christianity; and thirdly Catholicism' (p. 112). This is also how he explained the order of his beliefs to Bremond: God, Christ, Catholicism.[1] However, in the next three chapters we shall take these topics in the opposite order, the order in which Tyrrell came to accept them.

The fundamental reason for this mode of proceeding is precisely that implied in his choice of autobiography to make what amounted to a theological statement: Christian believing is more than the intellectual acceptance of a systematic theology, a point Tyrrell repeatedly emphasised. Like Newman, he used his autobiography to show that in believing 'the whole mind moves', although he sees his own as having moved much less rationally than Newman's.[2] He could only explain his Catholicism by explaining how he grew into it and through it found Christ and the Father.

Here there is only the faintest parallel with Arnold, though as we shall see Arnold warmed perceptibly towards Catholicism in the latter part of his life. At first sight the general area into which we are now moving – that of ecclesiology – does not offer much hope of fruitful comparison between Tyrrell and Arnold. Certainly, the Jesuit of whom it was said that 'the very word "Catholic" was music to his ears'[3] could have had little general sympathy with the erastianism of the son of Thomas Arnold. Nevertheless we have seen that he on one occasion declared himself 'not insensible' to Arnold's plea for erastianism because it brought the lay voice back into Church affairs;[4] and Arnold spoke of 'a Catholic Church transformed' as 'the Church of the future' (S VIII (LE) p. 110).

We have to shift the focus to find the convergence that exists here. What we saw in the previous chapter was a series of areas or attitudes in which such a convergence could be seen, but the effect was somewhat artificial as neither Tyrrell nor Arnold presented their thought in anything but a series of occasional writings. Plucking six general points out of their whole corpus, it was not possible to bring out the shifts and development in the thought of both writers, nor was it possible to embark upon a comparison of the way in which the points we discussed – about experience, conscience and conduct, immanentism, religion and science (both as a categorical and as a linguistic division) and the division of kernel from husk – were rooted in certain presuppositions about society. Both Tyrrell and Arnold worked with an organic conception of society: this immediately gives grounds for comparison, and for the suggestion that they had more in common than is usually allowed.

In order to avoid the most grotesque distortion, we should repeat that there is no suggestion here of Tyrrell's looking to Arnold for ecclesiological inspiration. Tyrrell's 'organic' caste of thought is certainly seen most clearly in his ecclesiology, but Arnold's emerges in his discussion of 'culture' and his social criticism. The obvious common ancestor of these two manifestations of 'organic thought' is Newman. One might almost say that Tyrrell is a follower of Newman to the right and Arnold a follower of Newman to the left – provided one remembers that in every way Tyrrell developed Newman's thought in a liberal rather than a conservative direction, so that the epitome of right-wing Newmanism was not Tyrrell but Wilfrid Ward. DeLaura writes of the 'miracle' that Arnold and Pater found in Newman, which was that

> this, the most powerful defender of the claims of religion upon the modern mind, was also the most adequate definer, in prose of incomparable lucidity and suavity, of an ideal of totality, comprehensiveness, inclusiveness, at a time when the image of the distinctively human was being either fragmented or radically reduced.[5]

For a time Tyrrell was similarly captivated. When he came to reject the terms in which Newman defended revealed religion he did not abandon the 'ideal of totality' as applied to the Church. Arnold never accepted Newman's defence of revealed religion, but still he took the cultural ideal so eloquently expressed in *The Idea of a University* (where Newman feels for the term 'culture' and does not find it)[6] and made it his own.

Since we are now concerned with 'wholeness' and the organic metaphor, we shall proceed somewhat differently from the way in which we have done in the previous chapter. We shall first examine Tyrrell's ecclesiology in an attempt to show how it is consistently informed by the image of the Mystical Body. Then we shall turn to Matthew Arnold's conception of culture. Finally, we look briefly at Tyrrell's fragmentary remarks on culture and consider Arnold's attitude to Catholicism.

The dominant theological picture of the Church in Tyrrell's writings is that of the Mystical Body of Christ.[7] This begins to emerge in *Nova et Vetera*, where he writes of 'one mystical body full of suffering' (p. 23), 'the Mystic Christ, i.e., Christ and the Church' (p. 138), 'one living, many-branched whole, one mystic Christ' (p. 145). In a section, significantly entitled 'Collective Praise', he writes of

the joy of that whole mystical body whereof we are members; of one living organism which sees itself with a million eyes, yet with but one vision; loves itself with a million hearts, yet with but one love; where the blessedness of the whole is more desired by each part than its own share in that blessedness.

(p. 275)

This is specifically written of the Church, but it is obviously a vision for the whole of society:

Natural reason and conscience convey to us the will of God, who is subsistent Reason, whose interest and aim is universal good and right order; and they impel us to live for a whole whereof we are but parts, and for a good whereof our particular good is but a fraction. (p. 405)

Thus we can see that the vision and calling which the natural man discerns by his natural faculties is given substance and stability when he perceives that it is realised in the Catholic Church.

In *Hard Sayings* there is a substantial essay on 'The Mystical Body' that elaborates these themes. The continuity between the historic Catholic Church and the incarnate Christ is an important concern, for it is this that gives the Church its authority to teach and its power to mediate salvation through the sacraments:

For the Catholic, Christ and the Church are not two, but one, as head and body are one, as husband and wife are one, two in one flesh...The Church is not all Head, nor all members, but the two together are one Christ and one Church, one mediator between God and man. (pp. 405–6)

Both to Christ and to the Church there are two aspects, of which we can only perceive one directly through our senses:

Who then shall weigh and measure and sum up in vain words the 'idea' of Him who is at once God and man, or the idea of that mystic Body, human and divine, earthly and heavenly, His Bride, the Catholic Church? (p. 398)

The whole is greater than what we see, and what we see ministers to the whole as sign and sacrament. In general terms, 'this world and the next are related as body and soul. The body is subordinate to the soul; but it is not its enemy, not even its slave, but its companion, its helper, its friend' (p. 274).

Tyrrell does not over-simplify the issue, and discusses the question of the visible and the invisible Church at some length:

Soul and body are at once distinct and in a sense co-extensive; whereas the invisible and visible Church are neither, some members being common to both, others belonging only to one. (p. 416)

Who then can be seen on earth to belong to the heavenly or invisible Church, the true Body? Tyrrell seems to give the broadest possible answer when he says, 'All those in whose hearts charity is diffused by the Holy Ghost; all those who give God and God's cause the first, if not always the only place in their affections' (p. 422). However, what he gives with one hand he half intends to take away with the other, when he writes, 'None, therefore, can be counted a member of the invisible Church who through any fault or negligence of his own remains outside the communion of the visible Church' (p. 431). With hindsight, we can see that this does not close, but rather leaves open, the issue. Tyrrell later leaves latitude for a person who finds the Church 'locally *or intellectually* inaccessible' (p. 434) to find salvation by direct incorporation into the invisible Mystical Body.[8]

Intellectual doubt about the grounding of Catholicism was not yet a serious issue for Tyrrell, but he was drawing close to the time of radical doubt. In *Hard Sayings* he does not transgress the bounds of contemporary orthodoxy. His fundamental vision is one of the organic unity of truth:

Truth, however seemingly many-membered, as apprehended piecemeal by us, in itself is one and simple. Let a single article of the Catholic creed be tampered with, and the whole fabric crumbles to ruin. (pp. 167–8)

Nevertheless, he is already flirting with the liberal reduction of Catholic doctrine that will shortly be forced upon him by what he will take to be the 'assured results' of New Testament criticism. In the same book he writes,

The history of the Christian era has been the history of the development of the dogma of the Fatherhood of God and the brotherhood of all men in Christ. (p. 333)

The attempt to reconcile this reductionist position with that of 'the integrity of Catholic truth', under the pressure of historical scepticism, is one to which the last ten years of Tyrrell's life were devoted. However much he capitulated to the doctrinal reductionism of Harnack and Arnold, he always maintained the vision of the Mystical Body. Before the vision had been too drastically split from what could be held to be historically founded in the teaching of Jesus and the self-understanding of the early Church, he wrote of the Church, 'Our faith in her is the effect of an impression produced on our mind and heart by her whole concrete reality' (p. 439). Even if the intellectual façade crumbled, the living structure would stand firm.

This organic vision for the wholeness of the living Church, for its continuity with Christ and for the integrity of its self-expression in the Creeds carries a number of important implications. Implicit in Tyrrell's ecclesiology, though not yet stressed, is the understanding that it is the whole Church which is the heir to Christ, the whole Church in which the living Christ speaks by his Spirit. Thus, Tyrrell wrote to Wilfrid Ward in March 1900,

I wish you wouldn't make the theologians an essential factor in the Church's life. I think it is rather in the subconsciousness of the faithful at large that God's spirit works.[9]

In *External Religion*, a series of conferences delivered in 1899, he took the same line with respect to the current distinction between *Ecclesia docens* and *Ecclesia discens*:

Some would almost seem to think that as we distinguish the *Ecclesia docens* from the *Ecclesia discens*, the Church teaching from the Church taught; so we should distinguish the Church active and militant, from the Church passive and quiescent; the former body being identical with the clergy and the latter with the laity – the clergy labouring and rowing; the laity simply paying their fare and sitting idly as so much ballast in the bark of Peter. Plainly this is a most false and pernicious analogy.   (ER pp. 123–4)

In *Hard Sayings* Tyrrell applies his thinking to the position of the clergy: 'The Catholic priest...is but the Church's delegate' (p. 404). He talks of 'the Christian republic not merely of today, but of the ages past', and when he talks of the Church who has sent this priest, 'whose mouthpiece he is' (p. 405) he means the whole Church, laity included, not just the Bishops. This is fundamental to his ecclesiology.

The issue of authority in the Church is not yet discussed formally, though Tyrrell's growing discomfort is evident in his private correspondence for 1899. In May he wrote to von Hügel, 'I confess I never felt my position more incongruous; but after all it is to the principles of an institution and not to their misapplication or denial that one is pledged in joining it.'[10] In giving advice to Bremond about his final vows, in the row over 'A Perverted Devotion', which blew up in early 1900, in his own problems with the hierarchy and with 'Jesuitism' generally, Tyrrell increasingly had recourse to the principles or spirit of the institution rather than their current application. Already, his organic view of society carried with it an outline position on the nature and function of authority:

The few are for the many and not the many for the few; the rich are for the poor and not the poor for the rich; the gifted for the needy and not the needy for the gifted. (HS p. 269)

This applies pre-eminently in the Church, but naturally in society as a whole:

In the mystical body of Christ [the Church] finds the archetype of all society, whose unity she accordingly concludes to be rather that of a living organism than that of an artificial aggregate of independent units bound to one another by the force of self-interest. (p. 242)

This will be the area of overlap with Arnold's view of society.

External Religion builds upon the ecclesiology we have outlined. Here Tyrrell is dealing with the '"Extension of the Incarnation" in the Church and in the individual' (p. 1). Again, 'the hierarchic visible Church' is regarded as 'the sacrament, the outward and effectual sign of that invisible union in Christ of all souls in Heaven and on earth, in whom the love of Divine goodness holds the first place' (p. 56). Again there is the *caveat* that will soon prove so significant,

To be organically incorporated with the visible Church as its member, is, *for those whom* ignorance or impossibility does not excuse, a *sine qua non* of incorporation into the communion of saints.[11] (p. 56)

Within the visible communion of saints there is a kind of 'clerisy', the educated *majores*,[12] whose function is 'steadily and quietly to check the growth of superstition; just as' — and here Tyrrell draws close to Arnold and also shows himself a man of his time — 'it is the function of the better classes in society to maintain standards of good taste and good judgment in a thousand matters, and so resist the downward influence of the uncritical majority' (p. 118). However, this in no way derogates from the essential position of the laity in the Church:

The layman is not a mere civilian in the *Civitas Dei*; for the Church is altogether and perpetually a militant state; and her victory requires and is measured by the exertion of each single one of her members, from the greatest to the least. (p. 125)

It is important to recognise that for Tyrrell the layman plays an essential part not only in the prosecution of the truth but in determination of the truth.[13] In 'The Relation of Theology to Devotion' (*The Month*, 94 (1899), 461–73; FM1 pp. 228–52), which von Hügel welcomed as 'the finest thing you have yet done',[14] Tyrrell makes the important distinction between 'the concrete language of revelation' and 'the abstract character of certain theological conclusions', which are secondary and inevitably to some extent artificial. The Christian 'deposit'[15] should be sought not in the words of the latter (as he had formerly maintained) but in the mental concepts that constitute the former:

This 'deposit' of faith, this concrete, coloured, imaginative expression of Divine mysteries, as it lay in the mind of the first recipients, is both the *lex orandi* and *lex credendi*.   (*The Month*, 94, p. 467)

Tyrrell's position is further elaborated a little later:

The 'deposit' of faith is not merely a symbol or creed, but it is a concrete religion left by Christ to His Church; it is perhaps in some sense more directly a *lex orandi* than a *lex credendi*; the creed is involved in the prayer, and has to be disentangled from it; and formularies are ever to be tested and explained by the concrete religion which they formulate.[16]   (p. 473)

For Tyrrell it always remained of cardinal importance that 'God has revealed Himself, not to the wise and prudent, not to the theologian or the philosopher, but to babes, to fishermen, to peasants, to the *profanum vulgus*' (p. 466). If one wants to know what God has revealed, the witness of the *whole Church* must be taken into account.

Tyrrell's view of 'the deposit' underwent a rapid change between 1899 and 1901. In 'Authority and Evolution, the Life of Catholic Dogma', which appeared in *The Month* for May 1899, he wrote,

To the Catholic, the language and symbolism in which Christ clothed His revelation was divinely chosen and approved...as conveying as much of the truths of eternity as we are capable of receiving in our present embryonic state of intellectual development. Every letter of that deposit is therefore treasured.   (*The Month*, 93, p. 496)

Just over a year later, Tyrrell wrote two articles on 'The Mind of the Church' in which he clearly changed his position:

Thus by the 'deposit of faith' we do not mean any primitive document, nor yet that expression which the faith received in the mind of its first hearers; but the present-day expression of the faith, in which that former expression is at once lost and preserved as the child is in the man.   (*The Month*, 96 (1900), 237)

He adds the important rider, 'And the recipient of this deposit is the collective Mind of the Church' – bishops, priests, laity are all on a level.[17] By the time the article was reprinted in *The Faith of the Millions* Tyrrell had changed his position again.[18] Now he wrote:

Thus by the 'deposit of faith' we do not mean any primitive document, nor yet that expression which the faith received in the mind of its first hearers: nor yet the present-day expression of the faith, in which that former expression is at once lost and preserved as the child is in the man; but rather, those truths and realities which were expressed and seen less perfectly in earlier forms, more perfectly in later – as though viewed through an ever clearer and more transparent medium.   (FM1 p. 199)

In two years Tyrrell moved from considering the deposit of faith as the mental and verbal expression of the faith, to regarding it as the truths and realities themselves which were expressed.[19] This is a momentous shift. Now he argued that what the Church must guard is not words, not symbols, not even ideas, but what those words, symbols and ideas conveyed in the beginning and, hopefully (Tyrrell was obviously more sanguine than Arnold), continue to convey – a living Spirit. The Newmanlike empiricism[20] is by-passed; the balance between past and present shifts in favour of the present; the focus changes from the particularity of the original expression to the generality of what has always been expressed; the way is open to the radical bifurcation of religion and science. This important shift, in which Tyrrell drew far closer to Arnold and entered his most liberal phase, nevertheless left *the form* of his ecclesiology untouched. His ideal, though now cut loose from history, remained that of the Mystical Body. The gulf between the ideal and the real Church was to be emphasised for him in the ecclesiastical storms that broke about his head.

On 29 December 1900, the Bishops of England and Wales published a Joint-Pastoral Letter against liberal Catholicism.[21] It was in effect a call for unquestioning obedience to the hierarchy based on an ecclesiology that Tyrrell cordially loathed:

Two orders of persons, therefore, constitute, by the design of Christ, the visible Church. The small body of chosen men, assisted by the Holy Ghost, who represent the authority of Jesus Christ; and the large body of the faithful taught, guided and guarded by the Divine Teacher, speaking through the audible voice of the smaller body. Theologians call the one the *Ecclesia docens*, the other the *Ecclesia discens*.[22]

The *Ecclesia docens* originally consisted of Peter and the apostles, and afterwards the Pope and the Bishops in communion with him. They are 'in supreme command of the flock'.[23] The *Ecclesia discens* consists not only of the laity but also of ecclesiastics and even bishops 'in their individual and private capacity'.[24] The Church as Divine Teacher speaks through the Popes and the Bishops. What is not made clear is how the Popes and the Bishops arrive at their authoritative teaching. Nevertheless, the Joint-Pastoral was a clear enunciation of just that ecclesiology that Tyrrell had pilloried in *External Religion*, and in a fury he set about attacking it again.

Tyrrell's irate reaction was expressed in private correspondence, in letters to periodicals, and in an important article to which Lord Halifax agreed to put his name.[25] For nine months Tyrrell kept up the assault. He wrote to von Hügel:

The bishops have mounted on metaphors as witches on broomsticks and have ridden to the devil. It is the 'sheep and shepherd' metaphor that does the trick. The sheep are brainless, passive; their part is to be led, fed, fleeced and slain for the profit of the shepherd for whose benefit solely they exist.[26]

In a letter to *The Pilot* he complained that the theory implied in the Joint-Pastoral 'would destroy the organic unity of the Church by putting the Pope (or the *Ecclesia Docens*) outside and over the Church, not a part of her, but her partner, spouse, and Lord, in a sense proper to Christ alone'.[27] Such teaching was historically and theologically indefensible. It was the ugly fruit of a process that restricted the infallibility of the whole Church first to the Bishops and then to the Pope himself: '*L'Église c'est moi* is literally the Pope's attitude' (AL2 p. 160).

In an editorial that he wrote for *The Weekly Register* Tyrrell laid out the two positions side by side. His own 'amended Gallicanism' (which he could not defend explicitly in the editorial) he defined as

a somewhat democratic and complex conception of ecclesiastical polity, as contrasted with the simplicity of that monarchic conception which is just what drives into the Church those who are wearied with the unworkableness of so vague and unwieldy a rule of faith as that of ecumenical consensus.[28]

It was the view that we have already seen developed in his early work: the *whole Church* in its organic unity is heir to the promise and the authority of Christ. The title 'amended Gallicanism' was deliberately provocative. Tyrrell saw in Gallicanism proper[29] a valid protest against 'monarchical absolutism' but one which did not go far enough (AL2 p. 156). He fought for nothing less than a concept of authority based on the conception of the whole Church as the Mystical Body of Christ.

The controversy over the Joint-Pastoral Letter helped Tyrrell find a clear theoretical base for his later course *vis à vis* Church authority, which was essentially that of staying in even when the Church authorities wanted to push him out. Though he fell into disgrace, he would never leave the Roman Church of his own accord, and even when pushed out would remain a Catholic *in spe*. Since the visible Church, which remained for Tyrrell the sacrament of the Mystical Body, proclaimed its own nature and origin in a way that would ultimately preclude Tyrrell's own membership, he needed to develop his understanding of both the visible and the invisible Church. In *The Church and the Future* he tried to adapt his ecclesiology to the Biblical and historical issues that the Church as a whole would not face.

The key to his position is his conviction that it is the '"Spirit" of Christ which is the true "*depositum fidei*"' (CF p. 77)[30] – not a series of propositions, or even mental impressions, but an unchanging Spirit. This Spirit is evident in the life of the whole Church:

It is in Christendom collectively, and in its whole continuity, that its content and meaning are gradually spread out and developed, as it were, in the mystical body whereof Christ is the Head; more especially in the Saints and Masters of the Art of Charity, yet also in sinners and penitents and mediocrities. (CF p. 74)

It is the Spirit that provides the continuity between the life of Christ and the developed life and doctrine of the Church today:

It is not then precisely as a creation of Christ that Catholicism can claim to be divinely instituted, but as the creation of that Spirit which created both Christ and the Church to be different and complementary organs of its own expression, adapted to different phases of the same movement. (CF p. 64)

The living organ of this Spirit is the 'mind of the Church', which is expressed in the utterances of general councils. The test that such utterances do reflect the mind of the Church is not juridical but practical – their acceptance in the life of the faithful as expressive of the consensus.[31] The function of the Pope and the Bishops in Council is to mirror more explicitly to the faithful the truths by which they already live. If their statements must be subjected to the popular consensus, this applies *a fortiori* to the statements of those prophetic individuals (like George Tyrrell) who claim to be able to discern how the Spirit is working in the Body:

The *Sensus fidelium* is the rule to which each individual must be conformed, and by which even the prophets must be judged when they claim to have fully assimilated and transcended that rule in any particular point, or to have experienced and found expression for some new development and manifestation of the spirit of Christ. (CF p. 131)

However sound theoretically, the position is beset with practical difficulties. How can one identify the *sensus fidelium* if the Pope and Bishops no longer speak for it? As Tyrrell wrestles with this, he sounds less and less recognisably Roman Catholic:

As long therefore as the liberal Catholic believes himself to be in communion with the spirit of the whole Church, he need not trouble himself about the views of her officers for the time being, unless in some matter obedience to them would put him in a false position.[32] (CF pp. 142–3)

What price now communion with the visible Church? The balance seems to have swung in favour of communion with the invisible Church, in other words towards the individual conscience as opposed to what is presented as the expression of the corporate conscience. It is a measure of Tyrrell's loss of confidence in the Pope and the Bishops. The difficulty of the position is manifest. There is, for the disaffected 'liberal Catholic', no objective criterion of conformity to the Spirit and his professions of loyalty to the *consensu fidelium*, the actual expression of which he challenges, begin to sound extremely erratic. Arnold, the prophet of culture, faces exactly the same theoretical difficulty.[33] In fact it was more acute for him than for Tyrrell: to what norm could he appeal in criticising the culture of his day? When Tyrrell saw how close his position had become to that of the Liberal Protestant, he shifted his ground yet again.[34]

By the time he wrote the introduction to *Through Scylla and Charybdis*, Tyrrell saw the position he had formerly reached on revelation as a perilous one. He called it 'not a deeper and clearer explanation of the patristic notion, but another notion altogether' (TSC p. 10), since the patristic appeal had always been not to present experience but to a revelation in the past. In fidelity to the traditional stance, Tyrrell again accepted that there was a 'form of sound words' which could be called 'the deposit' (p. 86). However, he would never go back to seeing those words as being, as it were, specifically revealed. They were the primitive, instinctive choice of those men who had experienced the revelation of God in Christ. He now regarded the apostolic 'form of sound words',

not as a reflex, thought-out life-theory, but as the spontaneous self-expression of a profound religious experience; as a prophetic vision of the Kingdom of God directed to the orientation of the spiritual life, and enshrining a mysterious truth independent of those other truths used for its illustration.   (TSC p. 11)

The truth of the words is not scientific, nor is it poetic, but 'prophetic' – that is to say, if it is accepted and followed in life, it will produce conformity to the Divine Will. The purpose of the writings is pragmatic, not rationally informative. The revelation is the experience of God, but revelation can only be recognised as such if its prophetic expression conforms to the apostolic norm, and the test of this conformity is ultimately pragmatic – successive prophetic expressions of the same are informed by the original, normative expression and produce the same sanctity of life. The notion of 'prophetic truth', which Tyrrell had developed by 1904, and explicitly applied to the whole of Scripture, is thus an attempt to find his way between the literal and the 'poetic' functions of language.[35] He explained what he meant in *Lex Orandi*, and provided a commentary in the letters to Abbé Venard given in the appendix. This notion of 'prophetic truth' is the key to his mature view of religious language. It is this that allowed him to pick up again theological notions that he had discarded as literally meaningless or mistaken; now he returned to them in a new sense. Against this background, he redefined his allegiance to Catholicism.

From the time that he wrote *The Church and the Future* Tyrrell had obviously been troubled about the ethics of conformity.[36] The position became not better but worse, and some time between 1904 and 1906 he wrote,

As, one by one, the claims of the hierarchic Church dissolve under criticism, and as our attitude towards the official and theological defenders of those claims becomes one of opposition and indignant protest...we are driven more and more to content ourselves with a sense of spiritual communion with all lovers and martyrs of truth and conscience throughout the world in all ages, present, past and to come. (EFI p. 115)

The mistake had been to take the visible Church 'for the substance, whereof it is but the shadow or sacrament'. However, the position he was forced to take up as a 'liberal Catholic' appeared to the conservative more than self-contradictory. It was positively dishonest and disloyal. In some lengthy 'Reflections on Catholicism', published in *Through Scylla and Charybdis*, Tyrrell defends himself.

In this essay Tyrrell examines Catholicism not theologically but as 'a living concrete reality' (p. 73) or 'a living social organism' (p. 74). By now his theory of a functioning social organism had become more clearly defined. He had worked it out in *Religion as a Factor of Life* and developed its application in *Lex Orandi* and *Lex Credendi* together with numerous other letters, notes and jottings. From his long struggle with the inter-relation of mysticism, dogma and ethics comes a concise statement like this:

If our religion, our Christianity, is alive and growing, it must necessarily be ever evolving a complex system of feelings, determined by and determining an equally complex system of judgments, fructifying in a correspondingly complex system of impulses. (p. 38)

As we shall see, this account of a dynamic system is very close to the Arnoldian view of society, where 'culture' precisely corresponds to Tyrrell's 'complex system of judgments'. This convergence may seem surprising, since Tyrrell is explicitly defending Catholicism. However, we shall also see the extent to which Arnold expressed his sympathy for Catholicism – not as a dogmatic system, but as a historical religion, which is just the approach that Tyrrell takes in this essay.

For Tyrrell Catholicism is 'divine with the divinity of a natural process' (p. 77). Religion is a natural expression of human life and Catholicism is a religion among religions. Echoing Arnold, he describes Catholicism as having given 'a mystical and religious depth to ethical requirements' so that they are recognised as being the very 'Will of the Eternal' (p. 28; also p. 273). Catholicism transcends other religions because it is a 'religion of the whole man, body, soul, and spirit...that...makes us sensible of our solidarity with, and dependence on, the whole of humanity' (pp. 28–9). It is not a perfected but an ever-emergent synthesis. We can see here Tyrrell's clear identification of the natural with the immanent working of God, and based on this, the position that he will take on the fulfilment of the religions of the world in a 'transcendent Catholicism'. Catholicism is not superimposed on the religions or the civilisations of the world. A synthesis itself, 'it enters as an organic part into the whole process of civilisation with its multitudinous interests' (p. 29).

Catholicism is never static. The overall picture is one of organic growth and unity, but the underlying mechanism is that of uninhibited conflict. 'God in Nature works slowly and surely through the unimpeded struggle of opposites' (p. 26). Such 'warring interests' may be found in the individual body, the body politic, the Mystical Body:

In Catholicism we find the competing claims of [man's] intellect, his feelings, his heart, his senses asserting themselves more or less discordantly and, as it were, fighting their way towards an unattainable ideal of harmonious agreement.[37]

(p. 29)

This is exactly what happened with the pagan religion of Rome and the leaven of the Gospel, which never, anyway, existed in its pure form but always as a kind of reformed Judaism, or reformed paganism. It is the error of Protestantism to attempt to distil an unattainable essence of the Gospel and ignore the human forms of religious expression it has already leavened. Tyrrell stood with Erasmus and not with Luther. Catholicism does not break continuity with the past.[38] It looks for evolution rather than revolution. 'Nature does nothing in jumps' (p. 58).

Where then does one hear the voice of God calling his people on? For Tyrrell, the principle of authority is essential to Catholicism, and it turns on 'the subjection of the individual mind, will, and sentiment in matters of religion to the collective mind, will and sentiment of the community' (p. 58).[39] This he has often discussed, but he now speaks of it in a dialectical way that is sharply reminiscent of Arnold. 'It is the voice of the people, and not that of the populace, which is the voice of God' (p. 59), and, a little later, 'for those truths which are reached by reflection and inference, general consent is the worst possible guide' (p. 80). We are back with the problem of the prophet and the consensus. Tyrrell is not daunted:

The general life of a permanent community gives birth to a complex body of opinions, sentiments, and practical attitudes in regard to a thousand matters. In this body we can distinguish between the average and the best and the worst.

(p. 59)

Arnold thought so too. Tyrrell then goes on to talk of education 'under the influence of the very best that has been thought, and felt, and spoken, and written on every subject' (p. 60). These are Arnold's thoughts in Arnold's words. He appeals from the Church as it is to the Church as it will be through the influence of a vanguard of liberal Catholics[40] just as Arnold appeals from the nation as it is to the nation as it will be through the influence of the culturally enlightened.

In this essay Tyrrell does not concern himself with the historical issues raised by New Testament criticism. It is rather the process of history that interests him, drawing him into Arnold's orbit. On the specific history of Jesus he was moving farther away from Liberal Protestantism than ever. By the time he wrote *Christianity at the Crossroads* he had re-read Weiss and Schweitzer, and the renewed focus on Jesus as an apocalyptic prophet led him to write that 'Whatever Jesus was, He was in no sense a Liberal Protestant' (p. xxi). Nevertheless, Tyrrell's view of religion in general and Catholicism as a religion did not change. This is evident in the last section of the book where he discusses Catholicism and world religion, seeing in Catholicism the best hope for an emergent world religion based on the scientific study of the laws of religion in general.[41] However, he now stresses again and again the sheer strangeness of Catholic teaching, with its eschatological content and apocalyptic imagery, and he takes a stand against all reductionist accounts of such doctrine, calling for 'a frank admission of the principle of symbolism' (p. 103).[42]

In the context of Jesus's apocalyptic teaching Tyrrell acknowledges that the Church is to be seen as continuous with 'the "little flock", awaiting and preparing for the Kingdom' (p. 95). He maintains a firm hold on the historical continuity of Church tradition. In the context of his discussion of world religions, he returns to the imagery of the Mystical Body: 'Through the mystical body, animated by the Spirit, we are brought into immediate contact with the ever present Christ' (p. 275). Once more we have the stress on the organic unity of the Church; once more it is spoken of as sacrament. The Church is 'not merely a society or school' (p. 275) as it would be for the Liberal Protestant, but 'a mystery and sacrament: like the humanity of Christ of which it is an extension' (p. 275). This is exactly what Tyrrell had taught in his early books. His theological categories had not altered. What had altered was his understanding of theology as a whole, and how it was to be related to history. He now saw in the development of Catholicism not the evidence of a divine master-plan, or even a human one. It was 'the work of instinct and experience, rather than of design directed by a recognition of the laws of religion' (p. 279). Instinct and experience had served well in the past, though not, as the present was showing, well enough. It was for design, based on scientific observation and understanding, to serve even better in the future.[43]

Matthew Arnold's understanding of the Church had been developed in a profoundly different religious environment from that of George Tyrrell. The dominant influence of his father remained with him, however much he might reject his father's specific interpretation of belief, or might acknowledge his debt to Newman.[44] Writing to his mother on his father's birthday in 1869, he said, 'On the whole, I think of the main part of what I have done, and am doing, as work which he would have approved and seen to be indispensable' (*Letters* I p. 392).

Thomas Arnold frequently reiterated his belief in a national Church as an expression of the religious identity of the nation. He wanted a Church broad enough to include all shades of opinion, whatever modifications of Church of England doctrine this might entail. This was the very opposite of the purist and exclusive Tractarian position. Where the Tractarians fought for the independence (though not the disestablishment) of the Church, Arnold saw the Church as simply the Christian State in its religious aspect: 'Religious society is only civil society fully enlightened: the State in its highest perfection becomes the Church.'[45] He wrote of 'that great doctrine of the King's supremacy' which

declares the identity of the Church and State, when each has attained to its perfection; both desire to effect man's greatest good; but the Church during her imperfect state is deficient in power; – the State in the like condition is deficient in knowledge...But when blended into one, the power and knowledge become happily united; the Church is become sovereign, and the State has become Christian.[46]

This, of course, was an ideal; the reality in 1835 was very different:

But now, the true and grand idea of a Church, that is, a society for the purpose of making men like Christ, – earth like heaven, – the kingdoms of the world the kingdom of Christ, – is all lost; and men look upon it as 'an institution for religious instruction and religious worship', thus robbing it of its life and universality, making it an affair of clergy, not of people – of preaching and ceremonies, not of living – of Sundays and synagogues, instead of one of all days and all places, houses, streets, towns, and country.[47]

The sad state of the established Church was his reason for writing *Principles of Church Reform*, which appeared in the same year that Keble preached his Assize Sermon. Where Keble's call (the 'first word' of the Oxford Movement)[48] was essentially conservative, a defensive manifesto against 'National Apostasy' apparently led by the government, Arnold was pleading for 'a Church thoroughly national, thoroughly united, thoroughly Christian, which should allow great varieties of opinion, and of ceremonies, and forms of worship'.[49] In this way, the dissenters (though not the Quakers, Roman Catholics or Unitarians) might be comprehended, the Establishment strengthened, the State christianised. What he wanted was an organically united society, securely based on Christian principles expressed in the whole life of the nation. The distinction between 'sacred' and 'secular' would then be abolished.[50] Arnold stressed the Pauline image of the Church as the body of Christ.[51] He was totally opposed to the Tractarian stress on priesthood, whilst recognising the need for 'government' in the Church. Within the Church there could be no first- and second-class citizens. He wanted the whole national Church – the Christian State or Kingdom seen from the point of view of its Christianity – to be a particular realisation of that international Church, 'the Communion of all living Christians'.[52]

Much of this Matthew Arnold took from his father. When he read Stanley's *Life* of Dr Arnold, he wrote to his mother, 'On questions of Church, and of religious belief, (wishing only that he had sometimes begun a little further back) I could not have believed I should find anything to enjoy so fully and so fully to go along with.'[53] He and his father shared the same ideal of a Church, 'a great national society for the promotion of what is commonly called *goodness*' (S VIII (LE) p. 65), that would be organically one with the life of the nation. He shared his father's concern for the whole life of the nation, political, social and cultural, with a special concern for education. He wrote to his mother, 'I never touch on considerations about *the State* without feeling myself on his ground' (*Letters* I p. 381). Like his father, he was implacably and insensitively opposed to dissent. However, since the time of his father, the whole religious situation had changed. Although no believer in verbal inspiration, Thomas Arnold trusted the Biblical narratives almost naively. For him the Gospel history 'was the most interesting *fact* that has ever happened'.[54] For Matthew, the 'fact' was obscured by a layer of tiresome *Aberglaube* that had to be stripped away by the discerning critic. Nevertheless he was in essence simply extending his father's treatment of Scripture far beyond anything dreamt of in the previous generation.[55] Matthew's vision of the function of the Church in society came from his father, the man who brought 'such a torrent of freshness into English religion by placing history and politics in connection with it' (*Letters* I p. 311). He revered his father as 'the last free speaker of the Church of England clergy' (*Letters* I p. 177). Since he was not ordained he saw himself as that much freer to continue his father's unfinished work of social and theological criticism.

Matthew Arnold's own position on the Church is clearly articulated in a number of his essays, though it is never undergirded with explicit Scriptural references as was his father's. Like his father, he was indebted to Hooker and Coleridge, and in a number of ways he simply repeated his father's views. However, there also developed in him a sympathy towards the Roman Catholic Church that his father never had, for he saw in the functioning of the Catholic Church qualities complementary to those he found in the Establishment. Matthew Arnold never discussed in theoretical terms the functioning of the Mystical Body, but his thought is always informed by the organic ideal, something that must have been congenial to Tyrrell.

In February 1876, Arnold lectured on 'The Church of England' to an audience of London clergy (S VIII (LE) pp. 63–86). It cannot have been easy for the author of *Literature and Dogma* to stand before an audience of clergymen and speak in defence of the Church of England. However, Arnold wrote to his sister that he was 'much pleased' by his reception and that the address would 'do good by directing attention to substantials' (*Letters* II p. 128). This was really what he had tried to do in his theological books, and he had thereby given the impression of being an outspoken liberal. When he speaks about 'substantials' with reference to the Church of England, his line sounds like a most curious mixture of the radical and the conservative.

He stresses that the Church of England is 'a great national society for the promotion of what is commonly called *goodness*' (p. 65) and that since it is a national institution its cause is not simply that of the clergy but of the whole community. The promotion of 'goodness' is of vital importance to the whole nation – too important a matter to be left to private bodies, such as the dissenters, or to a particular grouping, like the clergy. In the current agitation for disestablishment Arnold finds one particularly disturbing feature: the alienation from the Church of England of those working-class leaders who are anxious for social and political reform. Arnold condemns the traditional alliance between the squirearchy and the Establishment in no uncertain terms: 'The Church shares and serves the prejudices of rank and property, instead of contending with them' (p. 74). His whole view of the Church as a national institution leads him to conclude that, 'It is necessary for the Church, if it is to live, that it should carry the working classes with it' (p. 75). This it will do if it recovers its vision for the Kingdom of God as a radical transformation of existing social circumstances. However, if Arnold recalls the Church to its revolutionary manifesto ('there is certainly communism in the Bible' (p. 72)) he also invests a good deal in the 'downrightness, plain honesty, integrity' (p. 80) of the English character, which resists deceit in religious matters and desires 'to get at the real truth' (p. 81). In effect he says, aiming his remarks over the heads of the listening clergy towards the dissenters, 'Do not judge the Church of England by its dubious record in promoting "goodness", but by the aspirations of individuals.' (He has Butler in mind at this point.) What Arnold preaches is a kind of inchoate Christian socialism, based on the vision of the Kingdom of God as realised in a national Church. His social observation is acute, his failure to understand the dissenters total, his reliance on keywords like 'goodness', 'grace' and 'peace' a frustration to all those who want to bring what he is saying into a sharp focus.

Arnold is the more confident in the Church of England because of its historical tradition. He wrote in a letter to M. Fontanès of his 'faiblesse pour les religions historiques' (*Letters* II p. 146). He speaks of the 'historic Church of England, not existing for special opinions but proceeding by development' (S VI (SPP) p. 85). He calls it a 'living thing' (p. 96) and praises its Englishness:

> The Church of England was meant, in the intention of those who settled it at the Reformation, to satisfy the whole English people and to be accepted by them. It was meant to include both Catholics and Protestants in a compromise between old and new, rejecting Romish corruptions and errors, but retaining from Catholicism all that was sound and truly attaching...The Church of England, in offering its formularies to Englishmen, offers them with the recommendation that here is truth presented expressly so as to suit and unite the English nation.
> (S VIII (LE) p. 95)

In a letter to his sister Arnold called the Church of England 'the one Protestant Church which maintained its connection with the past' (*Letters* II p. 131). It was to him, 'a great and imposing institution...for the higher spiritual life and culture of the nation' (S XI p. 341).

It can be seen that Arnold's conception of the Church, since it is implicitly controlled by the organic metaphor, is ambiguous in its expression of democracy. In words that look forward to Tyrrell's assault on the Joint-Pastoral Letter of 1900, he writes,

> Who are really the Church? Evidently the whole religious society, and not its ministers only. The ministers exist for the sake of the community to which they minister; the clergy are for the people, not the people for the clergy.
> (S VII p. 118)

On the other hand, he also sees the need for a 'clerisy' within society as a whole:

> We have always said that in this country the functions of a disinterested literary class — a class of non-political writers, having no organised and embodied set of supporters to please, simply setting themselves to observe and report faithfully, and looking for favour to those isolated persons only, scattered all through the community, whom such an attempt may interest — are of incalculable importance.
> (S VII p. 92)

These are the cultured élite who raise the tone and temper of the general life of the nation. Arnold followed Coleridge in making it clear that they were not to be identified with the clergy but 'the whole body of men of letters or science' (S III (EC1) p. 51).

Arnold's thinking on the Church, whether the Church of England or the Roman Catholic Church (of which we shall say more later) only becomes explicit after he had written *Culture and Anarchy*. However, his concept of 'culture', that most slippery of his terms, is best approached via his ideas on society and the establishment. Although he rarely discusses the two together, Arnold's concepts of the Church and of 'culture' are stereoscopic. The two come into focus when organically related in the life of the Christian nation. The national Church exists to promote 'goodness' (the practical, moral life); 'culture' (the reflective critique of the life that is lived) works towards the same end, though not in a narrowly hebraistic way. Arnold writes of culture as 'the study of perfection' and claims that such study leads us 'to conceive of true human perfection as a *harmonious* perfection, developing all sides of our humanity; and as a *general* perfection, developing all parts of our society. For if one member suffer, the other members must suffer with it' (S V (CA) p. 235). The Pauline metaphor of the Body is never very far away when Arnold writes of 'culture'.

'Culture' is bound to support establishments, because it is a religious establishment that fosters and expresses 'totality': 'One may say that to be reared a member of a national Church is in itself a lesson of religious moderation, and a help towards culture and harmonious perfection' (S V (CA) p. 239). To be a member of an establishment is to stand within a spiritual and intellectual tradition:

Instead of battling for his own private forms for expressing the inexpressible and defining the undefinable, a man takes those which have commended themselves most to the religious life of his nation. (S V (CA) p. 239)

All this the nonconformists lack, whereas,

Establishments tend to give us a sense of a historical life of the human spirit, outside and beyond our own fancies and feelings...they give us leisure and calm to steady our view of religion itself...and to enlarge our first crude notions of the one thing needful. (S V (CA) pp. 243–4)

That is to say, establishments do not just promote 'goodness' (as the nonconformists in their hebraistic zeal tend to do) but they promote 'goodness' and 'culture'; morality with balanced critical reflection. It is important to Arnold that such reflection takes place within a tradition that has a lengthy history, and embraces all members of a society.

The religious basis of Arnold's concept of 'culture' is half concealed by the way in which he addresses himself to particular problems of his fragmented society. His vision is profoundly humanistic. He does not call men out of society, but he calls on society to become itself – a transformation to be promoted by the cultured clerisy. It is typical of Arnold to take a Biblical text – 'Estote ergo vos perfecti' – as an epigraph to *Culture and Anarchy*, and there can be little doubt that he sees his work as a serious attempt to apply the Biblical injunction to his own society. However, the England of his time is riven by discord and dissent. It is a society urgently in need of harmony.

The first requirement is courage to face the situation as it is, and then breadth of vision to see what it might be. Then there must be an intelligent application of that understanding towards the betterment of the common life. 'Culture' is what the well-stocked mind brings to such a process of critical reflection, and it is the process of reflection itself, not as a detached, intellectual activity, but as an active and committed movement towards the betterment of society. Arnold is looking for a quality of intelligent commitment that he finds neither in the Christians, whether the hebraistic dissenters or the torpid establishment, nor amongst the barbarian aristocracy, the natural initiators of change, nor amongst the philistine free-traders of the middle class, and certainly not in the uneducated populace. His ideal was one that would bring these disparate religious and social groupings into one. He was talking about both an attitude and an activity. His first term was 'criticism' – as in 'The Function of Criticism at the Present Time'. His second was 'culture'. A third was 'civilisation'.

Arnold has been criticised for the way in which he depicted the relation of culture and religion, apparently making religion a department of culture.[56] One classic expression of this criticism is that of T. S. Eliot:

> Arnold gives the impression that Culture (as he uses the term) is something more comprehensive than religion; that the latter is no more than a necessary element, supplying ethical formation and some emotional colour, to Culture which is the ultimate value.[57]

There are times when Arnold gives precisely this impression. For example, he writes,

> Culture, disinterestedly seeking in its aim at perfection to see things as they really are, shows us how worthy and divine a thing is the religious side in man, though it is not the whole of man.   (S V (CA) p. 252)

At other times it is clear that Arnold's criticism is not intended to put religion as such in its place, but the narrow practice of religion which he calls Hebraism. Arnold is feeling for a term that will express his vision for the integrated fulfilment of the individual and of society. The term 'religion' is denied him because of what it connotes in the society of his time; a term like 'perfection' is not so limited. In working for a balanced ideal, says Arnold, 'culture goes beyond religion, *as religion is generally conceived by us*' (S V (CA) p. 94).[58] The qualification is all-important.

The religious nature of the critique applied by 'culture' is clear as soon as one begins to examine Arnold's choice of words at all closely. For example, Arnold says that culture turns 'a stream of fresh and free thought upon our stock notions and habits' (S V (CA) p. 233). This was just what he saw his

father as having done, when he called him 'the last free speaker of the Church
of England clergy' (*Letters* I p. 177), and said that his greatness consisted 'in
bringing such a torrent of freshness into English religion' (*Letters* I p. 311).
He also said of 'perfection' that it was not possible while the individual
remained isolated:

The individual is required...to carry others along with him in his march towards
perfection, to be continually doing all he can to enlarge and increase the volume
of the human stream sweeping thitherward.   (S V (CA) p. 94)

Over a decade earlier he wrote of his father that what made him great was
'that he was not only a good man saving his own soul by righteousness, but
that he carried so many others with him in his hand, and saved them, if they
would let him, along with himself' (*Letters* I p. 42). This is also the theme
of 'Rugby Chapel' (especially lines 124–7, 140–4) where Dr Arnold as Good
Shepherd develops into a Christ figure of sorts. The point indicated by such
precise verbal echoes is this: for Matthew Arnold the epitome of the cultured
man was not the 'gentleman' of Newman's *Idea of a University*, not, as David
DeLaura thinks, Newman himself,[59] but a figure no less *religious* than
Newman: his own father. Never would Dr Arnold have accepted that religion
at its best was but an element in any higher synthesis, but he would have agreed
that religion 'as religion is generally conceived' is a very one-sided affair.

At this point we can glance back to the work of George Tyrrell. In *Religion
as a Factor of Life* Tyrrell dealt with this same issue: the place of 'religion'
in the perfecting of the whole man. Whilst he explicitly rejects Arnold's
'sentimentalism' – he mistakenly thinks that for Arnold the function of
religion was merely to awaken certain aesthetic emotions (p. 4) – he actually
draws quite close to Arnold without knowing it. Tyrrell recognises explicitly
'religious' activity or language to be a clearly defined area of activity of
language in general, but at the same time acknowledges that true religion must
permeate the whole of life. So he speaks of religion as the 'head' which
regulates the whole 'body' of our will-life. In what he takes to be opposition
to Matthew Arnold he writes,

Thus we conclude that religion is not the mere 'religionising' of conduct by
ethical reflection, vigilance, and self-examination – this is, at best, a fruit of
religion; but that it is a distinct life apart – in harmony indeed with the life of
conduct, or of thought, or of outward activity, but not simply a spirit infused
into them.[60]   (p. 36)

The religious life is not subsumed under the general life of society: it is both
fulfilment of and a critique of those other aspects of living which themselves
e open to religion. In the way that it operates it is thus analogous to Arnold's

'culture'. Tyrrell argues for religion as a distinct human activity (it is not everything that we do) but he is opposed to splitting off one aspect of life from the totality. Religion, like 'culture', has a double aspect – the speculative and the practical (RFL p. 13); the emphasis clearly falls on practice (p. 32). With 'culture' Arnold's tendency is to stress the speculative, and it is against this that critics like T. S. Eliot react.

Lionel Trilling perceptively called *Culture and Anarchy* 'the book that was to be the keystone of [Arnold's] intellectual life'.[61] All through the book, Arnold is working with the model of an organic society:

Because men are all members of one great whole...the expansion of our humanity, to suit the idea of perfection which culture forms, must be a *general* expansion. Perfection, as culture conceives it, is not possible while the individual remains isolated. (S V (CA) p. 94)

We have examined the basis of Arnold's humanistic vision in Christian tradition, and where his debt to Newman has often been stressed[62] I have tried to show the deeper debt to his father. John Dover Wilson sees a clear link between the Arnold of *Culture and Anarchy* and Baron von Hügel, whose writings, he suggests, 'would have interested him beyond measure, for he would have found in them his own ideas developed, articulated and clarified'.[63] In broad terms one could say that Tyrrell would have interested him in the same way.

In Arnold's later writings he came increasingly to use the term 'civilisation' as he had earlier used 'culture' – a term which he sometimes identifies more narrowly with knowledge acquired by reading.[64] He defined civilisation as 'the humanisation of man in society' (S VIII (ME) p. 286) and emphasised that such civilisation involved 'the power of conduct, the power of intellect and knowledge, the power of beauty' (p. 292). Once more, this is for Arnold a Christian ideal: the organic union of the social body, when the social body and the Body of Christ are one – 'Mankind are called in one body to the peace of God; that is the Christian phrase for civilisation' (S IX p. 18). 'Civilisation', like 'culture', was a term that Tyrrell sometimes picked up and discussed.

We have now seen something of the way in which Arnold used a number of key terms: how he talked about the Church of England, about 'culture', and about 'civilisation', and how his use of these terms can be related to the organic metaphor which underlies so much of his thought. This metaphor, which speaks of both society and the Church as a living body is, as we have seen, fundamental to Tyrrell's understanding of Catholicism. This common structure underlies Tyrrell's occasional use of Arnoldian language.

So, in the early works Tyrrell sometimes speaks of 'culture' and 'civilisation'. In 'A More Excellent Way', dated February 1896, he wrote, 'culture and civilisation is not sanctification; and a certain height of sanctity is compatible with low culture', but he stressed the commitment of the Catholic Church to the 'full development of man's capabilities' (FM1 p. 12). In *Nova et Vetera* he wrote, 'Civilisation and culture may be pagan or agnostic; but Christianity is never stably founded in barbarism and darkness' (p. 267). In *Hard Sayings* there is a discussion of 'modern progress and civilisation' in largely Arnoldian vocabulary. Tyrrell criticises a material interpretation of culture (p. 276), speaks of the 'Power that makes for Righteousness' (p. 276) striving against the current 'tendency', and of the Church as 'not only the ally but in some sense the mother of true civilisation' (p. 277). He concludes, rather flatly, that 'Civilisation is a good thing; one of God's helps to salvation' (p. 279). Arnold of course would say true civilisation *was* salvation[65] and he would have argued against Tyrrell's conviction that this life is 'chiefly a school of suffering' (p. 276). At this early stage Tyrrell's writing is contained within the bounds of orthodoxy and therefore somewhat cautious. Though it is clear from the vocabulary of this passage in *Hard Sayings* that he has Arnold in mind, he neither uses the terms in an Arnoldian way nor fashions an explicit critique of Arnold.

On the other hand an early letter to von Hügel shows Tyrrell's genuine openness to the culture of his time:

It seems to me a thing beyond any question that the study of nature and art, of science and history, of all that can open the mind and give it more matter to put into its conception of God, is an essential condition of spiritual development.[66]

This would have pleased the Baron, not least because, whilst showing cultural sensitivity, it implicitly seeks to safeguard the transcendence of God. In a later essay on 'Dogma', written between 1904 and 1906, Tyrrell shows his awareness of the hermeneutical tension between the common culture of a society and the individual engaged in critical reflection:

The public mind, sentiment, custom, morality, of a people or society, is an educational instrument and standard for the individual mind, which must be formed upon it and characterised by it in order to be capable of any critical reflection by which the said public standard may be improved and developed.

(EFI p. 122)

By this stage Tyrrell has a far deeper sense of tradition as the historical culture of a society, and of the way in which the critic of any dogmatic expression of Church tradition cannot appeal to any extra-historical source. In the current situation, to use Blondel's term, the 'extrinsicist'[67] defence of dogmatic statements cannot be met by any other form of extrinsicism. From the time of *Lex Orandi* it was clear that Tyrrell saw dogma as the expression of the public Christian 'mind, sentiment, custom, morality', not as supernaturally revealed information. Like Arnold, he stands within the hermeneutic exchange between the individual and a living historical community. Significantly, the section of the essay in *Essays on Faith and Immortality* is entitled 'organic continuity'.

This essay has no specific reference to Arnold. We have seen that the 'Reflections on Catholicism' at the beginning of *Through Scylla and Charybdis* are manifestly indebted to Arnold. When Tyrrell writes of religion in 'From Heaven or of Men?' his earlier transcendentalism is abandoned, and the approach is frankly Arnoldian:

If a religion is to influence and leaven our civilisation and culture it must be recognised as a part of it, as organically one with it; not as a foreign body thrust down into it from above, but as having grown up with it from the same root in the spirit of humanity.   (TSC p. 383)

The problem now is not how to integrate religion with society, but how to establish that it can provide an authoritative critique of an immanent process.

In less dangerous areas Tyrrell was prepared to make Arnoldian judgments from an early stage. There is often a touch of Arnold's snobbery about what he says: he talked of 'the vulgarising tendency of modern life upon the masses' and of the Church's patience with 'the civilised Philistine' (FM2 pp. 132–3). He referred to the 'frank philistinism of the supposition that knowledge, apart from its useful consequences, is nothing worth' (FM1 p. 96) and talked about the 'British Philistine of the nineteenth century' (p. 99). In *External Religion* Tyrrell wrote that 'it is the function of the better classes in society to maintain standards of good taste and good judgment in a thousand matters, and so to resist the downward influence of the uncritical majority' (ER p. 118). He complained to von Hügel that 'the tendency of modern Catholicism is to salvation neither by faith nor by works but by machinery'.[68] To Bremond he wrote at the end of 1899 that 'The "message of the Anglo-Saxon" *as such* is the gospel of comfort, of commercial progress at the expense of every other kind of progress.'[69] To Ward he wrote of his belief in a 'clerisy':

It is plain that the 'one man one vote' fallacy must be avoided; that opinions are to be weighed as well as counted; that in regard to questions still in dispute the numerical majority is sure to be wrong; and the few pioneers, right; that even in the worlds of science or history or art there is an *Ecclesia Docens* and *Discens*.[70]

In 'Medievalism' it is clear that he sees 'philistinism' as a danger for the Modernist:

A credulous enthusiastic faith in the thoughts and tendencies of to-day may be excusable and necessary as a revolt against a similar faith in those of the thirteenth century. But the similarity is there, and the difference is only between philistine and philistine.

(Med. p. 169)

In this sense Tyrrell himself, like Arnold, was something of a philistine.

Arnold described himself as a 'liberal of the future', Tyrrell as a Catholic *in spe*. Tyrrell's judgments sometimes show an Arnoldian élitism. For instance, he wrote in 1898:

The true Liberalism is really for the very few who are capable of thinking widely, deeply, and temperately; whereas, for the great majority, who form the receptive and conservative element of society, and who have neither leisure, ability, nor education, they must take their thought ready-made from others.

(The Month, 91 (1898), 456)

Once more the ideal of the 'clerisy' looks coldly élitist. However, Tyrrell's stance was thereby all the closer to Arnold's. Arnold would also have delighted in his critique of popular liberalism in every aspect but the commitment to dogma:

If to be a 'Liberal' is to be a utilitarian of the vulgarest type; if it is to have a secret contempt for anything that savours of mysticism...if it is to be dead to the 'liturgical sense', and to have lost all love and reverence for what has come down to us through the ages; if it means playing fast and loose with dogmas which martyrs have died for...then be our soul with the narrow-minded.

(FM1 pp. 83–4)

Tyrrell himself would later have repudiated only one part of these remarks: that about dogma. Even in that area his soul was with Arnold during a critical period, and not with the martyrs of the menology.

There is one sense, which we have not yet considered, in which Arnold's soul was very much with Tyrrell. A. O. J. Cockshut finds Arnold to be 'nearer in spirit' to the Catholic Modernists than to a Protestant modernist like Dean Inge.[71] It is really very striking that there develops in Arnold's works a strain of marked sympathy for Catholicism, particularly as he grows older. He obviously found the dogmatic system of the Catholic Church simply impossible but he retained an immense respect for its poetry and mysticism. David DeLaura draws attention to an early note:

Newman in his letter to Jelf. Le siècle tend vers je ne sais quel inconnu – and the Church of Rome appears alone in possession of this inconnu – giving, *elle eule*, un essor libre et régulier aux sentiments intimes d'adoration, de mysticisme, e tendresse, et à tant d'autres sentiments qui peuvent s'appeler plus spécialement atholiques.[72]

When Oxford whispered 'from her towers the last enchantments of the Middle Age' (S III (EC1) p. 290), she spoke of the antiquity, the universality, the sensuousness of Catholicism, which Arnold discussed in 'Eugénie de Guérin' (S III (EC1) p. 97). Yet he could see no reconciliation between the 'multiplication of dogmas, Mariolatry, and miracle-mongering' (p. 97) and the modern spirit. Nevertheless, Arnold admits, 'the style and circumstance of actual Catholicism is grander than its present tendency' (p. 97). He looks back to medieval Christianity which, in its poetry, lived 'by the heart and imagination' (S III (EC1) p. 230). The Christianity of Francis is to be transcended by the 'imaginative reason' but the *attrait* of the poetry and the mysticism ensures for the Christianity of Francis a sympathetic handling. In *Literature and Dogma* Arnold commended Catholicism for its hold on Jesus's 'secret' of self-renouncement, whereas Protestantism held onto the 'method' of inwardness and sincerity (S VI (LD) pp. 351–2). The accuracy or inaccuracy of such a statement is not the point here: once more Arnold held up the ideal of reformed Catholicism as the necessary complement to enlightened Protestantism.

In his travels on the Continent Arnold saw Catholicism at close quarters. In 1861 he wrote to his sister from Italy:

> The R.C. Church is *here* a great obstacle; you know I am not its enemy, but here in Italy it seems to me utterly without future, untransformable, unadaptable, used up, and an almost fatal difficulty to the country.   (*Letters* I p. 281)

In 1871 he was in Switzerland and wrote to his mother of 'religion, such as it is, entering into the whole life of the people, so unlike the Protestant cantons' (*Letters* II p. 62). By 1874, he speaks more positively, writing to M. Fontanès:

> My ideal would be, for Catholic countries, the development of something like old Catholicism, retaining as much as possible of old religious service and usages but becoming more and more liberal in spirit.   (*Letters* II p. 114)

The Preface to the second edition of 'Higher Schools and Universities in Germany', published in the same year, contains an important and sympathetic discussion of Catholicism with particular application to Ireland (S V pp. 90–130). Arnold is impressed by the record of Catholicism as a religion of the people:

> Who...has seen the poor in other churches as they are seen in Catholic churches or common soldiers in churches as they are seen in the churches of Rome? And why? Because the attaching doctrine of the equal share of Christians in the beauty and glory of religion, which all churches preach, the Church of Rome makes palpable.   (S. VII p. 10)

Two more years, and he wrote, 'A Catholic Church transformed is, I believe, the Church of the future' (S VIII (LE) p. 110). What Arnold foresaw was a Catholicism that would transform itself from a dogmatic religion to a poetic one. He was particularly concerned about the illiberal policy of a Protestant establishment that refused to the Catholic people of Ireland a Catholic university. He recognised accretions and superstitions in Catholicism: these are the dangers that go with a truly popular religion. He saw the dangers of ultramontanism and sacerdotalism,

> But when Ultramontanism, sacerdotalism, and superstition are gone, Catholicism is not, as some may suppose, gone too. Neither is it left with nothing further but what it possesses in common with all the forms of Christianity, – the curative power of the word, character, and influence of Jesus...It is left with the beauty, the richness, the poetry, the infinite charm for the imagination, of its own age-long growth.   (S VIII (ME) p. 333)

Arnold's last word on Catholicism is thus optimistic and sympathetic:

> I persist in thinking that the prevailing form for the Christianity of the future will be the form of Catholicism; but a Catholicism purged, opening itself to the light and air, having the consciousness of its own poetry, freed from its sacerdotal despotism and freed from its pseudo-scientific apparatus of superannuated dogma.
>   (S VIII (ME) p. 334)

The natural home of Arnold's humanistic Christianity is reformed Catholicism; the natural home of reformed Catholicism is the Christian State. It was a vision that seemed far from realisation in his own day. No wonder he wrote:

> Will there never arise among Catholics some great soul, to perceive that the eternity and universality, which is vainly claimed for Catholic dogma and the ultramontane system, might really be possible for Catholic worship? But to rule over the moment and the credulous has more attraction than to work for the future and the sane.   (S VIII (LE) p. 162)

He might have been speaking of Tyrrell, drawn from 'the very fringe and extreme outskirts of Christianity' by the mystery and ritual into lifelong conflict with those in authority over what he saw as renegade Catholicism. There can be little doubt how much Arnold would have appreciated him.

We have come a long way since we began to examine Tyrrell's ecclesiology. What I have tried to show is that the form of that ecclesiology – securely based as it is on the image of the Mystical Body – is identical with the form of Arnold's thought about the integrated society, and that Arnold's thought is itself informed by the same Christian imagery. Since both think of Church and society respectively *as a body*, not in primarily hierarchical or institutional terms, both use the language of participation, democracy and equality. However, since the bodies they are considering are so far from being what they ought to be, they also plead for a clerisy that will reflect to the society in critical form its own highest expression. They both struggle with the position of the prophet *vis à vis* the institution, and with the problem of authority, but belief in an immanent progressive force sustains their optimism. It blinds them to the totalitarian shadows cast by some of their ideas.

Tyrrell obviously did not learn to think this way from Arnold. The sources of his ecclesiology are much, much more deeply in St Paul, Aquinas, Newman, von Hügel and others. Far more than Arnold he struggled with the transcendence of the object of Church worship and for him the visible Church remained the sacrament of the transcendent invisible Church. He could not confidently identify Church and State in history. In 1907 he wrote to Kitty Clutton that 'Church is to State what Faith is to Science – greater not in the sane but in a different order.'[73] He was struggling far too intensely with the heteronomous application of Church authority to share Arnold's genial Anglican trust in the State as the agent of the corporate 'best self'. If Tyrrell had ever faced the question he would probably have made some tart reference to the Inquisition and called Arnold naive. Tyrrell was for the separation of powers this side of the eschaton – though the logic of his final position on symbolism should have brought him to a sacramental view not just of the Church but of the State as well, and thus closer to Arnold.

Where Arnold and Tyrrell are most often at one is in their attitude to particular historical problems. Both are anxious to read the development of the tradition aright, and convinced that the official seers are blind guides. It was Arnold who wrote,

For more than two hundred years the main stream of man's advance has moved towards knowing himself and the world, seeing things as they are, spontaneity of consciousness...[but the hebraisers] have made the secondary the principal at the wrong moment, and the principal they have at the wrong moment treated as secondary. (S V (CA) p. 175)

How Tyrrell (thinking of Jesuitism) would have agreed with that!

In chapter 3 we saw six areas of fundamental convergence between Tyrrell and Arnold, but without the material presented in this chapter the effect was inevitably somewhat two-dimensional. Since both Tyrrell and Arnold are so aware of the functioning of historical societies, it is necessary to know what they say about society before one can put other points of convergence in context. Despite all we have said in this chapter it remained true that Tyrrell was most at home with Arnold when he was overtly critical of him. On the evidence presented in this chapter, I would say that Bremond underestimated considerably when he wrote that a third of Tyrrell was in Arnold, and that he confused the issue by pointing to *Literature and Dogma*. It would have been still more outrageous and more shrewd to mention *Culture and Anarchy*, but then Loisy would have missed the point.

6

Christology:
the parting of the ways

In a brief book entitled *Modernism: Its Failure and Its Fruits*[1] Maude Petre summarised the unquestioned assumptions of the Catholic understanding of Christ with which she had grown up. At the head came:

the historical fact of the Resurrection:...if we could not be sure that the dead body of Christ actually rose from the tomb, the very foundation of our faith was insecure. Secondly, we were taught that Christ definitely affirmed His own Divinity...Thirdly, in virtue of the Hypostatic Union, He possessed, even as man, a certain omniscience...If He spoke, in [the Gospel] records, as though He only possessed the knowledge of His own time, that was in no way because only such knowledge was present to His mind, but because He had to speak to men in their own language. Fourthly, the Church was His direct foundation; her hierarchy and her sacraments were His direct institution: every one of her definitions was, explicitly or implicitly, included in His teaching.

She goes on to show, principally from the works of Loisy, though she might almost as well have done it from the works of Tyrrell, how all these hitherto unshakeable facts were questioned in the name of historical science by Modernist writers.

The atmosphere in which Matthew Arnold grew up would have been rather different. Certainly, the 'historical fact' of the resurrection would not have been questioned, nor would the explicit claims to divinity of the Johannine Christ. However, his father was a historian and open to the historical study of the Bible, especially study of the Old Testament and the Early Church. On the other hand, there is very little evidence that critical scholarship influenced his thinking on Christ. Nevertheless, the emphasis of his teaching was always on the moral rather than the scientific pre-eminence of Jesus, and in rejecting Newman's view of apostolic succession, he stressed continuity of obedience to Christ's command rather than any historical continuity of episcopal ordination, as constitutive of the Church. Thomas Arnold's position allowed a great deal more room for manoeuvre under the pressure of historical and Biblical criticism than the Roman Catholic position, but it was unstable. It would not be easy to hold the line on the resurrection or the divinity of

Christ as the critical pressure increased. Matthew Arnold, who saw no line to hold, simply argued that the Church had a knack of selecting the wrong issues on which to fight. It was obvious that traditional Christology was a nonsense; a radical reappraisal of religious language was necessary. Once people no longer looked for the referent of religious expressions 'out there' as though God were the object of science, they would realise that the thrust of religious expressions was moral, and their function to inspire not to inform.

At the end of his life George Tyrrell feared that he had conceded too much to Matthew Arnold's position and that his work had been dominated by the 'Liberal-Protestant Christ'. 'Civilisation', he declared, 'can do (and has done) all that the purely immanental Christ of Matthew Arnold is credited with.'[2] He judged himself unnecessarily harshly. His work was never 'dominated' by the Christ of Liberal Protestantism. What distinguished his Christology, as Maude Petre recognised, was that 'he clearly and positively faced the problem' (AL2 p. 388). It was not a problem mediated to him by Arnold, but by von Hügel and Loisy, who directed him to the historical work of scholars like Harnack, Weiss and Sohm. Just as with Loisy himself, Tyrrell had very little intellectual support in his quest for a synthesis between the Catholicism that he knew, loved and wished to retain, and the historical criticism which raised such urgent questions. We shall see in his work the constant strain of piloting himself between the Scylla of unyielding scholasticism and the Charybdis of omnivorous immanentism. It is his continuing concern with the sacramental and the symbolic that suggests a way through and that clearly differentiates his approach from that of Arnold. Even when most sympathetic to the radical conclusions of historical scholars, Tyrrell sought to differentiate himself from the position of an Arnold or a Sabatier. He fought consistently to preserve what he saw as most essential about Catholic Christianity: Christ as the sacrament of the transcendent Power we call God; Christ as the incarnation of essential humanity (in itself a transcendent concept); and the continuity between Christ and the Church. We shall find in this chapter that Christology is an excellent area for testing the relation between Tyrrell and Arnold. Arnold read the signs of the times boldly and applied his reading to the transformation of the Churches. Tyrrell was equally sensitive to changes in the intellectual and cultural atmosphere, but there was much more about Catholicism that he wanted to preserve − not least the incarnational form of Christology. We shall see to what extent he succeeded.

Nova et Vetera was intended as a book of informal meditations. Tyrrell comments in the introduction on the way in which his work focusses 'on the humanness of Christ and his Church' though not (he is still very circumspect) 'neglecting to give due emphasis to the Divinity of our Saviour' (p. viii). He acknowledges that

it is only by uncertain analogies that the life of a Nazarene carpenter of two thousand years ago, possessed of unthinkable supernatural prerogatives, with a mission of universal redeemer of humanity, can be positively applied as a pattern to the very unsupernatural man and woman of decadent civilization. (p. 376)

Unerringly, he finds the human point of engagement with the Christ of Catholic orthodoxy and though he does not explicitly deny, he simply omits to refer to the more bizarre conclusions of scholastic teaching. He is neither coldly intellectual, nor is he sentimental, yet a mystical passion is linked with sharpness of mind and clarity of human perception throughout. Hence the freshness that so attracted von Hügel.

A meditation on 'consubstantial with the Father' (pp. 78–83) is also a discussion of the nature of love. Tyrrell says of the hypostatic union that 'this is no barren or fruitless dogma to those who have dwelt on the mystery of Love' (p. 78). A meditation on union with God speaks of the 'Eternal Son' who 'uses the Sacred Humanity as an instrument whereby to render to the Father the love of a human heart' (p. 84). The Eternal Son is compared to 'one who descends into the slums to study and understand and ameliorate the life of the oppressed masses' (p. 196) and one thinks of Robert Dolling whom Tyrrell loved so much.[3] This remark occurs in a meditation on 'The Mediatorial Office', where the material on Jesus's 'comprehensive and experimental knowledge of sinful man' develops into a discussion of *the priest's comprehensive sympathy*: 'some seem to have a natural gift of discernment – many-sided men with a strong, sympathetic affection; but we all have a root of it within us which we can develop' (p. 197). That is typical of Tyrrell's way of talking about Christ. He is drawn to a Christ that is priestly but human, in fact the archetype of all that is best in himself.

External Religion is a series of conferences on 'the supernatural God-made religion of the Incarnation' (p. 28). The critical problems are not yet apparent, so it is a simple and uninhibited account of the religion of the incarnation. Again von Hügel read it with delight (and sent a lengthy criticism).[4]

The key idea is that of the correlation between 'the internal Christ of our conscience' and 'the external and visible Christ, the Word Incarnate' (p. 35). The one calls for the other: each complements and defines its counterpart. More than this, the whole drama of the life, death and resurrection of Christ is played out both internally and externally, so that by the historic life of Christ we find the meaning of internal struggles and strivings. Thus,

His whole life within us is a life of poverty, labour, and sorrow; of agonizing and struggling for dominion over the heart He has created to be His kingdom ...The Crucifix is the collective sin of the world made visible...The Resurrection...is the outward counterpart of that inward resurrection of Christ in the soul when conscience, quickened from the dead by grace, reasserts itself once more and reigns victorious in the penitent heart.   (pp. 32–4)

Through God's grace, the drama of the divine life in the human soul has been enacted by Christ in the world;[5] we have been given the external religion that we need. Von Hügel commended 'the truly splendid teaching about the immanental and the historic, external Christ, and their proper functions and relations'.[6] At this stage, Tyrrell still had a firm hold on the divine side of the religion of the incarnation and he could say that 'every deed and event of His mortal life was prophetic; was as it were a sacrament or symbol of the mysteries of the Kingdom of God' (p. 31). Jesus, then, is not only the perfect correlate of every man's flickering experience of the divine, but the sacrament of the Kingdom of God, as the Church, his Mystical Body, continues to be for those who come after.

   Oil and Wine deals with the same themes at a deeper level. So, Christ is spoken of as 'the Human Conscience Incarnate' (p. 96), to which (a hint of Arnold) 'our better self is always more responsive, our worse self always less responsive' (p. 98). Tyrrell approaches Christ by the same human route:

Those who know the nature of the human mind, will see that there is no way to the knowledge of the Father but by Him; that we must conceive God human-wise or not at all; that the object of our love must be, not merely a personality but a human personality; and that therefore the highest humanity is the highest image we can possess of the unimaginable divinity.   (p. 103)

However, there is in *Oil and Wine* a marked stress on organic unity: the organic unity of the human race, of the Mystical Body, of the body of Christian doctrine and so on. Tyrrell writes of 'the somewhat organic nature of God's entire work' (p. 99), and though this enables him to handle the atonement and the resurrection with assurance it has its dangers. Tyrrell rejects talk of Christ's being looked upon as a separate individual 'punished' for the sins of others. He is one with humanity – with the sin of the guilty and the expiation of the saints:

The deeper we enter into and realize the truth of our corporate unity with the whole race, present and past, the liker we are to Him who so realized it that He bore all the sins and sorrows of the world as though they were His own personal sins and sorrows.   (p. 118)

This is unexceptionable, but the danger comes when the 'as though' of the final clause appears to drop out, so that Christ becomes in all things, so included, one with men. This Tyrrell never said nor intended to say. However, he seemed to say at times that since Christ is ontologically one with all men, men are ontologically one with God: God is (already) all in all. Thus Gabriel Daly can speak of a passage in *Oil and Wine* (pp. 220–1) on God's life in ours as 'ostensibly the most monistic of any to be found in Tyrrell's writings'.[7] He is right to point out in explanation that Tyrrell is offering 'a mystical meditation not...[a] theological analysis'. If the meditation stimulates his readers to live the Christ-life, Tyrrell is not too bothered about overstatement. More seriously, the monistic tone sometimes destroys the sharp focus on the particularity of Christ's human experience, about which Tyrrell wrote in *Nova et Vetera*. Nevertheless, in *Oil and Wine* the work of Christ is presented by a characteristically vivid analogy:

Christ's task as Revealer is comparable, without any exaggeration, to that of one who should endeavour to reveal the visible world of form and colour to a race void of the sense of sight and of all language derived from or appealing to that sense. (pp. 74–5)

This is the germ of the idea worked out in *The Civilizing of the Matafanus*.

Although a mere pamphlet, *The Civilizing of the Matafanus* deserves extended consideration because it is, apart from *Christianity at the Crossroads*, Tyrrell's most important Christological statement. It brings together in allegorical form almost all the issues so far raised. It turns on an unshaken belief in the validity of a Christology of two natures and links this brilliantly with the growth of the Church and the development of doctrine. The story concerns an initially unsuccessful attempt to bring 'civilisation' (linked specifically with the name of Matthew Arnold – pp. 24, 35) to the primitive Matafanus. There is an extended discussion of the difficulty of communication between the civilised philanthropists and the uncivilised tribesmen, and therefore the need for a mediator. It is by hypnotism that such a mediator with 'the double experience in one personality' (p. 34) is to be created. The hypnotiser must be someone with a comprehensive understanding of the values and nature of civilisation; the hypnotised must be an intelligent Matafanu, acceptable to his own people. Such a tribesman is found in Alpuca, who is duly hypnotised and thus imbued with the entire contents of the hypnotiser's intelligence, memory and imagination – all his experience plus 'an imperative and irresistible impulse to communicate this great body of knowledge and light to the Matafanu tribe' (p. 36).

Tyrrell said of his allegory that 'the argument is rather closely knit and very little has been said without deliberate design'.[8] So, it is not unfair to press it a little. There are repeated references to the difficulty of communication, and the inadequacy of the Matafanu language to contain the concepts which Alpuca – with his vision for 'civilisation' – wishes to impart:

> He had to endure the anguish of being forced by a passionate appetite for self-revelation to try to give utterance to a conception so wide, lofty and deep, in a medium so narrow as the language and imagery of a people but lately advanced beyond the lowest stage of savage ferocity and darkness... Surely this were apparently as hopeless as the endeavour to render a Beethoven's sonata on the Jew's harp, or to reproduce Raphael on a stable door with a lump of chalk.
> (p. 46)

The problem is exactly that 'omniscience' about which, in exaggerated form, Maude Petre had been taught. Tyrrell is still prepared to do his Christology 'from above' – though in the context of an allegory that reminds us we have no option, in attempting to understand the incarnation, but to use words and images 'from below'.

This is the context in which Tyrrell places a discussion of miracles. The unsuccessful effort to communicate causes Alpuca intense suffering. In the attempt to explain his status as a denizen of two worlds, he is forced to use 'miracles', not to show his power as thaumaturge and thus compel some sort of wondering belief in himself, but as an illustration of that 'natural knowledge' in the 'civilised world' of which he is struggling to speak. Tyrrell had no time for the contemporary apologetic which relied on demonstrating the divinity of Jesus by means of miracles and fulfilled prophecy:

> In the case of Alpuca, it was his moral pre-eminence and absolute integrity that won for him, in the eyes of those capable of appreciating it, an implicit belief in the reality of his claim to a knowledge or science of which they were not yet capable, owing to the unprepared state of their minds.
> (p. 40)

We are not surprised that Alpuca finds himself under immense internal strain because of his dual personality, and at odds with the priests of his tribe because he threatens their authority. He has to reconcile himself to the fact that it is only after his untimely death that the Matafanus who accept his teaching will grow into an understanding of its import:

> Were we to sum up in one word the whole *reality* which it was the mission of Alpuca to reveal, it would be 'Civilisation'; and the power of apprehending this perfect ideal... would depend precisely upon the degree of imperfect civilisation attained by the people in question.
> (p. 57)

Tyrrell goes on to discuss the developing understanding of Alpuca among the Matafanus after his death. The loyally 'orthodox' fail to appreciate the inevitably symbolic nature of Alpuca's teaching and take it far too literally. This is a step backward, which leads to further distortion:

During this same period of declension, it became more prominently important to establish the claims of Alpuca to be the possessor of special knowledge than to enter into the substance of that knowledge. (p. 61)

Tyrrell pleads for a sense of religion as a life to be lived.

In can be seen that *The Civilizing of the Matafanus* meets three of the four points of Maude Petre's childhood teaching about Christ: Alpuca knows, if he does not flaunt, his membership of another and higher order of being, his 'divinity'; he has 'a certain omniscience' and has to economise in revealing his knowledge; he leaves behind him a 'Church'. If he is not raised from the dead, it can at least be said that his spirit lives on in that Church, though Tyrrell would not yet want to apply the allegory in that way, for what he has written is a brilliant miniature life not just of Jesus, but of the Church as well. Inasmuch as he deals with Jesus, he is uncompromising in his incarnationalism, and yet sensitive to the psychological dilemmas which he saw as implied by a 'two-natures' Christology. In theory, the story turns on the 'civilisation' that is brought, through Alpuca, to the Matafanus. In practice, the story is about Alpuca as the incarnation of that civilisation. This is Tyrrell's way of exploring the meaning of orthodox Christology. The problem he now faced was that he found it historically insupportable.

This is really the turning point: no longer able to express an acceptable liberal Catholicism, Tyrrell's thought divides. On the one hand, he was reading more and more deeply in the critics, tossed about by Harnack, Sohm, Weiss, Loisy and Schweitzer, and ready to push the conclusions of radical historical scholarship to their limit. The change of course here was immediately apparent to those who discovered the real identity of Hilaire Bourdon, author of *The Church and the Future*. On the other hand, Tyrrell was trying to recover the religious meaning of religious language, and incidentally to protect religious statements from the vicissitudes of historical scholarship, whilst at the same time acknowledging their openness to verification. This he worked out in an appendix to *Religion as a Factor of Life* and in *Lex Orandi*.

The appendix to *Religion as a Factor of Life* concentrates on the Creed. Tyrrell tries to get behind the intellectualised statement to the practical value of that statement:

The oneness of all men with one another in Christ; and their oneness with God through Christ, is the foundation of all practical and affective religion as summed up in [the] duty of Charity; and this is the religious value of our belief in 'Jesus Christ – His only Son – our Lord'. All that is added in the Nicene and Athanasian creeds as to the precise nature of the hypostatic union...is but protective of the simple truth, that Christ is God, whose religious value is, as we have said, quite distinct from its metaphysical value. (p. 63)

95

He goes on to spell out the 'religious value' of the belief that Christ is God: 'If "Christ is God" my will and conduct must be shaped in certain ways in relation to Him' (pp. 63–4). This is how Tyrrell now approaches the statements of the Creed. He distinguishes between their historical and their religious value. So, he argues that the historical facts of Christ's birth are neither here nor there; the importance of the belief in Mary's virginity lies in the attitudes and behaviour it inspires. 'God has spoken the spiritual truth in the language of bodily facts' (p. 66). Tyrrell at this point does not deny the virgin birth, though he speaks of it as 'subject to the fluctuations of historical certainty' (p. 66). However, the escape route is prepared, and should it come to the decisive abandonment of the historical affirmation then the religious affirmation will survive:

Even granting that criticism could weaken or wholly upset the *factual* character of the Gospel narrative, our faith would none the less be in Christ, 'who was conceived by the Holy Ghost, and born of the Virgin Mary'; of whose spirit these beliefs are a genuine development. (p. 67)

He takes the same line with the resurrection, hotly denying that we are 'to pass from the evidence of the resurrection to a belief in Christ's claims to be the Son of God' (pp. 68–9). He argues that in I Corinthians 15 Paul was 'not proving Christ from the resurrection, but proving the resurrection from Christ' (p. 69). The resurrection *has* to be true – regardless of 'history' – because it conforms to 'the whole economy of the Incarnation' (p. 69). It externalises and objectifies what we know to be true in our experience. Therefore it is a truth of the will-world, a religious truth – and the truths of religion are more important than the truths of 'history'. At this stage, it is true, Tyrrell maintains a toehold in history: it is 'religious materialism'[9] rather than historical credulity he is actually attacking – but, for the present, attack is the best form of defence.

As he saw it, the faith was under attack from two sides, and it was necessary to fight on both fronts at once. On the one hand there was the 'religious materialism' of contemporary Catholic apologetic, which actually produced a form of monophysitism, because there was no way that a Christ so obviously supernaturally endowed could be a real man. On the other hand, there was the reductionism of the Scriptural critics whom Tyrrell was avidly reading for their historical insight, but whose scientific rationalism precluded any Christology higher than some form of Arianism. In broad terms, Tyrrell was struggling with the problem of doing Christology 'from above' or 'from below'[10] and finding neither approach adequate for the maintenance of that firm belief in the incarnation which was for him not the conclusion but the presupposition of Christology. Thus, he wrote in *Lex Orandi*:

No relation of closeness that...falls short of that of personal identity between
the God-Christ and the Man-Christ can lend the same emotional and practical
value to the life at Nazareth and the death on Calvary. (p. 152)

Some of the few comments that Tyrrell ever made on the hypostatic union
are to be found in his correspondence with von Hügel at the time von Hügel
observed and then entered the Christological controversy between Loisy and
Blondel.[11] Von Hügel had outlined to Tyrrell what Tyrrell called 'the need
of the two-fold Christ – subject and object – glorified and terrestrial' and
Tyrrell had gone on to refine von Hügel's position on 'concupiscence':

When you deny 'concupiscence' to Christ I need a distinction. There is natural
and blameless passion whose absence were a defect; and there is a passion which
is the fruit of past carelessness or sin, personal or ancestral. To deny the former
to Christ is open to the same objection as docetan views as to his knowledge.
Are not ignorance and passion the two roots of our temptations? and how is
Christ tempted as we, how is his sinlessness conceivable, if he lacked either root?[12]

Von Hügel liked and accepted the point. Shortly after, Tyrrell responded again
with an important discussion of von Hügel's conception:

I suppose our psychology and metaphysic is, and will be for ever, too imperfect
to reach down to those very roots of reality in which the answer to the God–man
problem lies hid and we must be content with a plexus of mutually exclusive
and yet mutually complimentary similitudes and with the faith that their
unthinkable synthesis exists somewhere...If we accept scholastic dichotomy
(soul + body = human person) it is almost impossible to escape Nestorianism or
to show that in Christ there was not a human as well as a divine personality.
If we accept trichotomy (body + soul + spirit or person = human person =
me + I) then we can say that a Divine Spirit or Ego assumed a non-personal
human nature (i.e. soul + body, which as related to the Divine Spirit becomes
the *me* of that I). *Ignoramus et ignorabimus.*[13]

The really characteristic touch is in the last phrase. Tyrrell's heart was not in
any kind of logical approach to the hypostatic union. In a sense, he had not
the patience. For von Hügel the Council of Chalcedon 'bequeathed us the
most satisfying of all the possible formulae';[14] though he humoured the
Baron, Tyrrell simply could not see the need for contorted explication of an
obvious antinomy. Such explication was demonstrably a source of serious
misunderstanding. Once you have said that Jesus is God, you have ensured
the dynamic of the Christian life.

At this time Tyrrell was reading Loisy avidly. He wrote in November 1902
to thank him for the gift of *L'Évangile et L'Église*, and continued to believe,
as did von Hügel, that Loisy did not impugn the divinity of Christ by his
searching critical work. In June 1903 he wrote to Maude Petre:

Loisy does not touch remotely the strict dogma of the Hypostatic Union; but only its etceteras and appendices *sc.* that Christ *as man* always enjoyed the facial vision of God and drew upon his divine omniscience in virtue of a continuous revelation; that he possessed, besides, an infused knowledge of the realm of nature and religion. The *Kenosis* doctrine means that he, as it were, pulled down the blinds against some of these sources of light from without – against nearly all, says Loisy; against scarcely any, say the Fathers. He shared all our groping and darkness and uncertainty and blameless ignorances – to me, that were more than his sharing mere physical pain and weakness. The theological Christ lived in a blaze of absolute certainty about everything – like a Roman Cardinal.[15]

Loisy managed to maintain a tenuous orthodoxy by distinguishing sharply between statements of faith and statements of history. He claimed that the doctrine of the hypostatic union, being a statement of faith, was untouched and untouchable by the strictly circumscribed work of the historian. However, this meant, as Tyrrell saw, that the cognitive value of statements of faith was very much thrown into question. Loisy in effect denied that the problem had anything to do with him, since he was working *historically*. Tyrrell, as a theologian, tried to meet the challenge.

In *The Church and the Future* the influence of Loisy's historical conclusions is pervasive. Tyrrell first set out the case against Catholicism as officially stated, and showed how this position had been eroded by 'the scripture critics, and the ecclesiastic historians, and the students of comparative religion' (p. 15). The loss of confidence has been catastrophic: 'If Jülicher is even approximately right, as it is hard not to allow, then the real Christ vanishes into the background, and the gospels give us only a somewhat blurred shadow of His personality and teaching' (p. 25). Once he has faced the worst, he attempts a restatement that will meet the objections of the most sceptical critic. This is how he summarised it to von Hügel:

I regard the 'Catholicising' of Christianity as a *per se* result of the Spirit of Christ, and not as a perversion or accident;...I apply the '*quod semper*, etc.' test in a *practical* way *sc.* Beliefs and institutions which are universally proved, experimentally, to foster the Christian spirit, *ipso facto* are proved to be true to that spirit. And by the Christian spirit I mean that spirit which spoke from the beginning in the prophets and men of faith and found its most docile organ in Christ... The Spirit of Christ rather than Christ himself is the creator of the Church.[16]

Set out like this one immediately sees the danger that the Spirit is God in a way that Christ is not; the position is Arian.

The advantage of such a position is that it frees Christ to be a man of his time – above all an apocalyptic prophet with a unique message:

It is impossible not to see that the central and inspiring theme of Christ's message was his own proximate advent in Glory as the Son of Man or Messiah, to judge the world, to overthrow the kingdom of Satan, and to establish the Kingdom of God. (p. 44)

Of course, on the timing of the Parousia Jesus was wrong, due to the immediacy of his prophetic enthusiasm. We can further see now that he and the Early Church were mistaken to take the religious imagery so literally. As Tyrrell had written in *Religion as a Factor of Life*, the real criterion of such beliefs is, 'Do they bring the will into a right attitude Godwards?' (RFL p. 74). Jesus simply did not foresee the development of the Church:

Indeed to suppose that Christ foresaw the whole future history of his Church, all the conflicts that would arise from the paucity and obscurity of his utterances; all the doubts that a clear word of his would have solved; all the controversies that have split Christendom into fragments and cost the spiritual destitution of countless millions – and that, foreseeing all this clearly, he deliberately wrapped, or even left, the truth in obscurity is, from an apologetic standpoint, antecedently irreconcilable with a belief in his goodness, wisdom, and pity. (CF pp. 61–2)

The Jesus that Tyrrell now depicts is intensely human, of perfect moral integrity, and of limited knowledge. He is the most 'docile organ' of the Spirit of God.

Two unpublished essays in *Essays on Faith and Immortality*, both written between 1904 and 1906, take this approach to Christology further. The first is simply entitled 'Christ' and recapitulates the points we have so far covered: Christ could and did err in knowledge; what he had to communicate was a spirit not a theology; he alone was God-possessed in an absolutely unresisting fashion; his words were prophetic not scientific; he took traditional material and imbued it with new meaning:

If...one had to 'formulate' the originality of Christ's mind, one would be inclined to find it in the first and decisive recognition of the true relation between the letter and the spirit; and in the bodily transfer of all the intellectual apparatus and imaginative symbolism of theology to the service and worship of Conscience.
(p. 50)

That sounds like Arnold, and Tyrrell was now as close to Arnold christo-logically as he was ever to come. In 'The Spirit of Christianity' he declares that Jesus himself never dreamt of founding a new religion or of seceding from Judaism (p. 64) and he goes on in purely Arnoldian vein:

What he taught was not a new religion, but a secret, a method, a spirit; a return to inwardness; a return to the end and intention of the Law and the Divine Legislator, whom he revealed as a Father, not as a despot. (p. 65)

Jesus brought about a return to the spirit of true Judaism; what Tyrrell and Arnold wanted was a return to the spirit of true Christianity – though the concept meant something quite different to each of them.

Once more, at the very time he was drawing closest to Arnold, Tyrrell tried to differentiate himself from him specifically. Part One of *Lex Credendi* is an extended discussion of 'The Spirit of Christ' in which he declares that we cannot know what the spirit is; we can only know it by its effects. He will not become involved in a metaphysical discussion. In fact, he had already involved himself in such a discussion when he wrote *Religion as a Factor of Life*, which was much indebted to Blondel and turned on the Augustinian conception that 'we are nothing else but wills' where 'will' is 'only another name for the free personal *ego*' (LO p. 32). In the end we do not know how it is that the will moves in a certain direction, but we speak of 'the spirit' that moves it. In *Religion as a Factor of Life* Tyrrell wrote:

Religion as an activity of the individual soul is simply the movement of its will-attitude in relation to the Divine Will and to all other wills so far as accordant with the Divine Will. (p. 12)

In *Lex Credendi* he speaks of the spirit as 'primarily a sense, feeling, sentiment, or instinct' (p. 12) and he wants to make it clear that this is expressed in every aspect of human life, ethical, intellectual and aesthetic. He is concerned with the conformity of the whole person to Christ, and takes the Lord's Prayer as a model for the human response to God. Such a response can be spoken of both as a response of spirit to Spirit, and of will to Will. The advantage of the terminology of the spirit is that it emphasises Tyrrell's constant opposition to 'religious materialism'; the advantage of referring to the will is that it underlines the ethical aspect of the religious response.

The Christology of *Lex Credendi* is primarily that of the responsive will. The metaphysical depth of the hypostatic union is shrouded in mystery but we can see the effect of this union in the life lived by Jesus:

To be permanently and absolutely the voluntary instrument of [the] Divine enthusiasm; to be so completely and perfectly wielded by God's Will that the action and effect must be called simply Divine, all separate personality being merged indistinguishably in that of the Infinite Spirit; to be subject to it as the hand or foot is to its owner – is the moral manifestation of that mysterious hypostatic union which entitles Jesus to be called the Son of God in an unique and incommunicable sense. (LC pp. 22–3)

The point is repeated a number of ways:

Here, as throughout, we speak of Christ's moral and spiritual relation to the Father; not of the metaphysical relation of personal union, which is its mysterious, inscrutable root. We speak of that faultless, unbroken unity of will, which practically merged all distinction of agency and made His spirit-life as much a part of the Divine Life as the life of any member is part of that of the whole body. (LC pp. 106–7)

It is a union that is potentially open to any human being. When Tyrrell writes on the Lord's Prayer he writes about the 'Not-self' that resists us. In his discussion of the ethical struggle and the ethical victory of Jesus, in his speaking of the conscience as the instrument by which we determine the will of God which we either accept or oppose, he sounds very like Arnold.

What must be emphasised is that in all this period of experiment Tyrrell never considered that he was denying the hypostatic union: he was merely trying to find new ways of expressing the essential truth of the incarnation as he had experienced it. So, he criticises the Christ of the New Theology because he does not conform to the Christian's experience:

This Christ is certainly not the Christ of ordinary Christian feeling, life, and experience; He is not the God to which, as to its Centre and Rest, the finite spirit is drawn with a profound sense of dependence and awe mingled with trust and confidence.[17]

However much his theology carelessly or mistakenly subordinated Christ to the Father or the Spirit, it is clear that Tyrrell's devotion never did. It was a certain paradoxical devotional security that made him at times quite careless. Thus he wrote to Houtin in 1907:

I would never deny the divinity of Christ, or the Atonement, or the Real Presence etc. etc. partly because they symbolise real religious experiences; partly because it would enlist protestant sympathy on the side of Rome. Other symbols might do as well; but these are in possession.[18]

What sounds like extreme theological carelessness is exactly that: it was the devotional and religious import of the traditional Christian symbols that mattered. Such cavalier treatment of the intellect left a sick and troubled man heavily reliant on his feelings. At times he felt like an atheist.

Certainly Tyrrell questioned whether he was not spiritually bankrupt at the end of his life. He mentioned to Loisy a paper he was writing for *The Hibbert Journal*, which appeared shortly after his death. With characteristic self-denigration he wrote, 'I am incompetent to speak on critical points and have no Christology of my own to propose.'[19] This was true only inasmuch as Christology rests on metaphysics, with which Tyrrell was very much out of sympathy. It was also true that Tyrrell was heavily dependent on scholars like Loisy for his opinions about the New Testament, but it was not true that he was unable to construct a Christology of his own, as his last book showed.

In his article on the state of the question, 'The Point at Issue'[20] Tyrrell immediately commits himself to the *Nicene* formula:

The Nicene formula marked a climax in the exaltation of Jesus. We cannot exalt him above God. His Godhead may be made more intelligible, but any formula

that excludes the Nicene is another doctrine, and not a more developed
re-statement. (p. 5)

Once more he commits himself to the incarnational form of Christology. In
the article he shows the development of the term 'Christ' from the Jewish
concept 'Messiah' to the Second Person of the Trinity made man, and then
asks the question whether the predicate 'Christ' as interpreted by the Creeds
agrees with the subject Jesus as interpreted by criticism. First he discusses the
predicate 'Christ'. He pinpoints a key area of confusion in the accepted
interpretation of the Church's teaching about the Divine Sonship. This
confusion is based on the discrepancy between the theological and the popular
use of the term 'person'. The popular understanding is of:

a separate spiritual individual, a separate mind, will, and energy...Hence, when
our creed tells us there is but one personality in Christ, we interpret it almost
inevitably as meaning a union of natures, a mixture or confusion of divine and
human attributes in a third hybrid nature that is a blend of both; we imagine
a man whose mind is omniscient, whose energy is omnipotent. Our language
is orthodox but our mind is monophysite. (pp. 9–10)

Theologically, the term 'person' as applied to Jesus was

simply a word to express the solution of a difficulty that could not be solved;
an *x* to symbolise a missing link by which Godhead and manhood might be
united without confusion of natures.[21] (p. 14)

This comes about because of the sheer impossibility of reconciling (1) that Jesus
was an incarnation of God (2) that God is numerically one (3) that Jesus was
a personality distinct from his Father. In terms of the normal use of language
Tyrrell accuses the orthodox formula of being simply incoherent. If we are
too much influenced by contemporary use of the term 'person' we shall be
monophysite; if we insist on the duality and separateness of the divine and
human natures we tend to imagine a duality of persons and so fall into
Nestorianism.

In his discussion of the historical Jesus, Tyrrell points out, as he has
frequently done before, that the hypostatic union did not *necessarily* imply
miraculous gifts of knowledge, goodness, and power, and that testimony to
such gifts could not prove the hypostatic union, which is 'a transcendental
truth' above historical proof or disproof. This is important because renewed
emphasis on Jesus's eschatological teaching had brought out his humanity :
a Jewish prophet of the first century. Weiss and others 'have left us a Jesus
whose inspiration and enthusiasm were entirely religious, mystical, and
transcendent, but in no sense liberal or modern-minded' (p. 15). Tyrrell
concludes that 'such a Jesus would have been far more in sympathy with

102

orthodoxy than with liberalism' (p. 16). *Christianity at the Crossroads* is an account of how this is so.

This final Christological statement contains both a vigorous reassertion of the transcendence of God (von Hügel seems to have forgotten this when he later criticises Tyrrell for a lack of emphasis upon the transcendence of God)[22] and a restatement of Tyrrell's belief in Christ as conscience incarnate. Here he set out his final 'Modernist' position, distinguishing it explicitly from neo-scholasticism, from Newmanism and from Liberal Protestantism. For the first time Tyrrell writes at length on the historical Jesus, leaning heavily on the work of Weiss, Loisy and Schweitzer. Thus, for Jesus, 'His Messianic consciousness was the main determinant of His action and utterance... His Christhood was the secret, the mystery of His life' (pp. 46–7). In his earthly state he probably regarded himself as the promised Son of David and the 'suffering servant' who was to be glorified eventually as the Son of Man. He was concerned to preach not his own glory, but to proclaim the coming of the Kingdom. Everything is coloured by immediate expectation of the end, which he himself intended to precipitate by his provocation of the powers of Evil to a final assault upon himself when he went up to Jerusalem. For the latter part of his life he actively sought the death that he predicted on the basis of his own resolve; on the basis of his messianic self-consciousness he expected the resurrection. The roots of Catholic doctrine lie in the apocalyptic vision of Christ – an uncompromisingly transcendent vision. As Tyrrell expounds the apocalyptic understanding of Jesus he writes with a sense of real release, of release from the misunderstanding to which his adoption of Liberal Protestant methods had opened him; of release from the tentative nature of his own former conclusions, and the fear that the 'assured results of criticism' might produce a Jesus like the Jesus of Harnack. The key to Tyrrell's synthesis is 'a frank admission of the principle of symbolism' (p. 103), which is now made easier for two reasons: the imagery of apocalyptic is patently imaginative, and therefore less likely to be taken as an attempt at literal expression; and the continuity that exists between the imagery accepted and used by Jesus and that retained in Catholic doctrine is demonstrable. This continuity of imagery links with continuity of experience (and of course development in under-standing) to form a complex but undeniably unified tradition. Tyrrell's Christology is, then, traditional if it stops short of orthodoxy:

The faith in His own Christhood that Jesus, by the power of His personality, was able to plant in His Apostles, has been continually reinforced by the experience of those who have found Him, in effect, their Redeemer, the Lord and Master of their souls, their Hope, their Love, their Rest – in short, all that they mean by God. For them He has become the effectual symbol or sacrament of the transcendent, through which they can apprehend the inapprehensible – the Eternal Spirit in human form. (CCR pp. 183–4)

Thus if any brought up like Maude Petre had turned specifically to *Christianity at the Crossroads* for a fresh expression of their childish faith, they would have found more comfort there than in most of Tyrrell's books, but in an entirely new mode. On the resurrection, he writes that 'there can be no doubt as to the appearances of Jesus to His Apostles after death' (p. 146) but he had not changed his attitude to the question of resurrection as an historical question, which he had succinctly expressed elsewhere:

They believed and therefore they saw; they saw and therefore they believed; faith and vision were organically one and correlative, as the real object and its mirrored reflex or shadow. (EFI p. 59)

Now, on Jesus's attitude to his own divinity, Tyrrell writes of 'messianic consciousness' and 'messianic secret', though adding,

It would be at least hard to show that, whatever Catholic theology may mean by the doctrine of a hypostatic union from the very first of [the] two natures, that doctrine is excluded by the notion that Jesus was *made* the Christ only by His glorification after death. (CCR p. 81)

The omniscience of Jesus is, of course, rejected. He speaks in the apocalyptic language of his own time because he is a man and a prophet of his own time, but we have seen that in Tyrrell's estimate that did not detract from his divinity. The Church, if not his institution as such, was the continuation of the corporate life of that 'little flock' he gathered round him.

It is the last section of the book that is in many ways the most interesting and the most frustrating. Here Tyrrell states his convictions on the relationship between Christianity and other religions, turning his religious philosophy, as developed in *Lex Orandi*, to account with respect to religion in general. He depicts Catholicism as a potentially universal religion on the basis of his 'Spirit' metaphysic and Christology. With respect to Christology this is actually a step back, for the effect is to leave the apocalyptic Jesus of the first half of the book, who became, in the Church's developed understanding, the Catholic Christ, lying uneasily alongside the immanent, spiritual Christ in whom the yearnings of the world's religions are fulfilled. The tension is unreconciled.

Tyrrell's Christology was criticised both during his lifetime and after. Loisy saw two persons in Tyrrell's Christ[23] and criticised his concessions to Protestantism.[24] Blondel found Tyrrell too concerned with the interior movement of Jesus's human soul and his prophetic vision; not enough with 'une vie incarnée dans la perfection de l'Homme-Dieu et proposée du dehors à nos besoins intimes'. He felt that Tyrrell should have seen the life and acts of Jesus as *constitutive* of the supernatural order.[25] Dean Inge savaged *Christianity at the Crossroads* in *The Hibbert Journal*[26] and roundly declared that 'it is impossible to make the Messianic idea the centre of Christ's teaching'. William Barry wrote:

In a short but decisive correspondence I elicited from Tyrrell that Jesus of Nazareth need not have known Himself to be the Eternal Son of God. That was too much for me...So far as I can judge, Tyrrell was falling away from positive beliefs altogether when the end came.[27]

Joseph Crehan roundly asserted that Tyrrell was at the end of his life left with 'Nothing'.[28]

Both Crehan and Barry go beyond the evidence in concluding that Tyrrell was falling away from positive belief at the end of his life. Inge's review is the angry response of an uncompromising Protestant of a Platonist turn to an uncompromising statement of the eschatological roots of Catholicism. Although he asserts that Tyrrell's Jesus was 'a man who believed himself to be a demigod' this is a hellenising travesty of what Tyrrell says about messiahship. The thrust of his criticism is against Tyrrell's reading of history, not his critique of the hypostatic union. Loisy and Blondel come nearer to the mark because they have more sympathy for what Tyrrell was trying to do, although Tyrrell was more radical than either of them. It is clear that Tyrrell tried different Christological approaches as he perceived the problem more sharply, and that some were more successful than others. At times he is clearly subordinationist, at times monist, at times, as Loisy saw, Nestorian. The impression that is left is one of ceaseless experiment about certain fixed points.

The heart of Tyrrell's Christology lies in the attraction of 'that strange man on his cross who drives one back again and again',[29] the recognition that in his living and dying he speaks to the depths of the human personality which responds intuitively to the externalisation of its own highest aspirations; the belief that this same Jesus was more than the acme of humanity: he was the sacrament of the transcendent God; the affirmation of continuity between the life and teaching of Jesus and the life and teaching of the Church. All of this was in *External Religion* and, much transformed, all reappeared in *Christianity at the Crossroads*. These positive beliefs, and the negative belief that the hypostatic union was a mystery, a truth 'fringed with darkness', to be contemplated, not solved, provide a thread of continuity in all his work. Such a thread may look very weak to Tyrrell's militantly orthodox critics; when one compares his Christology with that of Arnold it has a certain tough conservatism.

105

For most of our survey of Tyrrell's Christology Arnold has simply dropped below the horizon. This is because what he said would have appealed to Tyrrell as far as it went – he avoided religious materialism and focussed sharply on Jesus as a credible human figure – but it never went far enough. To adore the Eternal Son of God would have been 'utter blunder' for Arnold, whose liberalism was in many ways the epitome of all that Tyrrell fought to avoid: he found it attractive but reductive. So, during the period when he was most attracted to Liberal Protestant methods, Tyrrell remained as keen as ever not to come to Liberal Protestant conclusions.

In 1867, Arnold published his poem 'Obermann Once More'. After twenty years the poet re-encounters an Obermann who discussed the religious history of the world: the emptiness and accidie of the pagan world, the novelty of Christianity, and the subsequent erosion of belief which has left a post-Christian world deprived of joy and hope.

> 'Ay, ages long endured his span
> Of life – 'tis true received –
> That gracious Child, that thorn-crown'd Man!
> – He lived while we believed.
>
> 'While we believed, on earth he went,
> And open stood his grave.
> Men call'd from chamber, church, and tent;
> And Christ was by to save.
>
> 'Now he is dead! Far hence he lies
> In the lorn Syrian town;
> And on his grave, with shining eyes,
> The Syrian stars look down.'   (lines 165–76)

When the poem was published it was assumed in some quarters that Arnold had used Obermann as a mouthpiece for his own religious opinions, but this he vigorously denied. He concluded a letter on the subject,

[Obermann] retains, because I meant him to be true to the reality, an aridity and crudity in his language which savours of the French Revolution and its vehemence of negation and opposition, and which certainly, were I writing directly for myself, would not be mine.

That Christ is alive is language far truer to my own feeling and observation of what is passing in the world, than that Christ is dead.[30]

But Arnold had not yet begun to explore who Christ might be and in what sense he was alive. This he did in a series of prose works published through the seventies.

106

Arnold showed himself prepared to stray into religious matters in *Essays in Criticism* but the first trailer for his Christological views is to be found in *Culture and Anarchy*. Here he attacks Puritan interpretation of the Bible. 'No man', he says, 'who knows nothing else, knows even his Bible' (S V (CA) p. 184). In the course of a discussion of the Pauline notion of resurrection he emphasises that Paul's stress is on rising to a new life before the physical death of the body and not after it. Arnold approaches Christ by means of Pauline theology:

The idea on which we have already touched, the profound idea of being baptized into the death of the great exemplar of self-devotion and self-annulment, of repeating in our own person, by virtue of identification with our exemplar, his course of self-devotion and self-annulment, and of thus coming, within the limits of our present life, to a new life, in which, as in the death going before it, we are identified with our exemplar – this is the fruitful and original conception of being *risen with Christ* which possesses the mind of St Paul.   (p. 183)

This is the key to Arnold's entire Christology. He begins from the resurrection in Pauline experience and in the experience of the believer:

Christ's physical resurrection after he was crucified is neither in point of time nor in point of character the resurrection on which Paul, following his essential line of thought, wanted to fix the believer's mind. The resurrection Paul was striving after for himself and others was a resurrection *now*, and a resurrection to *righteousness*.   (S VI (SPP) p. 52)

Arnold draws heavily on Romans, where he finds Paul's teaching to be that Christ died to 'blind selfish impulse' and lived the life of obedience to 'the eternal moral order'. He is the pattern with whom the believer must be identified.

Arnold does not doubt that Paul accepted the physical miracle of the resurrection. However, he believes that this is but the surface-level of his theology, and it is in this context that he places his own lines:

> Below the surface-stream, shallow and light,
> Of what we *say* we feel – below the stream,
> As light, of what we *think* we feel – there flows
> With noiseless current strong, obscure and deep,
> The central stream of what we feel indeed.   (p. 51)

Paul's originality, says Arnold, lay in his search for 'a moral side and significance for all the processes, however mystical, of the religious life' (p. 51), so it was inevitable that he would treat the resurrection in this manner. In support of this hermeneutical strategy Arnold quoted II Corinthians 5. 16 as Bultmann was to do after him: 'though we have known Christ after the flesh, yet now henceforth know we him [so] no more'.

In *God and the Bible* he takes the same line with Jesus's predictions of his resurrection in the Fourth Gospel.[31] He finds the resurrection announced by Jesus to be 'clearly spiritual' (p. 315), but the disciples interpreted this in a physical sense:

> His disciples were misled...by something Jesus actually did say, which had not really the sense that he should physically rise from the dead, but which was capable of lending itself to this sense, and which his disciples misunderstood and imagined to convey it. (S VII (GB) p. 317)

Belief in a physical resurrection led the disciples to miss the real meaning of Jesus's words. Arnold is positive that such events as the physical resurrection of Jesus do not actually happen, and therefore seeks to account for the primitive Christian belief in a physical resurrection. He offers little explanation beyond the suggestive power of Jesus's (misinterpreted) words, undergirded by the transforming power of individual moral experience as experience of Christ. This is the weakest point in his argument. Arnold's last word on the resurrection occurs in 'A Comment on Christmas' (S X p. 230) where he refers to the resurrection story as 'poetry'.

Arnold is, then, waging his own campaign against religious 'materialism' much as he believes Jesus and Paul did before him. He wants to bring the believer's experience of death and resurrection to the centre: death first, and then resurrection. He calls the doctrine of *necrosis* 'Paul's central doctrine, and the doctrine which makes his profoundness and originality' (S VI (SPP) p. 47). This is the real *imitatio Christi*: to follow Jesus in his renunciation of every impulse to sin. Identification with Jesus in his renunciation of evil gives the power to the believer to do the same. Arnold clearly suggests that experience of resurrection is given to the believer during his life as it was to Jesus during his: if you participate in dying to sin, 'you rise with him to that harmonious conformity with the real and eternal order, that sense of pleasing God who trieth the hearts, which is life and peace, and which grows more and more till it becomes glory' (p. 48).

At this point Arnold himself raises the question of Jesus as an example of such death to self:

> The real worth of this mystical conception depends on the fitness of the character and history of Jesus Christ for inspiring such attachment and devotion as that which Paul's notion of faith implies. (p. 48)

What Arnold means by faith he has already described as 'a new and potent influence' in the life of Paul who found that 'the struggling stream of duty which had not volume enough to bear him to his goal, was suddenly reinforced by the immense tidal wave of sympathy and emotion' (p. 43). Faith is defined as 'a power, pre-eminently, of *holding fast to an unseen power of goodness*' (p. 44) and for Paul the key to this is 'identification with Christ' (p. 44). It is not clear that, despite the ecstatic language of union which Arnold borrows from Pauline theology, 'to be attached to Christ, to embrace Christ, to appropriate Christ, to be identified with Christ' (p. 45) can mean anything more than following in his footsteps, inspired by his example to experience certain fundamental human experiences that he experienced in greater degree, and which he described – to the confusion of his contemporaries except the incisive Paul – as dying and rising. A central theme of Arnold's Christology is, then, the exemplary nature of Jesus's life, his renunciation of sin and the moral resurrection thus brought about. This is explored in *Literature and Dogma* at greater depth.

Arnold talks there of the *method* of Jesus, which he approaches through certain well-known words of Jesus which amount to: 'Let a man *disown* himself, *renounce* himself, die as regards his old self, and so live' (S VI (LD) pp. 292–3). Jesus's method (and Arnold is not always very clear about this) appears to be the depiction of 'two lives': the real, which we attain by obedience to conscience (this is what Arnold means by 'righteousness') and an illusory, impoverished 'life in this world' (pp. 292–3). The first is life lived in conformity with the will of God; the second is life lived in conformity with the distorted, human will. The *secret* of Jesus is that dying to self which Paul described as *necrosis*, but is peculiarly the secret of *Jesus* because 'although others have seen that it was necessary, Jesus, above everyone, saw that it was *peace, joy, life*' (S VI (LD) p. 296). So, Jesus shifted the emphasis away from all the exuberant detail of future eschatology which had captivated the literalistic understanding of his countrymen, and which Arnold called '*Aberglaube*', back to the ethical struggle and its immediate, experiential results:

From his countrymen's errors about righteousness he reverted to the solid, authentic, universal fact of experience about it: the fact of the higher and lower self in man, inheritors the one of them of happiness, the other of misery. He possessed himself of it, he made it the centre of his teaching. He made it so in the well-known formula, his *secret*: 'He that will save his life shall lose it; he that do lose his life shall save it.' And by his admirable figure of the *two lives* of man, the real life and the seeming life, he connected this profound fact of experience with that attractive poetry of hopes and imaginings which possessed the minds of his countrymen. (S VIII (LE) pp. 155–6)

Again and again, Arnold stresses the joy of renunciation. He believed this to be a 'fact' of moral experience, empirically verifiable, accessible to all who would undertake the experiment: 'Man sincere, man before conscience, man

109

as Jesus put him, finds laid down for himself no rights; nothing but an infinite dying, and in that dying is life' (S VII (GB) p. 145). Here above all, Arnold's stoicism meets his Christianity. A. O. J. Cockshut puts it succinctly: 'For Arnold the Resurrection is contained in the Crucifixion – or rather is contained in the joyous Christian acceptance of it.'³² 'Conduct' and 'experience' are two words that Arnold uses again and again in his attempt to put the centre of religion where it should be: the life of man lived now. He is vehement in his rejection of intellectual conceptions which detract from this.

Future eschatology is dismissed as '*Aberglaube*', extra-belief, belief beyond what is certain and verifiable; it is pure poetry and in no way science. To mistake it for science, or as an attempt at describing in detail how things will be, is to fall into that error against which *Literature and Dogma* is a sustained polemic. It is to materialise religion. This estimate of apocalyptic imagery clearly divides the Tyrrell of *Christianity at the Crossroads* from the Arnold of *Literature and Dogma* and this is naturally reflected in their Christology. In searching for a 'symbolic' interpretation of such imagery Tyrrell wanted to maintain its content with respect to a transcendent God and his future action. He had once been much closer to Arnold and even in 1908 wrote,

I dislike the view which makes the feverish apocalyptic spirit *essential* to Christianity. I regard the illusion of Christ and His Apostles – the cataclysmic power and the Jewish content which they gave to the idea of the Kingdom – as irrelevant to the essence of the Gospel.   (SL p. 116)

This was Arnold's sentiment entirely. In his last book, however, Tyrrell acknowledged that Christian teaching was inextricably bound up with apocalyptic imagery. If such imagery was to be interpreted *symbolically* that meant there could be no successful attempt to disentangle some essence of the Gospel that by-passed such imagery entirely. So, Tyrrell came round to writing in *Christianity at the Crossroads*:

I feel sure that the apocalyptic Heaven, with all its colour and music, and light and happiness, is a truer symbol of man's spiritual aspirations than the cold constructions of intellectualism, in that it escapes a false antithesis of the spiritual and the phenomenal, and recognises the one as an inseparable correlative of the other.   (CCR p. 207)

What Arnold allowed as a concession – the poetic expression of 'scientific' reality – Tyrrell now embraced as an epistemological necessity. The ground rules for his hermeneutic are demonstrated in his long central chapter on 'The Apocalyptic Vision of Christ'. We cannot follow this in detail here, but simply note that he seeks at every point to differentiate himself from the pure immanentism which he sees as characteristic of the Liberal Protestant (with whom he would identify Arnold):

If we agree with Liberal Protestantism in taking symbolically what the early Church took literally, we differ in taking it at all as symbolic of transcendental values and not of the moral order in this life. (p. 145)

Arnold, of course, takes the line that we cannot talk about 'transcendental values' except in the language of poetry, language 'thrown out' at a vast reality.

In sweeping away metaphysics, Arnold sweeps away traditional Christology:

That Jesus Christ was the divine Logos, the second person of the Trinity, science can neither deny nor affirm. That he was the Jewish Messiah, who will some day appear in the sky with the sound of trumpets, to put an end to the actual kingdoms of the world and to establish his own kingdom, science can neither deny nor affirm. The very terms of which these propositions are composed are such as science is unable to handle. But that the Jesus of the Bible follows the universal moral order and the will of God, without being let and hindered as we are by the motions of private passion and by self-will, this is evident to whoever can read the Bible with open eyes. It is just what any criticism of the Gospel-history, which sees that history as it really is, tells us; it is the scientific result of that history. (S VI (SPP) p. 42)

This does not leave very much except 'poetry' and the imitation of Christ: 'The fundamental thing for Christians is not the incarnation but the imitation of Christ' (S VI (LD) p. 146). It also leaves a dilemma in the interpretation of Jesus. Either Jesus, as a man of his time, was duped by the transcendent imagery of contemporary Judaism and the modern critic is wiser than him in this respect, or Jesus saw to the ethical heart of contemporary imagery and let himself be misunderstood by his contemporaries, perhaps knowing that a later generation would understand him better. This Arnold accepts.

The picture that emerges is thus at least consistent. Jesus stands firmly in the Jewish tradition, but as a reformer who resists the materialism of current religious thought. He is not a worker of miracles ('miracles do not happen') nor a supernaturally endowed prophet. His appeal is entirely that of transparent integrity and moral pre-eminence. Arnold talks frequently of his '*epieikeia*', his 'mildness and sweet reasonableness' (S VI (SPP) p. 115) which was 'a new way of putting things' with 'an air of truth and likelihood' (S VI (LD) p. 219). This was demonstrated in that Jesus 'put things in such a way that his hearer was led to take each rule or fact of conduct by its inward side, its effect on the heart and character' (p. 219). Arnold links this with the 'method' and 'secret' of Jesus:

111

The conjunction of the three in Jesus, – the method of inwardness, and the secret of self-renouncement, working in and through this element of mildness, – produced the total impression of his 'epieikeia', or sweet reasonableness.

(S VI (LD) p. 300)

Arnold clearly saw this as the appropriate model for Christian apologetic; he criticised Butler because he lacked it (S VIII (LE) p. 28) and he tried to make it his own.[33] He wrote that

The most important and fruitful utterances of Jesus, therefore, are not things which can be drawn up as a table of stiff and stark external commands, but the things which have most soul in them; because these can best sink down into our soul, work there, set up an influence, form habits of conduct, and prepare the future. (S IX (EC2) p. 303)

The link between the believer and Christ is one of moral unity, through belief in the same ideal and participation in the same experience. As far as Jesus himself is concerned, it is the life that he lived, not metaphysical statements about his Eternal Sonship, that truly inspire the believer to accept his divinity:

For us, who approach Christianity through a scholastic theology, it is Christ's divinity which establishes his being without sin. For Paul, who approached Christianity through his personal experience, it was Jesus Christ's being without sin which established his divinity. (S VI (SPP) p. 40)

We have seen that he wrote in the preface to the popular edition of *Literature and Dogma*, 'The fundamental thing for Christians is not the incarnation but the imitation of Christ' (S VI (LD) p. 146).

Arnold's whole approach to the interpretation of Christ was summarised in a little essay he wrote in 1885, called 'A Comment on Christmas': 'The solid fact of history marked by Christmas is the birth of Jesus, the miraculous circumstances with which that birth is invested and presented are legendary' (S X p. 223). In discussing the 'legend' and the 'miracle' accompanying the birth of Jesus, Arnold says that they have 'their virtue of symbol' – a term he uses rarely. Before making clear what he means he drives home the point that those who originally retold the legendary narrative had no notion of taking it symbolically, as we must do. Such legendary treatment was at the time 'the popular homage to a high ideal of pureness' (p. 224). The 'pureness' of Jesus is the underlying truth of which the miraculous story of the Incarnation is the symbol. The same hermeneutic can be applied to almost all the Christian festivals:

There is hardly a fast or a festival of the Christian year in which the underlying truth, the beneficent and forwarding idea, clothed with legend and miracle because mankind could only appropriate it by materialising it in legend and miracle, is not apparent. (p. 230)

We take as poetry what was once taken as fact. Understanding this, we are free to honour Jesus for his moral integrity, his conformity to the natural moral law, rather than for any supposed working of wonders. Arnold calls him 'an absolute': 'we cannot get behind him and above him, cannot command him' (p. 232). He is uniquely fitted to be the founder of a great religion. Arnold summarises:

Therefore, when we are asked: What really is Christmas, and what does it celebrate? we answer: The birthday of Jesus. But what, then, is the miracle of the Incarnation? A homage to the virtue of pureness, and to the manifestation of this virtue in Jesus. What is Lent, and the miracle of the temptation? A homage to the virtue of self-control and to the manifestation of this virtue in Jesus. What does Easter celebrate? Jesus victorious over death by dying. By dying how? Dying to re-live. To re-live in Paradise, in another world? No, in this. But if in this, what is the kingdom of God? The ideal society of the future. Then what is immortality? To live in the eternal order, which never dies. What is salvation by Jesus Christ? The attainment of this immortality. Through what means? Through faith in Jesus, and appropriation of his method, secret, and temper.

(S X p. 234)

With this statement of Arnold's before us, it is instructive to return to an important letter that Tyrrell wrote to von Hügel in February 1907, because it illustrates precisely how they could draw so close and yet remain so far apart. Tyrrell writes about the Virgin Birth:

Its denial as historic fact involves that complete revolution in our conception of what dogma is for which Loisy and Le Roy are preparing the way – a 'kill-or-cure' remedy to which...we are simply *forced* by the results of the historico-critical method.[34]

(SL p. 56)

Here he is absolutely at one with Arnold, who foresaw the need for the 'revolution' forty years earlier. Tyrrell argues, as Arnold did, that 'to take away the affirmative reasons for the Virgin Birth is to prove it false – as historic fact'. The point here is that history deals in probabilities; the Virgin Birth must, by any canons of experience, be improbable; historians will say it did not happen. Tyrrell, though, wants to ask a further question which Arnold does not ask. Speaking as historians we may confidently say that the Virgin Birth is untrue – but is there another sense in which it is true? In fact, an affirmative answer to this second question raises a third question which Tyrrell does not really face. If the Virgin Birth is true in some non-historical sense, does that truth modify our first conclusion; should it in fact modify our view of history? It was a question of which Blondel was well aware; but then Blondel was a philosopher who turned his attention to history.[35]

Tyrrell explains his position on the second question clearly, and should be quoted at length:

I distinguish sharply between the Christian revelation and the theology that rationalises and explains it. The former was the work of the inspired era of origins. It is prophetic in form and sense; it involves an idealised reading of history past and to come. It is so to say, an inspired construction of things in the interests of religion; a work of inspired imagination, not of reflection and reasoning. It does not develop or change like theology; but is the subject-matter of theology. Of that symbolic and imaginative construction the Virgin Birth is an integral part. It is an element of a complete expression. But it must not be broken off and interpreted alone. All the elements conspire to express one thing – the Kingdom of God.   (SL p. 57)

What Tyrrell says of this 'whole' is immensely suggestive in the light of later developments in hermeneutics – about which I shall say more in chapter 8:

It gives us the *world* of our religious life.   (*Ibid.*)

Arnold would have accepted this, understanding this 'world' to be one of pure poetry, a stimulus to ethical effort and no more. This is in some part what Tyrrell says here: 'My faith is in the truth, shadowed by the whole creed and in the direction it gives to spiritual life – in the Way, the Life, and the Truth.' Where Tyrrell differs from Arnold is in his acknowledgment (which never wavered) that there was some truth shadowed by the whole Creed. However dim his apprehension of that truth, and however much his attempt to state the truth-value of the Creed sounded like Arnoldian 'sentimentalism' he was not satisfied with such a reduction, and had developed beyond it in the use he made of apocalyptic in *Christianity at the Crossroads*.

A further point from the same letter distinguishes Tyrrell and Arnold. Tyrrell is not prepared to admit that the Virgin Birth and the resurrection are on the same level: 'the historicity of [the] passion is all-important, the factualness of [the] resurrection equally so'. Tyrrell's point here is that certain religious values are dependent on the realisation in history of the images and symbols which convey them. He speaks in a different way of the passion and the resurrection because the historical mode in which two such events would have been realised could not be identical. He side-steps the question here of what phenomena an unbeliever might have witnessed at the tomb of Jesus on the first Easter Sunday. Yet it is essential that the Church should be able to say of the resurrection of Jesus on that day that 'it happened'. This is not true for Arnold. For Arnold, the Church *did* say this, not so much because of events after the death of Jesus, but because of the life he lived before his crucifixion.

At the end of his life Dean Inge wrote that George Tyrrell had once said that some day nothing might be left of Christianity except the Pauline Christ mysticism and the law of love; and confessed that he had himself been moving in this direction.[36] If so, he was moving towards Arnold and away from the Tyrrell of *Christianity at the Crossroads*. However, Arnold's reduction of Christianity was even more harsh than that which Inge attributed to Tyrrell, because it was not so much the law of love, but the law of self-renunciation that he stressed. On the other hand, he wrote so eloquently of this as a life of joy that many of his readers must surely have failed to observe the austerity of what he was offering. Much of what he did offer: a pre-eminently attractive Jewish Jesus concerned more with righteousness than with metaphysics, Tyrrell accepted. On the other hand, Tyrrell became increasingly suspicious of a Jesus who stood above his own time intellectually, and was consciously misunderstood. That was too like the practical docetism of popular Catholic belief. He chose to replace the intellectual superiority of Jesus with the messianic consciousness stressed by Wrede and Weiss. In Christology as in every other field we see Tyrrell, having broken away from the restraints imposed by scholasticism, flirting with the obvious Liberal Protestant alternative, but speedily drawing away from that also.

In the field of Christology it is Tyrrell's sheer lack of indebtedness to Arnold that is striking. Where Arnold put a line through the doctrine of the Incarnation and called it of secondary importance, Tyrrell fought to find and express the meaning of the Incarnation in terms that would meet the demands both of history and the tradition. In Christology more than in any other field their contrasting strategies stand revealed. Yet even here it would not be unfair to say that a third of Tyrrell was in Arnold. He himself feared that it was so, and the fact that he did bears witness to his continuing conviction that if he lost the Incarnation he lost everything.

7

God, and 'the Power that makes for Righteousness'

For both Tyrrell and Arnold the question of God was central. Moreover, they often expressed themselves in similar terms. We have seen in chapter 3 that Arnold gave Tyrrell a phrase for God: 'the Power that makes for Righteousness'. In that earlier discussion (pp. 33–5) it was clear that Tyrrell played on or alluded to the phrase from 1899 on, that it reappears in a number of his most important books, and is specifically debated with Hakluyt Egerton (Arthur Boutwood) in 1908–9. In a preliminary way, we saw that for Tyrrell the phrase always carried connotations of personal being,[1] because 'the Power that makes for Righteousness' was for him a phrase describing the human experience of a personal God. Egerton argued that Tyrrell could not logically move from the experience of such a Power to the assertion that the Power was personal. Tyrrell took issue, with what success we shall see.

Arnold, in his use of the phrase, blocked off the question of the personal nature of God. What we experience is no more (and no less) than a 'power, not ourselves, that makes for righteousness'. Tyrrell tended to omit 'not ourselves', whereas for Arnold the phrase was incomplete without those words. Surprisingly, then, it is Arnold who has the more secure hold on the transcendence of God – the 'power' is 'a power, *not ourselves*' – whilst Tyrrell has by far the stronger hold on the personal nature of God. Arnold simply argues that the Jews thought of this Power in anthropomorphic terms, and that the evidence for any attribution of personal being to God is lacking. More than that, since the anthropomorphism of the Jews was a product of their religious immaturity, we, in more enlightened times, should let such notions drop. Despite considerable sympathy with much that Arnold was saying, Tyrrell for reasons that we shall explore, did not accept this conclusion at all.

These, then, are the questions to be covered in this chapter. Although a considerable proportion of the discussion will turn upon a phrase, we should note that this is not the only phrase that Arnold or Tyrrell used when they wanted to speak about God. Even though Arnold spoke of 'that stream of tendency by which all things seek to fulfil the law of their being' and Tyrrell spoke of 'the Absolute', it remains true that the preferred term for God was virtually identical in both writers. We begin by looking at Arnold's thoughts on God, and then proceed to the more wide-ranging and self-consciously exploratory work of Tyrrell. We shall find one major difference between the two: although Tyrrell, like Arnold, respected the rights of 'mystery', he did not give up on metaphysics. Certainly, he turned his back on the Aristotelian framework in which he grew up, but he substituted an experimental metaphysic of the spirit and the will. Sometimes he compromised the transcendence, the personal nature or the tri-unity of the Christian God. Where Arnold did this with insistent abandon, Tyrrell's stance was both more conservative and more interrogative. Already, the evidence of chapter 3 has shown that it was as important to Tyrrell to distance himself from Arnold as to draw on him. What Arnold actually said we shall now examine.

When Mary Arnold read her brother's first book of poems in 1849, she commented,

I felt there was so much more of this practical questioning in Matt's book than I was at all prepared for; in fact that it showed a knowledge of life and conflict which was *strangely like experience* if it was not the thing itself; and this with all Matt's great power I should not have looked for.[2]

Mrs Ward finds in this comment 'an interesting proof of the difficulty we all have in seeing with accuracy the persons and things which are nearest to us',[3] but that is very commonplace. It may be that Mary was making a much finer remark, deftly pointing out a deficiency in Matt's poetry which has often been noted subsequently: he seems to write about something which is not quite experience, or experience a little distanced. When he writes to his sister Jane he is quite self-deprecatory:

My poems are fragments – *i.e.*....I am fragments, while you are a whole; the whole effect of my poems is quite vague and indeterminate – this is their weakness...I shall do better some day I hope...Do not plague yourself to find a consistent meaning for these last, which in fact they do not possess through my weakness.[4]

In a sonnet, published at that time, he praises Sophocles because he 'saw life steadily, and saw it whole'[5] as he could not. The quest for *wholeness* was, in fact, a fundamental theme of Arnold's entire life, expressed both in his poetry and his prose.[6] When wholeness was lacking, whether in himself or in society, he clearly felt pained and diminished: 'Who prop, thou ask'st, in these bad days, my mind?'[7] The guarantor of the wholeness of the society in which he had grown up had been the Christian God, experienced above all through the words of the Bible and the moral integrity stressed by his father. However, this God already seemed remote to Arnold by the time he reached Balliol. What was immediate was duty, aspiration, necessity, change, and with that a 'something that infects the world',[8] which is all that Arnold knew of God for the moment.

If God is gone, experience as a cohesive continuum is threatened, and this Arnold will not have. His poems speak eloquently of the catastrophic shock that the old world-view and the old culture have sustained, and of the corresponding confusion in the minds of men. They speak also of the elements of permanence and continuity that seem to suggest some teleological force at work behind the manifold of experience. Nature, no more man's 'alma parens', becomes a fickle but dominant mistress:

> Man must begin, know this, where Nature ends;
> Nature and man can never be fast friends.
> Fool, if thou canst not pass her, rest her slave![9]

It was a hard doctrine, too hard to live by. The emotion that turns what is 'strangely like experience' into 'the thing itself' is much more prominent in a stanza from 'The New Sirens':

> Where I stand, the grass is glowing;
> Doubtless you are passing fair!
> But I hear the north wind blowing,
> And I feel the cold night-air.
> Can I look on your sweet faces,
> And your proud heads backward thrown,
> From this dusk of leaf-strewn places
> With the dumb woods and the night alone?[10]

In an explanation of this poem, Arnold wrote to Clough of his 'conscientious regrets after the spiritual life' despite the fear that it is 'hard and solitary'.[11] The poem is a kind of 'Lead Kindly Light' *à rebours*, with sirens for angel faces and darkness for light. Nevertheless, in only the previous year (1848), when Clough was on the point of resigning his fellowship, Arnold closed a letter to him: 'God bless you: there is a God, but he is not well-conceived of by all.'[12]

There is one poem, written between 1863 and 1867,[13] which deals with exactly this point. In 'The Divinity' St Bernard is depicted as maintaining

> ''Tis God himself becomes apparent, when
> God's wisdom and God's goodness are displayed,
> For God of these his attributes is made.'[14]

Arnold stands this on its head:

> *God's wisdom and God's goodness!* – Ay, but fools
> Mis-define these till God knows them no more.
> *Wisdom and goodness, they are God!*[15]

Robbins points to the influence of Spinoza on this sonnet and on 'The Better Part', and notes that if they were indeed written in 1863 they were written in the same year as Arnold's essay 'Spinoza and the Bible'.[16] In that and other essays Arnold began to hint at the way in which he now thought of God.[17]

In the *Essays in Criticism* (First Series) Arnold is only beginning to approach the religious problem and what he has to say is said obliquely, with reference to Spinoza or Joubert,[18] Colenso or Stanley. Prominent among these is Spinoza upon whom Arnold wrote three separate essays. The third, and most considerable, 'Spinoza and the Bible', includes a critique that very neatly draws out the issues with which we are concerned. Arnold commends Spinoza because 'his whole soul was filled with desire of the love and knowledge of God, and of that only' (S III p. 179), but he also makes it clear that Spinoza did not mean by 'the love of God' what the Hebrew and Christian religions have meant by the phrase: 'Spinoza's ideal is the intellectual life; the Christian's ideal is the religious life' (p. 178). Arnold is critical of a contemporary writer who tries to make of Spinoza an atheist using theistic language, but on the other hand he maintains the distinction between the God of Spinoza and the God of Augustine just as sharply. Precisely what Spinoza did understand by 'God' is not made clear. Nevertheless the thrust of Arnold's essay is plain: since the context in which we can most profitably talk of 'God' is that of obedience to the law of reason (reason here being not merely an intellectual, but fundamentally a moral concept), many of the traditional attributes of God are no more than powerful fictions. The stage is set for Arnold's attack on the improper use of anthropomorphism, though as yet he reserves his own position.[19] In a letter to his mother (*Letters* I p. 179) Arnold denies that he held the same doctrines as Spinoza. Nevertheless, when he came to handle religious issues at length the influence of Spinoza's *Tractatus* was everywhere apparent.

Two other influences are apparent in a review of *Selections from Theodore Parker's Unpublished Sermons* that Arnold wrote in 1867. Parker was an influential American Unitarian, of whose theism Arnold is sharply critical, because it does not measure up to the demands of what Arnold calls 'the scientific intellect':

The idea that the world is in a course of development, of *becoming*, towards a perfection infinitely greater than we now can even conceive, the idea of a *tendance à l'ordre* present in the universe 'groaning and travailing in pain together', this the scientific intellect may accept, and may willingly let the religious instincts and the language of religion gather around it. But the idea of a 'Great Director', or 'Wise Engineer', to use Parker's language, who has set this movement a-going on a foreknown plan, and who sits *outside* of it watching its operation, this the scientific intellect can at the present time no more admit than the idea of a God

119

who turns himself into a sacrificial wafer or who foredooms a large proportion of the human race to hell. (S V p. 83)

To a remarkable degree, the whole of Arnold's religious programme is laid out in this extract. The pain and indignation are unmistakable. Arnold is pleading for *adequate*[20] conceptions of God, such as those he found in the depressive Obermann, with his '*tendance à l'ordre*', to which Arnold returned in *Literature and Dogma*.[21] Goethe is another fruitful source when he says that 'Man..."calls the best he knows, *God*"' (p. 83).[22] As we have seen, Arnold's poem 'Divinity' says more than this, or says this more strongly, when it asserts that Wisdom and Goodness *are* God. Here he goes on: 'the God of the Pantheist, the Positivist, and the Theist is alike the best that each of them knows'. Theodore Parker falls short of the best by any criterion and is dismissed with the faint praise that he is at least ahead of the worst (the God of Calvinist Puritanism). What is evident from this review is that Arnold is again in middle ground: the God of traditional Christianity, with his crude anthropomorphic attributes, cannot be taken seriously any more, but the question remains: there is a referent of supreme importance for talk about 'God' and this referent is known to every man who takes the question seriously. Arnold (like Spinoza) is no atheist.

Inexorably, Arnold moves nearer to an extended treatment of the question of God. 'Culture', he tells us in *Culture and Anarchy*, 'demands worthy notions of reason and the will of God' (S V p. 92). Culture is an attempt 'to draw towards a knowledge of the universal order which seems to be intended and aimed at in the world, and which it is a man's happiness to go along with or his misery to go counter to, – to learn, in short, the will of God' (p. 93), and it is more than that, for it involves the attempt to make it *prevail*. Arnold grants that the Greek and the Hebrew approaches to life are both founded on 'the desire, native in man, for reason and the will of God, the feeling after the universal order, – in a word, the love of God' (p. 165), but he makes an important distinction:

While Hebraism seizes upon certain plain, capital intimations of the universal order, and rivets itself, one may say, with unequalled grandeur of earnestness and intensity on the study and observance of them, the bent of Hellenism is to follow, with flexible activity, the whole play of the universal order.   (p. 165)

Already, in his essay on Spinoza, Arnold acknowledged that the Old Testament conception of the will of God saw that will as characteristically revealed in the particular. For him this is not so. *Culture and Anarchy* is an essay on the meaning of 'the will of God' in his own time: it is determined by reason (in the broadest sense), promoted by culture, thwarted (often enough) by religion. Still, Arnold does not yet grasp the nettle: who, or what, is God? Like Spinoza, he comes at the question not as one of pure metaphysics, but through the interpretation of the Bible.

In writing about religion, Arnold opened himself to exactly the charge that he had pressed against Colenso: that his work was negative, destructive, unedifying. The thrust of *St Paul and Protestantism* is against those Calvinist notions of God that sprang from Biblical language taken at its most literal, against God as a 'magnified and non-natural man' (p. 10). Arnold is searching for the least inadequate way of speaking about 'that universal order which the intellect feels after as a law and the heart feels after as a benefit' – for this is what he takes 'God' to be. When he speaks of 'that *stream of tendency by which all things seek to fulfil the law of their being*' (p. 10), he is trying to get behind the word 'God' by using language that he thinks 'men of science' will understand and accept. What his words mean (he would want to say 'refer to') remains obscure.[23] Later, he speaks of the importance that Paul attaches to 'God as moral law' (p. 30). To serve God is 'to follow that central clue in our moral being which unites us to the universal order' (p. 31). Conforming to *the will of God* is conforming to the moral order (p. 32). Arnold sometimes identifies the moral order with God himself and sometimes with what God wills. However, it becomes increasingly apparent that the God with whom Arnold is concerned cannot *have* a will. It may be that it, or he, *is* will, but there is not enough evidence to warrant an analogy between this God and the human being as willing agent.

Arnold also notes that the Hebrews apprehended God as 'the source of life and breath and all things' (p. 36). He links this with 'the necessary, mystical, and divine world, of influence, sympathy, emotion' (p. 38). When he quotes Paul's reference to 'the power that worketh in us', we see foreshadowed the 'power, not ourselves' and, linking this with 'God as moral law', see the origins of 'the power, not ourselves, which makes for righteousness'. However, in *St Paul and Protestantism* he did not use this phrase and offered no extended discussion of the problem of God. Rather, he discussed problems of Pauline exegesis abutting on the problem of God, and problems of nonconformity. With hindsight, one can see perfectly clearly what he was saying about God, but Arnold had not yet commanded the attention of his contemporaries on the subject.

With *Literature and Dogma* the situation changed. Here was a book that tackled directly the meaning of dogma, the nature of God, the future of Christianity. What Arnold has to say on the question of God is concentrated into the first chapter, where he attempts to clear the ground for his later critique of contemporary Christianity. The chapter (and the book) is really a sustained polemic against traditional metaphysics as a confusion of literary language with scientific. Once terms like '*personality*,[24] essence, existence, consubstantiality' (S VI p. 195) have been swept away, we can get down to what we really know about God, and what we really know is that which 'comes forth in our consciousness' and is acknowledged to be verifiable.[25] Not language, but *experience*, is central to the knowledge of God.

Although dismissive of theological language, Arnold remains concerned with the relation between language and experience.[26] He plays in this chapter with two notions of God, neither of which is really new to his readers, both of which are now drawn out more fully. The first is the famous 'power that makes for righteousness' (with or without the 'not ourselves') (p. 183). The second is 'the stream of tendency by which all things seek to fulfil the law of their being' (p. 189). Arnold himself uses both descriptions of God (or, more accurately, our experience of God) almost interchangeably, though he indicates that the first goes beyond the second and that one can move from acknowledgment of the second to understanding of the first by a study of the Bible. Broadly, the first is a religious definition and the second a scientific, though both are verifiable in experience. In one he is referring to what the heart feels after; in the other to what the intellect feels after. 'Imaginative reason' is fulfilled in 'God'.

Arnold is trying not to go beyond the evidence, and, once the incontrovertible evidence has been agreed upon (he was always sanguine about this), to build. His approach to Israelite religion is to

> take their fact of experience, to keep it steadily for our basis in using their language, and to see whether from using their language with the ground of this real and firm sense to it, as they themselves did, somewhat of their feeling, too, may not grow upon us; and that what we are saying is true, however inadequate.
> (p. 200)

Here is his whole strategy in all its strength and weakness. He is a divider of the certain from the uncertain, of fact from feeling, of science from religion, of belief from *Aberglaube*. Yet he will not give up the 'poetic' language of the Bible that he values so much. Because of his sensitivity to this language, Arnold is at his best when trying to make something of the Israelite 'fact of experience' which is not, of course, a 'fact' (i.e. a datum that natural scientists would recognise) at all. When he begins to explore the Israelite consciousness he does it with a hatchet, for his presumption is that the anthropomorphic depiction of God can be isolated as having been added to a primary intuition of creatureliness and of the call to righteousness. The two are as clearly isolable as religion and theology in Tyrrell's mature thought. The 'Eternal that makes for righteousness' came to be 'a mere magnified and non-natural man' (p. 215). In *God and the Bible* Arnold ackowledged that the two were more closely linked from the beginning. This is all to the good, for the move that he is making is towards what would now be called phenomenology. This, not science, whether natural science or the science of history, is the way forward. In *God and the Bible* he is forced to pay closer attention to the Israelite consciousness of God (S VII pp. 214–15), to the experience as experienced. In the end, however, he retracted nothing, for he remained confident of his critical ability to discriminate between the essential and the inessential.

In prescinding from the questions of traditional metaphysics and turning to anthropology, Arnold was pointing to a number of questions perennially raised by human existence: the ourselves and the not-ourselves, the encounter with moral demand, the phenomena of time and change – questions that have traditionally been answered in the West by postulating the personal God whom Arnold wants to exclude. What Arnold finds in terms of progress, the inevitable fulfilment of laws of being, the rewards of righteousness, seems to us chimerical, but the questions remain, and the possibility that there can be *some* valid induction from the way in which they are encountered is intriguing. Arnold pointed out in *God and the Bible* that he did not deny the existence of a personal God: 'All we say is that men do not know enough about the Eternal not-ourselves that makes for righteousness, to warrant their pronouncing this either a person or a thing' (p. 160). The real challenge to the theologians was not to say the same old things louder, which many of them did, but to pay closer attention to experience (closer even than the poet Arnold) and to articulate the Christian doctrine of God less crudely, showing how the doctrine related to the texture of experience. Most of the theologians simply condemned Arnold out of hand.

In Arnold's own words, the first of the objections to *Literature and Dogma* is that 'its conclusions about the meaning of the term *God*, and about man's knowledge of God, are severely condemned' (S VII (GB) p. 150).[27] These he deals with in the first three chapters of *God and the Bible*, the most concentrated (and involved) discussion of the question of God in all his writings. He takes nothing back; he merely states his own case more sharply in the face of (selected) hostile reviewers. In turn, he deals with what he takes to be the supports for the theory of the 'magnified and non-natural man': metaphysics and morals and experience. Each time he fails to meet the thrust of objections, ending his chapter more or less where he ended in *Literature and Dogma*.

On the question of miracles, Arnold gives the impression of being less than dogmatic. He does not say, as he later did in the Preface to the popular edition of *Literature and Dogma*, written in 1883, '*Miracles do not happen*'; he says that we simply do not know on *a priori* grounds whether miracles are possible or impossible. This being so, we have to accept that the overwhelming majority of people do not now believe the miracle-stories of the Bible. By the end of the chapter Arnold has reverted to a more assertive tone:

Only a kind of man magnified could so make man the centre of all things and interrupt the settled order of nature in his behalf as miracles imply. But in miracles we are dealing, we find, with the unreal world of fairy-tale. Having no reality of their own, they cannot lend it as foundation for the reality of anything else.
(p. 172)

An open *a priori* has become a closed one. Arnold's original question had been 'Are we to affirm that God is a person who thinks and loves because miracles compel us?' (p. 163). His answer is 'no' because there *are* no miracles to compel us. In making the climate of opinion his explicit standing ground, he was on ground that could easily shift under his feet. He does not deal with the question of the characteristics a miracle would have to have in order to allow or even compel the valid inference that a personal God exists. He leaves to the theologians the preliminary work on 'personal being' and 'personality' that would have to be done if such language, with all its modern connotations, were to be reapplied to God. For Arnold, miracles, 'the magnified and non-natural man', metaphysics and theologians are all part of an impossible and outdated package.

Arnold is at his worst when trying to cut a swathe through traditional metaphysics: tortuous, repetitive, uncomprehending. He makes great play with Descartes and his attempt to find a sure grounding for metaphysics (implicitly recognising a kindred spirit), but he rejects the term 'being' – which he takes to be central to metaphysical language, and reduces, by dubious etymological jugglery, to 'breathing' – because he finds it incapable of adequate definition. Just as with 'verification', Arnold's concepts of definition are crudely empiricist, and largely unexamined. The model with which he works is that of clear ideas impressed upon our minds by material objects in the world. Abstract concepts should conform as much as possible to this empiricist ideal:

The moment we have an abstract word, a word where we do not apprehend both the concrete sense and the manner of this sense's application, there is danger. The whole value of an abstract term depends on our true and clear conception of that which we have abstracted and now convey by means of this term.
(p. 188)

His conclusion is that 'when we talk of the *being* of things, we use a fluid and literary expression, not a rigid and scientific one' (p. 193). This will not serve as a verifiable basis for religion, and so metaphysics are to be discarded.

Arnold is back with *experience*, cutting away metaphysics with the best of the logical positivists. He deals with Paley and the like in less than a page:

We do not know from experience that an infinite eternal substance, all-thinking and all-powerful, the creator of all things, makes ears and buds. We know nothing about the matter, it is altogether beyond us. When, therefore, we are speaking exactly, and not poetically and figuratively, of the ear or of a bud, which we see working harmoniously and well, all we have a right to say is: It works harmoniously and well.   (p. 198)

(Not even, one is tempted to ask, that it is 'fulfilling the law of its being'? – if one dare use the term 'being' after its reduction to 'breathing'.) What Arnold has in mind here is the use of metaphysics to *prove* that the personal God exists; he rightly says that such proofs do not get off the ground. However, he fails to consider that there might be other uses for metaphysics: to answer questions like 'Given that societies have tended through history to depict God in personal terms, how would the existence of such a God be demonstrable?' For Arnold this is simply a non-question. His scorn for metaphysics betrays him into a somewhat two-dimensional account of experience, and certainly one cut in two by the dichotomy between science and religion. Again, the appropriate answer might have been for metaphysicians to reconsider the uses of metaphysics at that time. Since the orthodox theologians tended to dig themselves in, Arnold was betrayed into a position that often looked more like agnostic sensationalism than revitalised Christianity.

In a third chapter Arnold deals with a number of objections to his notion that the 'power that makes for righteousness' – rather than the God of Abraham, Isaac and Jacob – was central to Israelite experience, and that the existence of this power – as power – can be proven experimentally. We have seen in chapter 4 of this book the shifts to which Arnold was driven by Secrétan's assertion that righteousness does not in this world lead to happiness. Arnold reasserts that 'joy and happiness are the magnets to which human life irresistibly moves' (p. 234), but this does not meet the objection that in experience happiness does not follow *righteousness*. Arnold's call would have been more compelling if he had paid more attention to what he meant by 'joy', 'happiness' and, particularly, 'righteousness'. At this point he abandons his empiricism and talks in terms of 'reason', 'the moral law' and 'the will of God'. He assumes the cogency and the compelling nature of the Biblical concept of 'righteousness' because he finds it to be in accord with nature: to live in accord with righteousness is to follow the law of nature which is what we mean by 'the will of God'. The Bible, one understands, indicates what is meant by 'righteousness', but it indicates what we already know. At root, Arnold believes that we understand what righteousness is because the moral law is written on the heart of everyman. This is the sort of language Tyrrell understands and frequently uses, when he talks of Jesus as 'the human conscience incarnate'. Where Arnold made a sharp distinction between the human experience of 'righteousness' and the anthropomorphic conceptualisation which was so often its correlate, Tyrrell tried to hold the two together, and argued for the cognitive import of the dogma that Arnold despised. Tyrrell's case was that of a minimalist: such conceptions had in the past been productive of good works. The fact that he was prepared to make it at all is indicative of a fundamental difference between himself and Arnold.

Arnold's later works add nothing to what we have already seen. The essay on Butler in *Last Essays*, however, provides for us a convenient summary of the position he has taken all along, without the wearisome repetition of Arnoldian catch-phrases. Arguing against both Butler and his Deist opponents, Arnold says,

> The proposition that this world, as we see it, necessarily implies an intelligent designer with a will and a character, a quasi-human agent and governor, cannot, I think, but be felt, by any one who is brought fairly face to face with it, and has to rest everything upon it, not to be self-demonstrating, nay, to be utterly impalpable. Evidently, it is not of the same experimental character as the proposition that we *are* rewarded and punished according to our actions.
>
> (S VIII (LE) p. 52)

He deals in turn with four major areas of Butler's argument in support of such a God. On traditional metaphysics he comments, 'Religion must be built on ideas about which there is no puzzle' (p. 53). How crude and limiting Tyrrell would have found that! The arguments from analogy are dismissed, at root, because they go beyond our experience. Butler's arguments from miracles and the fulfilment of prophecy are dismissed as they were in *Literature and Dogma*: 'men's knowledge increases, their point of view changes, they come to see things differently' (p. 55).[28] In a revealing sentence, Arnold concludes, 'After reading the *Analogy* one goes instinctively to bathe one's spirit in the Bible again, to be refreshed by its boundless certitude and exhilaration' (p. 57). It is as though he were saying 'I know the Bible speaks to me as the *Analogy* does not. If I could be sure that some part of what it says is undeniably true,[29] I could draw upon it all, interpreting the unknown by the known.' He did not see that any other strategy was possible for his contemporaries, nor did he see the dangers implicit in his own boldly reductionist approach.

All along, Arnold is the prisoner of his own divisive method. He sees the value of words like 'spirit', 'power', 'culture' and so on, and uses them freely, but he tries to justify himself with an empiricist epistemology that really has no place for them. A consistent application of his own principles would exclude *a priori* not only the 'magnified and non-natural man', but 'the power that makes for righteousness' as well. Arnold's commitment to conscience, feeling, poetry and religion is at war with his commitment to empirical verification. His God is a 'something that infects the world', which could best be made explicit not in an all-out war with traditional or received metaphysics – though doubtless the Churches of his time, both established and nonconformist, were such an obvious target that the temptation to restrict his critique to banter and polemic was overwhelming – but by a closer attention to the texture of experience. The work of Arnold is of permanent value because he points in this direction – towards *experience* – but in the end he offers nothing that one could recognisably call a 'god'.[30]

This is not true of Tyrrell, to whom we now turn. In 1909, 'Hakluyt Egerton' published a critique of *Through Scylla and Charybdis* under the title *Father Tyrrell's Modernism*.[31] Tyrrell himself put his finger on the difference between his position and that of Egerton, when he replied to Egerton in a lecture delivered at King's College, London, on 26 March 1909.[32] Tyrrell wrote,

> The great question between us is as to the character or nature of Revelation. Does it consist in certain divine statements; or in certain spiritual experiences about which *man* makes statements that may be inspired by those divine experiences, yet are not divine but human statements? (*The Heythrop Journal*, 12 (1971), 130)

Egerton criticised Tyrrell particularly for claiming to describe moral or mystical experience when he was in fact *interpreting* such experience in a theistic way. Egerton does not deny that we experience moments of 'renewing strength' when we feel the influence of a power that lifts us up 'above our disappointments, above our questionings, above our sins',[33] but he does deny that such experiences tell us anything about a specifically personal God. If we are to learn about a personal God, it will be by revealed statements, the truth of which may seem more likely in the light of the sort of experiences to which Tyrrell refers, but which is not implicit in the experiences themselves. Egerton's position on experience is very close to that of Arnold,[34] though Arnold, of course, denies the revelation in which Egerton believes. In refuting Egerton Tyrrell also refutes Arnold.

Tyrrell was always fair in dealing with critics who were fair to him, and he hears Egerton's question perfectly clearly: 'What right have I, asks Mr Egerton in effect, to say that the Power making for Righteousness which is given in experience, is God or from God? Is it not simply an anonymous impression?' (p. 142). How, in other words, does Tyrrell dare to go beyond

Arnold? Tyrrell has already argued in his paper that 'we only know real causes in and by their effects'. This, says Tyrrell, is precisely how we know 'the Power making for Righteousness'. However, he also agrees with Egerton that 'the Power' cannot be identified with the personal God directly from our experience. The theistic interpretation of experience such as that described by Egerton is only one legitimate interpretation. This Arnold would have agreed with, though wanting to play down the possibility of traditional theism as unnecessary and misleading.

However, there is another arm to Tyrrell's argument. He will not prove the existence of God via the propositions of theology, but maintains that 'all we need do is to prove to men that they necessarily believe in him; that they affirm him in every movement of their spiritual and moral life' (p. 143). For Tyrrell the experience of 'the Power making for Righteousness' is that of 'spiritual will drawing our wills into union and personal relationship with itself'. He concludes:

If experience gives us a Power that makes for Righteousness it gives us God – it gives us, not a statement or an idea but a thing, a term of action, of obedience, worship, self-sacrifice, about which we more or less spontaneously frame ideas and statements. Experience is revelational. It reveals God as every cause is revealed in and with its effects; it reveals Him not in a statement but in the moral and religious impulse that proceeds from Him. (p. 144)

Tyrrell's fundamental point is that the Power which we experience does not only call forth our obedience, as it might do if we were merely aware of some superior *force*, but it calls forth our *worship*, and that which we worship is God.[35] Strictly speaking, it must be acknowledged that 'God' is not necessarily personal, but this is not the way we function as human beings. The experience he speaks of is such that it produces mental constructs which become 'a common language of self-utterance' (p. 146).[36] This is how the Creeds are formed. They are not supernaturally revealed statements, as Egerton might say, but they are constructed by men driven to speak in a certain manner about their experience. They live or die as they promote or impede spiritual life and they are the appropriate medium for supernatural revelation to the degree that they promote the experience from which they sprang in the first place.

Arnold, as we have seen, makes no distinction between the natural and the supernatural, largely because he can only think of the supernatural in an interventionist sense. For him, what is revealed is what is most truly *natural*, and vice versa. We discover what is natural by the methods of natural science, which turn on experimental verification. Tyrrell, in holding onto the distinction between natural and supernatural, works with an entirely different model of revelation, most succinctly summed up in the motto of Cardinal

Newman, *'Cor ad cor loquitur'*.[37] He takes the model of interpersonal communication, which does not turn on experimental verification, though such verification may have its part to play, but on shared meanings, intuition, community of vision and action. This is possible only where one has a metaphysic of wills, but not with the dogmatic agnosticism of a truly empiricist epistemology. We have seen the strict limits of Arnold's views on God, and that Tyrrell acknowledges the justice of what he has to say within those limits. He is most sympathetic to Arnold's ethically slanted phraseology. However, he will not let himself be fettered and he develops a doctrine of God along quite other lines. To understand these we need to go back to *Nova et Vetera*.

We need first to look at Tyrrell's doctrine of God in the phase when his Thomistic orthodoxy was crumbling and he was turning to Newman, when his writings were mainly devotional and orthodox, if they sailed a little close to the wind. Although the way ahead was clearly uphill, Tyrrell knew where he was going for the time being, and the landmarks were still plain. He was persistently critical of the way in which the most well-trodden paths of his time obscured some of the most important aspects of the divinity – often, paradoxically, by making them too plain.

'How should we think about God?' is perhaps the central question of *Nova et Vetera*. Again and again, Tyrrell's concern for 'worthy conceptions of God' (p. 53) breaks through. One pre-eminent function of Jesus is 'to drive from men's minds all harsh, cruel, narrow, unworthy conceptions of their God and Maker' (p. 231). 'Many "safe" people', writes Tyrrell, 'will be damned for their mean conceptions of Almighty God' (p. 320). Like Arnold, he is suspicious of 'gross, anthropomorphic caricatures' (p. 232) but he sees that we cannot conceive of God in any other way than by putting together the best that we know of humanity (p. 238). Pantheism is rejected (p. 83); God is both immanent and transcendent: 'the soul of our soul and life of our life' (p. 255). He brings human beings into the life of the Trinity, where personality finds its origin and fulfilment (pp. 78–83). The God who emerges from these meditations is a God who is radically involved with humanity, who uses the (free) human heart 'as an instrument to love Himself' (p. 385) not in any mechanical or exploitative sense but in a free union of wills. It is typical of Tyrrell to have written, 'We mostly love God far more than we think' (p. 105).

In *Hard Sayings* Tyrrell has an essay on 'God in Conscience' (pp. 45–68) which is preceded by an epigraph from Newman[38] and much indebted both to the second 'University Sermon' and *The Grammar of Assent*. There is no mention here of 'the Power that makes for Righteousness'. Rather, the pressure to do right that we feel in our conscience is connected first with our attraction towards 'ultimate and complete happiness' (Arnold would have been happy with that) and secondly with 'the urgency of the Divine Will' (p. 47), which for Tyrrell is central to all that he writes about the activity of God. 'Every thinking creature', he writes, 'is sensible, at least dimly and confusedly, of being dependent on some personal power which has put him into this world' (p. 49). We have seen that Tyrrell continued to maintain this against Hakluyt Egerton in 1909. He talks of 'the pressure of will against will, and person against person' (p. 51). 'It is as bringing us into will-relations with God that conscience differs so generically from any other act of our mind' (p. 52). Already, the outline of Tyrrell's final position on revelation is apparent in what he says of conscience: 'Here it is that God speaks to us; not indeed as man to man, but with a far closer and more intimate communing, whereby without words or symbols we are directly made conscious of His will' (p. 62). As in *Nova et Vetera*, he does not stress, but rather assumes, the transcendence of God. The emphasis here is on personal knowledge of God at a pre-rational level, its correlative ethical expression, and the illegitimacy of ethical or dogmatic extrinsicism. In September 1898 he wrote to von Hügel of the divine personality,

who is apprehended (*as every personality is apprehended*) rather by a certain *sense* or *gustus* than by any reasoning process; and the sensitiveness of this sense (which, I take it, is simply our whole moral and spiritual being regarded as attracting and attracted by its like, as repelling and repelled by its unlike) depends on the purification of the heart and affections, whereby they are brought into sympathy with God. (SL p. 46)

On December 31 von Hügel sent Tyrrell his criticism of *Hard Sayings*. He was delighted by the teaching 'as to the immanence of God, Heaven and Hell in each individual soul'. Although not one of the four chapters picked out for special commendation, the chapter on 'God in conscience' won his approval.

At each point in Tyrrell's early progress we can see parallels with Arnold: the concern for worthy conceptions of God, the reaction against crude anthropomorphism, the focus on conscience as that in which God makes himself known, the concern with ethics and with the mystery of God. In *Literature and Dogma* Arnold made his protest against 'our mechanical and materializing theology, with its insane licence of affirmation about God' (S VI p. 152).[39] For him, language about God was merely 'thrown out at' a vast reality, and he washed his hands of any attempt to understand so deep a mystery. For Tyrrell the term 'mystery' had a subtler meaning. Despite his concern with the humanity of God – learnt from Ignatius Loyola and proclaimed in the introduction to his first book – he was as deeply committed to the transcendence of God. Since God has revealed himself, we can talk about him confidently by symbol and analogy, but we cannot encompass so great a mystery in human language. Both rationalism and materialism are equally the enemies of a proper sense of mystery. The danger is that we should take our pictoral imagery or, more insidiously, our philosophical language, so seriously that we forget its provisional status (FM1 p. 237). Tyrrell believes we *can* penetrate to the heart of the Divine reality, but we must never think that we can express its transcendent profundity in anything other than an oblique or allusive fashion. Mysteries, for Tyrrell, are not riddles (FM1 p. 103) but 'truths fringed with darkness' (ER p. 113).

> The riddle is designed to hide the intended idea as carefully as verbal truth will permit; whereas the mystery is the result of an attempt to reveal as fully as possible in human ideas realities that are too big to fit into such narrow frames, except piecemeal. (FM1 p. 103)

In all these early writings Tyrrell was critical of the teaching and practice of contemporary Catholicism but he had not finally pulled down the edifice of scholasticism and begun to build again. By 1900, when he was living in Richmond, his thought had taken a new turn. The most important pointers to this new direction are in *Religion as a Factor of Life* and *The Church and the Future*, which turn upon a metaphysic of 'will' and of 'spirit' respectively. We shall now look at these, and then see how Tyrrell's new metaphysic is represented in *Oil and Wine* and *Essays on Faith and Immortality*. This whole phase of Tyrrell's thinking roughly corresponds to his time in Richmond. Not yet a 'Modernist' (the technical term had not yet been invented), he was rapidly becoming one.

Religion as a Factor of Life is concerned with the whole man and his experience of God, and with the distinctive expression of that experience in the different areas of human life, religion being at the head. '*Nihil aliud quam voluntates*', quotes Tyrrell from Augustine: 'We are nothing else but wills' (p. 2). Our relation to other wills is experienced as feeling; feeling and understanding are correlative, each fostered by the other, the more successfully as the action engendered, or the engendering will-attitude, with its correlative conceptual frame, correspond to reality. Within this anthropological framework Tyrrell speaks of our 'sense of the Absolute', that element of our experience

> that pervades and unites all the rest – the real Whence and Whither of all being and movement, whereof our own being and movement is an infinitesimal fraction. Prior to being gathered up into any distinct thought of the understanding about God or gods, this *datum* lies, as it were, fused through our total experience,

co-perceived with other perceptions,[40] but not perceived apart, and similarly, can give a religious modification to our other actions without giving birth to distinct acts of religion. (p. 6)

It is a sense of 'the ultimate and independent value of truth, goodness, and beauty, apart from all other consequences and advantages' (*ibid.*). The fact that this is securely located in human experience ensures the immanence of God. Tyrrell goes on to say that our 'understanding, for practical purposes, considers only the divine manifestations and effects, and cannot touch God in His reality' (p. 8). Knowledge of God as subject comes only 'in and through action and will'. Rather overstating his case, Tyrrell writes, 'Our will and affection are never directed to an abstraction, or an idea; but always to a concrete object; in the last analysis, always to a person, a will' (p. 11). It is clear that for him the subject of 'a will' must be personal, whilst for Arnold it might be some impersonal force like the Power we encounter, or 'the *Zeitgeist*'. Religion, then, can never, for Tyrrell, be reduced to ethics, or an inducement to moral behaviour ('morality touched by emotion'). God is personal by analogy with human personality: 'He alone is, therefore, all-personal, all-active; in no sense passive; determining everything, determined by nothing' (p. 51).[41] Our religious response is the response of person to Person, religion being the life of charity, or will-union with God. So, Tyrrell talks of prayer as Arnold could never do. Perhaps glancing at Arnold, he asserts that, 'Neither the God of the Hebrews, nor the gods of the Hellenes possess the requisite fulness characteristic of the Supreme Will, from whom, by whom, and in whom are *all* things' (p. 54). In this short, anonymous pamphlet Tyrrell spoke more eloquently of the relation between God and man, between transcendence and immanence, than in anything else he wrote, except for his early devotional work. There is never any doubt that the God immanent in the depths of human experience is truly transcendent, truly personal, and that the bond between God and man is one that consists of and must issue in charity.

Tyrrell was becoming aware that in the current intellectual climate, to confine himself to devotional works and metaphysics was in fact to duck the issue of authority. In the end, he had to face the question of the critical grounding and cognitive value of Biblical and ecclesiastical statements, just as Arnold had done. Appended to *Religion as a Factor of Life* is a brief essay in hermeneutics, his first attempt at an answer, in which he takes the Creed clause by clause. Now that he is aware how the historical facts and the symbolic expression of the faith may be attacked, Tyrrell, like Loisy, drives a defensive ditch between the scientific and the religious meaning of the credal statements. The Church, he says, is concerned with the religious, which has religious value as promoting will-union with God, even if historically proven wrong. It is a classic move towards the methods of Liberal Protestantism. Where his original essay did not necessarily imply the sharp division of religion and science, that break is now clearly made. Tyrrell was now arguing that one could say the Creed *as if* it were true in the accepted sense, knowing that truth lay *in* it, but not being able to say exactly where. God was no longer committed to the specific words, images and events as he had once been. These in turn retained their sacramental dimension only in a diminished and generalised sense. The net effect was predictable. Where there are no sharply defined material sacraments God 'in Himself' retires from the natural world. This was the hermeneutic whirlpool into which Tyrrell was being drawn.

Yet his basic beliefs about God had not changed. What he had lost – not through metaphysics, but through a hermeneutic infected with scientific positivism, which said that 'miracles don't happen' and 'eschatology is *Aberglaube*' – was the ability to say how he related the world of wills and the world of science, the transcendent and the immanent, referent and symbol, spirit and letter. He asserted that they *were* related, but had in fact drawn up the drawbridge on the former so that it could not be attacked through the latter. This is even more evident in *The Church and the Future*.

Part Two of *The Church and the Future* begins with a section entitled 'Religion as Spirit'. Again, Tyrrell stresses that religion is 'an affair of the whole soul' (p. 38) and talks in terms of 'will–certainty' (p. 41). He is in full reaction against the intellectualism of Catholic teaching. His real concern is with the problem of authority, and hermeneutics:

As Christians by profession, Catholics and Protestants alike take Christ as their supreme guide in religion. He being personally inaccessible, his mind and teaching must be sought in the Church, according to the Catholic; in the Gospels and dependent Scriptures, according to the Protestant.   (p. 42)

But how does one know 'the mind and the teaching of Christ'? By responding to 'the Spirit' which is here identified with 'the religious sense' (p. 45). Now, as we have seen in chapter 6, there is a danger that the Spirit begins to stand above Christ. Tyrrell asks to what extent Catholicism is 'the creation of that Spirit which created both Christ and the Church to be different and complementary organs of its own expression, adapted to different phases of the same movement' (p. 64). As the transcendence and the immanence of God fall apart, that which can bridge the gap is 'Spirit'. Tyrrell explicitly resists a monism of the Spirit. He speaks of 'the Divine Spirit' and 'the human spirit *as influenced* by that Divine Spirit' (p. 74), but the danger of monism is now obvious. Since language about the triune God that would provide a critique of such monism is now rendered provisional and pragmatic, where Tyrrell would once have said 'God is Spirit', he tends, from his grounding in the immanent activity of God, to say, 'Spirit is God'. This is particularly evident in Christology, where he speaks of 'Christ' or 'what has been committed to the Church to keep and to impose upon men' as 'a living spirit, *rather than a system of ideas*' (p. 73, my stress). Given the choice as stated, this must be true, but the choice is crude and dangerous, as Tyrrell himself later saw.

The period in Richmond was one of searching and uncertainty. Much of Tyrrell's writing is open to criticism for its unorthodoxy or self-contradiction. *Oil and Wine*, his next devotional book, is very different from the two devotional books that preceded it. Tyrrell himself wrote in the introduction to the edition of 1907:

> In avoiding the false 'transcendence' of Deism I may have drifted too near the Charybdis of Pantheism in search of the middle course of Panentheism; in urging the unity, I may have endangered the distinctness of souls. (p. ix)

Both Laubacher and Daly pay particular attention to chapters 41 and 42, Laubacher in an attempt to get at what Tyrrell meant by a 'Power that makes for Righteousness',[42] and Daly because, if Tyrrell is charged with 'immanentism', then these two chapters form 'the principal evidence for the prosecution'.[43] Tyrrell argues that God himself 'is not, in this life, a direct object of our mind; and if here we are to touch Him and be immediately united with Him, it is not in thinking about Him but in acting with Him' (p. 207). He declares that 'every good action of ours is His also' (*ibid.*) and talks of 'God acting in our action...mingling His life with ours so inextricably as to defy clear analysis or separation' (pp. 214–15). Just as in *Nova et Vetera*, Tyrrell suggests that 'the deepest and most fundamental appetite in the soul is God's love of His own life and action, temporal and eternal' (p. 220). Yet he clearly states that the human will is other than the will of God, though most itself when conformed to the will of God. If there is monism here, it is strictly held in check by distinguishing the love of God from the response of the human soul – which is ultimately grounded in the love of God. Tyrrell has already talked in terms of a '*process*' and some of his thoughts anticipate the thoughts of later 'process theologians', as David Wells has shown.[44] For instance, Tyrrell writes: 'God cannot *be* more than He is eternally, but this Society of God and creatures can grow to an ever greater fulness of being, even as a body and soul can grow, though in a sense the soul grows not' (p. 221). The more Tyrrell looked at God's commitment to the process of evolution, the more open he became to expressions of an increasing fulness in the divine life. At another point, Tyrrell writes of 'that buried treasury into which all consciousness present and past have poured their contributions' (p. 322). He suggests that 'somewhere, deep down, every other soul is vitally connected with our own, – is more or less remotely a part of ourself' (p. 323).

The link between this and God is not clear, but he writes of God in somewhat similar terms as 'the root whence all personalities branch out with a separateness that increases with every moment of their several lives' (p. 327). God's immanence in the process of Nature, of which man forms a part, is one of the major themes of the essays brought together in *Essays on Faith and Immortality*. Some of these, being drafts and jottings are more outspokenly heterodox than any other of his published works.

In 'God and Nature' (pp. 89–102) Tyrrell is clearly trying to accommodate theism to an evolutionary philosophy. An immanental approach is to be expected, but it is surprising to find him at times apparently identifying God and Nature: '"Immanuel" means, not only in-dwelling, but working *from within*; and God works in no other way than does Nature. Conscience is the key to it all. In us Nature, the whole, works as Conscience' (EFI p. 98). If Nature works as Conscience, is Nature then to be identified with God? Tyrrell does not want to say this. He talks of God working *in* Nature, but he cannot entirely exclude the monism against which he protests:

The precise relation between God and Nature, like that between Conscience and myself, is necessarily unthinkable and unstateable; it is not identity or diversity, not oneness or two-ness, since all these relations are between *objects*...'God is a spirit' – a '*power within us, not ourselves*, which makes for righteousness', *i.e.* which bids us subordinate our individual self and interest to an absolute and universal interest, which is that of our deeper, unknown, spiritual self. (pp. 98–9)

Tyrrell tries to protect himself against misunderstanding by quoting Arnold's phrase in full, even adding 'within us'. Two pages later, in sympathetic dialogue with Fichte, he is far less circumspect:

Enough to know that somewhere, somewhen, the Idea that works in our spirit will at last fulfil itself, nay, may have fulfilled itself millions of times; that it is our own spirit which is the one subject of all experience; that if it is 'I' who fail here and now, it is 'I' who succeed there and then; if I succeed there, it is because I have struggled, not only there, but everywhere, for success. (p. 101)

It is not at all clear how God links with the 'idea' mentioned here or with the transpersonal 'I'. The more Tyrrell is concerned with the whole of nature as an evolving system the more confused and confusing his thought about God becomes. 'We are constrained', he says, 'by necessity of thought to think of the whole of existence in terms of the highest category we know, which is that of self; to think of it, that is, as of a spirit which thinks and wills and works like our own' (p. 184). This 'spirit' of the whole of existence is not God (p. 194), but God works through it. The relation between it and God is ineffable. In trying to reconcile an evolutionary view of nature and the Christian God, Tyrrell first hypostasised Nature in this intermediary 'Nature-

Spirit', and later presented the Spirit more as Necessity. This first spiritualising of nature was a way of reclaiming the natural world for a Christ who remained ethically inspired and inspiring but was shorn of his cosmic rule. In speaking of the 'Nature-Spirit' was Tyrrell actually offering anything more than 'the stream of tendency by which all things seek to fulfil the law of their being'? Neither phrase excludes the existence of a transcendent God, lost in inscrutable mystery, known to all only in 'the Nature-Spirit', 'the stream of tendency'. What they offer *practically* is a closed universe, a sealed immanence. Tyrrell concludes an essay of 1904:

> The purest faith is that which believes that between God and Law there is no real opposition, no need that either should be stronger than the other; that Love is not so much above, behind, and over against the harsh-seeming law-bound workings of deaf merciless Nature, as identical with them, working in them and through them. (p. 234)

The latest of the essays in the book is 'Divine Fecundity', delivered as a lecture in March 1909. In the preamble Tyrrell acknowledges his debt to Bergson.[45] Writing under the shock of the Messina earthquake and the flatulent Christian comment upon it, he declares: 'Newman said that, apart from the phenomena of conscience and man's moral life, he could not see evidence of God in Nature. I would go further, and say that the evidence points rather to a Devil' (p. 252). Thus the benign 'Nature-Spirit' was smartly turfed out. In his private correspondence Tyrrell spoke of 'the Cat-theory of the universe' (SL p. 285): if there is a God, he plays with us like a cat with a mouse. In this article Tyrrell takes issue with all forms of bourgeois optimism:

> Is there the faintest evidence in favour of...an organic unity in which each has its part to play, each demands and is demanded by all the rest, in which not one is wasted, or fails to contribute to the realisation of a fore-ordained end? (p. 257)

In this perspective, the organic unity of Catholicism and culture is seen as provisionally and temporarily superimposed upon the struggle for existence. The 'Nature-Spirit' has given place to millions of competing organisms. God, 'or Nature if you like' (p. 265), is not omnipotent. He is bound by 'the necessity of universal fecundity'. Tyrrell admits the problems of making God subject to necessity, but argues that his is the only hypothesis consistent with the existence of God, the fecundity of nature and the pain inevitably involved in a competitive existence.[46] Only by suggesting some necessity can Tyrrell exonerate a God who is not positively evil from the suffering caused by a natural disaster like the Messina earthquake. Faced with 'the tragedy and the mystery of existence' Tyrrell doubts not God's love but his omnipotence. At the end of the essay he offers in summary form a list of the advantages in looking at the world in this Bergsonian light. He welcomes 'the enrichment

of the impoverished Christian consciousness by the restoration of that
provisional pessimism to which Christ opposed His message of a transcendental
Hope' (p. 277). 'Divine Fecundity' is an essay in 'provisional pessimism',
unrelieved by a hint of Christological hope. This lack of reference to Christ
is surprising, for surely this is where Tyrrell would have found resources to
hold together a transcendent, omnipotent God and a God bound by necessity?
'Divine Fecundity' cries out for Christology done from the side of God; in
Christianity at the Crossroads Tyrrell offered a Christ who proclaimed and
embodied eschatological hope, but not the suffering of God.

Tyrrell's last book is a Christology in the light of 'thoroughgoing
eschatology'. He is trenchantly critical of Liberal Protestantism because of its
tendency to minimise transcendentalism. He strove to show that transcendence
was of the essence of Christ's message and of the essence of Catholic teaching.
Whatever Jesus was, he was nearer to Catholicism than to Liberal Protestantism, which had turned first-century eschatology into nineteenth-century
humanism. Michael Hurley speaks of the 'chasm' that Tyrrell now put
between himself and the 'Adolf Harnacks and Matthew Arnolds of his own
day'.[47] In asserting the value of apocalyptic symbolism, Tyrrell once more
involved himself in the problem of hermeneutics. No longer was he looking
for the spirit behind all religious expression, but for the spirit of *that particular,
normative religious expression* used by Christ and endorsed by the Church. This
return to particularity did not destroy but restored the credibility of a
transcendent God for the very framework of the eschatology that Tyrrell now
endorsed was one of sharp transcendence. On the other hand, it was not a
transcendence removed from the affairs of men, for history *now* was
interpreted in apocalyptic terms, and the Son of Man proclaimed that others
could know the transcendent Father as he knew him. Accessible and yet hidden,
God could be known in the particularity of historic revelation, sacraments
and prayer.

Christianity at the Crossroads marked the end of Tyrrell's exploring. He did
not throw away what he had learnt from liberalism, but he found in the
rediscovery of apocalyptic a way into a symbolic framework other than that
of nineteenth-century Liberal Protestantism, which seemed only too clearly
discontinuous with historic Catholicism, and other than that of scholasticism,
which accommodated neither the spiritual nor the historic complexity of
human experience. It was such a framework that Tyrrell had been seeking,
since his conviction about the human experience of God altered very little
in the last decade of his life. Thus he wrote in *Christianity at the Crossroads*:

What we experience (be our creed or non-creed what it may) is a Power that
makes for Righteousness, *i.e.* that subjects us to an universal, super-individual,

super-social end, of which we have no distinct conception, and which we can only figure to ourselves in symbols and images. (p. 108)

In 1908, he wrote a long letter about his understanding of God, calling himself Sabellian, and claiming that his imagination was 'quite cured of the outside God'. He explained:

What I find in myself as the highest law and law-giver of my being, is a Divine Will or Ideal, which struggles to realise itself against a contrary and disintegrating tendency; and does so dependently on my co-operation. I recognise it as the same will which moves every living creature, and indeed the whole world, towards its proper perfection and highest development. Religions can help me to name it, to imagine it, to understand it, to converse with it. I learn to call it Conscience, my better Self, the Holy Spirit, the indwelling Christ.[48] (AL2 p. 413)

In 1904, he wrote to Edward Thomas:

The *direct-line* ancestry of our Christian God is to be sought, not in the theologies it has supplanted, but in the various stages of man's moral development, whereby he has come to recognise the dictates of his conscience as the expression of an Absolute Will, at once immanent and transcendent, and therefore has come to render to that Will the adoration formerly given to idols. (SL p. 13)

In chapter 3, we saw that he wrote to Bremond in 1899:

As for my faith, so far as it must necessarily be rooted in some kind of experience and not merely in propositions and principles accepted on hearsay, it rests upon the evidence of a Power in myself and in all men 'making for righteousness' in spite of all our downward tendencies; – that is the basis of my Theism.
(AL2 p. 73)

All his life Tyrrell struggled to express that fundamental knowledge of God which he found to be integral to his own experience, and he believed to be built in to the experience of everyman, could everyman but recognise it. Whatever metaphysical language he used – spirit, will, absolute, power – he remained convinced that God communicated with the whole man in his wholeness – not through the intellect alone. This is why he talks of 'feeling', 'conscience', 'intuition' and the 'subconscious' as areas in which God makes himself known, of 'action' and 'life' and 'conduct' as the field of expression of this knowledge of God. Finding God in nature became increasingly difficult; finding God in man, and primarily in oneself, was simply a case of recognising the God in which every man subconsciously believes 'by the mere fact that he believes in truth and right and disbelieves in falsehood and wrong', (SL p. 26). In this Tyrrell and Arnold were at one.

Tyrrell, then, was very much with Arnold as far as Arnold went, but Arnold did not go far enough. Tyrrell wanted a God to whom one could respond in love and worship and was prepared to experiment (not always successfully) with metaphysics, with language and with theology in order to find – or keep – him. He objected to Arnold's 'righteousness' as 'frigidly Anglican and respectable'. It produced

a sort of university God, a personification of the Nicomachean ethics...God must be righteous but He must be more...As intuition, or the 'illative sense', is to explicit reasoning, so is love to righteousness, and so is faith to ethical goodness. Love, or grace, is inclusively righteousness.   (SL p. 199)

There is the whole difference between them.

139

8

Conclusions

When Bremond said that a third of Tyrrell was in Arnold, he made an informed and informative comment, which scholars have rightly taken seriously. However, we should be on our guard: he said 'in ' not 'from' Arnold. I have not tried to go beyond Bremond and argue that Arnold was an important formative influence on Tyrrell. Much of this book has been a reading of the one against the other, to show where their interests converge and diverge, and to see what mutual illumination there is in looking at them together. We have examined two very different ways of doing theology that in a certain light may be made to look reasonably alike.

There was little in *Literature and Dogma*, the book which Bremond mentioned specifically, that Tyrrell could not have found elsewhere. Had he never read Arnold, he would have found the stress on experiential verification in William James, upon conscience as the mediator of the knowledge of God in Newman, upon immanent forces in Bergson; he would have found the sharp division between religion and science in Loisy, between kernel and husk in Harnack. All of these together (plus an emphasis on revelation as experience, the distinction between religion and theology, and a concern for the symbolic value of dogma) Tyrrell found in Sabatier. Nothing in Tyrrell's published works or private correspondence suggests that he read Arnold at all deeply or systematically. On the other hand, he undoubtedly turned to Arnold from time to time to illustrate some of the most important points that he made, and he respected Arnold as a radical Christian thinker who appreciated the revolutionary changes that had to come in the thought of the whole Church. Here Tyrrell and he were wholly at one. *Literature and Dogma* was the most articulate and successful blast against inflexible and insensitive religion in the nineteenth century. In swashbuckling style it made a number of polemical hits against those who denied the shift in religious consciousness that had overtaken Europe since the time of Kant and the Industrial Revolution. Arnold, then, gave Tyrrell nothing he did not already know, or could not learn better elsewhere. What he did give him was encouragement, and warning, on a path he was taking anyway, plus a form of words – 'The Power that makes for Righteousness' – which Tyrrell gladly adopted, on condition that nobody thought he was using them in the precise way that Arnold did.

It is not at the level of particular borrowing that Bremond's remark is important. Bremond's significant insight was that Tyrrell and Arnold belonged to what John Coulson has called 'a common English tradition'.[1] Coulson identifies in this tradition a common use of 'fiduciary' as opposed to 'analytic' language. Language is taken 'as it were, on trust'[2] within a living community where the meaning or meanings of words emerge. He traces the tradition back through Maurice, Newman and Coleridge, and glances behind Coleridge to the way in which words were used before the drive for 'scientific' precision in the later seventeenth and eighteenth centuries. He points up the links between the poets and the theologians in their common commitment to a 'sacramental' use of language. Coulson elsewhere paraphrases Arnold: 'A religion that turns its back on poetry and the imagination is under sentence of death.'[3]

On this, both Arnold and Tyrrell were agreed. Arnold's remarks about Catholicism as 'the religion of the future' turn on his perception of the poetic and imaginative resources there. His antipathy to nonconformity is antipathy to the lack of imagination, the lack of poetry, in that tradition. He wants religion to fulfil the valid longings of the 'imaginative reason', and this is precisely what Tyrrell found in Catholicism. The problems that Tyrrell later had were those not of a starved imagination, but an outraged reason.

Tyrrell's language is drawn from English literary tradition. As far as his prose is concerned the debts to Newman and Swift and Sterne are patent; his sensibility was formed by poets and spiritual writers like Dante, à Kempis and Loyola, and then by 'the common tradition' as expressed in Wordsworth, Tennyson and Browning. His friend Lawless may have overstated when he said that Tyrrell knew the whole of 'In Memoriam' by heart,[4] but there is no poem that he quotes as frequently to express the admixture of doubt and faith, tinged with loss, which is his most characteristic spiritual attitude. He does not show the same familiarity with Arnold, but that is not really to the point. The point is that Tyrrell is an heir to that common tradition of which Arnold was a member, where poets, novelists and spiritual writers fed one another in a way that hardly happens today. Tyrrell knew and loved the English poets; he also knew and loved Dante, à Kempis and Heine, as Arnold knew and loved them. Ironically, his closest companion here was not English at all; it was the Frenchman Bremond. When Bremond said that 'a third of Tyrrell' was in Arnold, I have no doubt that he was not specifically thinking in these terms, for he mentioned Arnold, with Jowett, as 'grands libéraux anglais'. However, his remark suggests that Tyrrell be read as an *English* writer, loyal to a tradition of language that retained its European roots and imaginative freshness from Coleridge to T. S. Eliot. It was the whole tradition that was opposed to 'religious materialism'.

Tyrrell and Arnold are both radicals. They are at one in what we might call 'the feeling of standing on Dover Beach', unable to move into a hinterland of desiccated unbelief, unable to immerse themselves in that 'Sea of Faith' which once,

round earth's shore
Lay like the folds of a bright girdle furled.[5]

Arnold wrote in a letter of 1882:

Events and personages succeed one another, but the central fact of the situation always remains for me this: that whereas the basis of things amidst all chance and change has even in Europe generally been for ever so long supernatural Christianity, and far more so in England than in Europe generally, this basis is certainly going – going amidst the full consciousness of the continentals that it is going, and amidst the provincial unconsciousness of the English that it is going.
(*Letters* II p. 201)

Tyrrell would have agreed wholeheartedly. 'Dover Beach' was not a poem he quoted explicitly, but he wrote in the introduction to *The Faith of the Millions* of 'the power of public opinion... passing over from the side of faith to that of doubt, dragging the fluent multitude after it as the sea is dragged by the moon' (p. vi). That is almost exactly what Arnold saw and described in 'Dover Beach'. At another time, he used an image that was later echoed by Tyrrell. Arnold concluded 'The Function of Criticism at the Present Time' by speaking of 'the promised land, towards which criticism can only beckon'. He went on, 'That promised land it will not be ours to enter, and we shall die in the wilderness' (S III (EC1) p. 285). Tyrrell, applying the Biblical words more specifically to his religious position, wrote to Maude Petre in January 1902,

As far back as 1896 I wrote on the title page of my Breviary: 'Thou shalt see from afar the land which the Lord God will give to the Children of Israel, but thou shalt not enter therein' – and from that conviction I have never swerved since long before that date. (AL2 p. 4)

Both Arnold and Tyrrell felt themselves exiles, 'between two worlds'. Moreover, there were times in Tyrrell's life when, faced by intolerable strains, all he could do was to adopt an Arnoldian pose of philosophic calm. In 1900, he wrote to Bremond,

I am afraid you allow yourself to be much tormented, and that you do not study the stars enough or try to calm yourself with the thought of how infinitely little all looks from there – this battle of microbes. I have come to regard my internal quiet of soul as more important even than personal religion, of which it is the first condition. (SL pp. 5–6)

That could be taken from any of Arnold's letters to Clough. On another occasion Tyrrell turns to the sea:

Undoubtedly it is the *calm* sea that, combined with the sense of space, fills up the notion of eternity. The fussy waves belong to senseless maniac Time, and make the sea measureable; they are a *fieri* not a *factum esse*. Calm is what all came from and goes to. 'Then shalt Thou rest through us, even as now Thou dost labour through us.'[6]

The Arnoldian tone is quite transformed by the touch of Augustine. It is typical of Tyrrell to stand on Dover Beach – or Tintagel cliffs – and feel as Arnold felt, but then to find, with Gerard Manley Hopkins his fellow-Jesuit, that,

> though the last lights off the black West went
> Oh, morning, at the brown brink eastward, springs.[7]

Such a moment is not yet. In the present darkness both Tyrrell and Arnold acknowledge that they must wait with whatever hope or fortitude they can muster.

Tyrrell's fear that he had conceded too much to the 'purely immanental Christ' of Matthew Arnold is symptomatic of his whole attitude towards Liberal Protestantism.[8] In 1904, having read Sabatier's 'very wonderful and inspiring book *Les Religions d'Autorité et la Religion de L'Esprit*', he asked himself, 'Am I implicitly a liberal Protestant; or is Sabatier implicitly a liberal Catholic?' (SL p. 89). He went on to cobble up a difference between himself and Sabatier because he needed to differentiate himself from an unacceptable position, however difficult it was to do so intellectually. He just knew that he was not facing in the same direction, and needed to say so. At the end of *Lex Orandi*, the book in which he drew closest to Ritschl, he wrote,

Herein we part company with those who would bid us look underneath all varieties and transformations of religious expression in doctrine or ritual for one and the same simple homogeneous sentiment of God's Fatherhood and man's brotherhood in Christ...this the kernel, the rest mere husk. (p. 213)

The reason he gives is both fascinating and significant:

Though variations of doctrinal and ritual expression may be governed and criticised by ascertainable laws, and may exhibit developments that are to be distinguished as false or as true to such laws, yet these are laws of thought, of language, or of symbolism, not of the life of religion. (*Ibid.*)

At the heart of religion is not a static essence but a dynamic *life*. Tyrrell was determined to defend the immanent logic of the religious system, the

143

co-determination of the symbols and the life in one developing whole. So, he wrote in the introduction to *Lex Credendi*:

The mind, indeed, may abstract, and analyse, and dissect; it may give a fictitious completeness to what are really fragments; but it is only the unbroken unity of the living whole which appeals to the heart – and Faith is of the heart. (p. ix)

This is worlds away from the epistemological dualism of Liberal Protestantism.

Concern with 'the whole' is characteristic of Catholicism, and it is characteristic of Tyrrell. More consistently than Arnold, he retained this concern: it is present from *Nova et Vetera* to *Christianity at the Crossroads*. In the first he wrote, 'Natural reason and conscience convey to us the will of God, who is subsistent Reason, whose interest and aim is universal good and right order.' (How like Arnold!) 'They impel us to live for a whole whereof we are but parts, and for a good whereof our particular good is but a fraction' (p. 405). The same concern, somewhat differently expressed, is present in *Christianity at the Crossroads*:

The transcendent is not the spiritual as opposed to the phenomenal; but the whole as opposed to an infinitesimal fraction of possible spiritual experience. Our spirit-life, our disinterested love of the universal Good, our unqualified worship of the Right in conduct, *thought and feeling*, is just the life of the Whole that is immanent in every part. (pp. 207–8, my stress)

The ethical thrust, and the concern to relate the part to the whole, is the same but the thought has been modified by Tyrrell's deliberate attempt to break free from Kantianism. He was always concerned for the integrity of the whole man and the whole truth: 'Not only the mind but the whole soul is the organ of truth'. He wrote (OW p. 39). Again and again, Tyrrell shows himself concerned with issues that have been illuminated by later philosophers of hermeneutics.

With the help of Paul Ricoeur, we can pinpoint the difference between Tyrrell and Arnold. Ricoeur distinguishes helpfully between two types of interpreter: there are those who see interpretation as the exercise of suspicion and those who see interpretation as the recollection of meaning.[9] The three masters of the school of suspicion are Marx, Nietzsche and Freud. For them 'to seek meaning is no longer to spell out the consciousness of meaning, but to *decipher its expressions*'.[10] On the other hand, there is the approach with which Ricoeur aligns himself: that of phenomenology, of attention to the object, of expectancy that the old symbols will speak again. Where do Tyrrell and Arnold stand with respect to this distinction?

When Arnold writes of God as 'the power that makes for righteousness' he is telling us that this is what we *really mean* when we talk about God; he isolates that element of our experience to which our words refer. To take Ricoeur's word, he is 'suspicious' of the word 'God', and he cuts it down to size. He is poet enough to see that this entails immense imaginative loss, but he does not draw back, 'for whatever is to stand must rest upon something which is verifiable, not unverifiable' (S VI (LD) p. 149). Nobody has expressed the danger of this position better than James Martineau, who anticipated the most famous line of criticism (against Liberal Protestantism) that Tyrrell ever wrote, in which he declared: 'The Christ that Harnack sees, looking back through nineteen centuries of Catholic darkness, is only the reflection of a Liberal Protestant face, seen at the bottom of a deep well' (CCR p. 44). Martineau complained that 'our age finds it easier to feel sure of what Religion is in man, than of what is *says* of God'. He says of religion that,

We are naturally averse to supposing that mere emptiness and illusion can have a dominant influence in the education of mankind: so we try to find some solid little nucleus secreted at the centre of this brilliant nebula, and to make out that, f *we* could not lodge there now, it has belonged, or is going to belong, to some less erratic and more habitable world; and we insist that, though in itself it cannot pretend to much reality, it may symbolically stand for a good deal, if we do but construe it aright.[11]

Then he sounds his warning:

What is the result? Much, I think, what we would expect, where the text is disparaged to glorify the interpreter: its thought is twisted into a mask, through which *his* eyes look out; and under the guise of ancient sage or prophet, we are confronted by the commonplaces of today.[12]

For Harnack Jesus is a Liberal Protestant. For Arnold, Jesus turns out to be a man of 'culture'.

However, we should not type-cast Arnold. He was actually torn. Prickett writes perceptively that 'Arnold's dependence on the "poetic" theological tradition of Wordsworth, Coleridge, and Keble, is ultimately fatal to the cause of demythologising.'[13] When it came to it, Arnold was confident that the language of great poetry, or of the Bible, would speak, without being sifted for ethical content and *Aberglaube*, morality and emotion. If the theologians had left the Bible to speak for itself all might have been well. As Arnold wrote in an introduction to Isaiah, chapters 40–66: 'It is by being apprehended *as whole*, that the true power of a work of literature makes itself felt' (S VII . 505). The basis of both Arnold's style and his critical method was not the deciphering hermeneutic of suspicion, but precisely the opposite: a belief that the right phrase or line would speak to the receptive ear, especially if repeated several times.[14] His choice of poetic 'touchstones' like '*In la sua volontade è nostra pace*' is governed by a belief in their symbolic import, the essence of beauty in a phrase. If you cannot see it, you are blind.

There are, then, two sides to Arnold. As a theologian he unashamedly practises a 'hermeneutic of suspicion', attempting to go behind theology to what it 'really' means. He thinks this is how scientists proceed, and he is trying to speak to a scientific generation. As poet, critic and humble reader of the Bible, he wants to let the texts speak for themselves. This is why Hutton gave him high marks as a literary critic and nothing as a theologian. Tyrrell is also torn, but inclines far more than Arnold towards interpretation as recollection of meaning. Hence his thumping reassertion of eschatology and of 'the principle of symbolism' in *Christianity at the Crossroads*.

If it was characteristic of Liberal Protestantism to exercise a hermeneutic of suspicion, it was characteristic of Catholicism to encourage confidence in the traditional expressions of Christianity. Although Tyrrell turned to Liberal Protestantism in the period when he was seeking a new understanding of Christianity, he did so reluctantly and suspiciously. Radical he may have been; a Protestant he was not. Intellectual honesty drove him from an untenable scholasticism. What he sought as a viable alternative did not exist, so he had to set about building it, and for this he was prepared to use whatever tool he could beg or borrow. It was inevitable that he should be attracted to the 'scientific' exegesis of Liberal Protestantism, and to the underlying epistemology. There was no viable alternative. The Liberal Protestant package deal never fulfilled the demands of the logic of the heart, for Tyrrell was wedded to Catholicism as a whole, rather as Arnold was wedded to 'culture' as a whole. The epistemological dualism of the Kantian tradition was in the end unacceptable to Tyrrell. He took up the apocalyptic framework of Weiss and Schweitzer because it offered a return to the source, but in a new mode: it accommodated the need for historical verisimilitude; it was isomorphic with Catholic teaching, in that it stressed the transcendence of God within the apocalyptic scenario; it had imaginative and ethical power, but called for patently symbolic reading of Christian doctrine. The last people in the world to understand Tyrrell's apparent switch were liberals like Inge and Rashdall[1] but in retrospect one can see that the adoption of this stress enabled him to find his way between the Scylla of scholasticism and the Charybdis of Liberal Protestantism. A sound hermeneutic of Catholicism had to be based not on an artificially imposed scholastic synthesis, but upon the synthesis of first-century apocalyptic, which provided the key to the later development of Catholicism. Tyrrell went back to the original symbols in the belief that they could speak to his own generation. 'How?', said the liberals, thinking of the kernel and the husk. 'Listen to them', said Tyrrell, with his concern for the whole.

When Tyrrell turned to first-century eschatology, he did not abandon what he had learnt from liberals like Arnold. He maintained his concern for history for ethics, for experience, but he was now able to reunite these with his concerns for religion, symbolism and tradition. Weiss and Schweitzer, by their stress on apocalyptic, brought home the *strangeness* of Jesus. For Tyrrell, Jesus was ever accessible because the human conscience responds to him intuitively, the more so as historical research sharpens our picture of the first-century prophet. The more the original picture is restored the less likely we are to distort the interpretation which is appropriate for today.

I believe that Tyrrell's stress upon the startling symbolic world-view of first-century eschatology, and his stress upon the continuity between Christian life and teaching in the first century, and Christian life and teaching today, is one of the most valuable things he has to offer – and it is this, precisely, which distinguishes him from Arnold. Arnold finds the continuity in moral response, Tyrrell finds it in religious life, and Tyrrell's position is strengthened by his insistence upon the place that the symbolic canopy of doctrine has to play in the life of the whole. I do not believe he solved the question of the cognitive significance of the symbols. The pragmatic answer, that on the whole they promote spiritual life, leaves as many questions as it answers, but the thrust of Tyrrell's work is to point a direction, to ask a question.

I have tried in this book to show in what sense Bremond's remark that 'a third of Tyrrell' is in Arnold was perfectly just, informed and informative, suggestive of an important perspective upon Tyrrell (that of 'the common tradition') and yet to be handled with care. I have suggested that their greatest convergence lies in reaction against intellectualist and rationalist apologetic (though Arnold was not free of it himself) and stress upon the experiential verification of Christianity; in stress upon the primacy of the ethical, of 'conscience' and 'conduct', in Christianity, though Tyrrell always resisted the reduction of Christianity to 'ethics plus...'; in the perception of an immanent teleological force in the world, though for Tyrrell this was not a force, but the will of a *person*; in the acceptance of a rigid distinction between 'religion' and 'science', though for Tyrrell this could only be provisional, acceptable while there was no agreed way of talking about the whole; in a particular concern with the linguistic bifurcation between science and poetry or prophecy; in an attempt to express the essence of Christianity, to distinguish the kernel and the husk, though here again Tyrrell struggled to dissociate himself at the earliest opportunity. I have tried to show how Tyrrell accepted these Arnoldian positions, but struggled to qualify or modify what he said, so that in the end the impression is not of differing emphases within a fundamental agreement, but of apparent agreement between fundamentally different positions. In chapter 5 the evidence for a convergence in ecclesiology and culture was set out, showing a common concern for the organic society as an expression of the life of the immanent spirit. It was suggested that Bremond might reasonably have picked out *Culture and Anarchy* as the text to which Tyrrell was closest, a choice that would have given a very different impression from Bremond's naming of *Literature and Dogma*. In the areas of Christology, and the Doctrine of God we again noted convergence, but here there is a much more emphatic parting of the ways which turned on Tyrrell's unswerving attachment to a divine Christ and a personal God. One general reflection from this study might be the profound difference that is made in theology where the form of the thought is determined by a belief in a triune, personal God. This was the form of Tyrrell's faith, however difficult he found it to express, however incomplete that expression when he did.

Was there a third of Tyrrell in Arnold? If one remembers the convergence of interest on the points that Arnold hammered home in *Literature and Dogma*, especially the key distinction between scientific and religious language, the wider attunement to doubt and faith in the contemporary world, the common concern with an 'organic' society and implicit self-appointment to the 'clerisy', the common concern for the 'Catholicism of the future', rid, at last, of 'spiritual materialism', the knowledge that they stood 'between two worlds', then the answer must be 'yes', not because Tyrrell took a third of his thought, or anything like that proportion, from Arnold, but because the area of common interest, the area that Tyrrell *recognised* in Arnold, must, if one is to speak in such Arnoldian terms, cover quite a third of all that Tyrrell has to say.

APPENDIX

Two letters to the Abbé Venard

Note

These letters, which explain Tyrrell's notion of 'prophetic truth' were written to the Abbé Louis Venard, who, as a young seminarist had become a keen student of Biblical exegesis under the influence of his teacher, Loisy. He later made an eirenic contribution to the debate between Loisy and Blondel over the relation between history and dogma ('La valeur historique du dogme', *Bulletin de Littérature Ecclesiastique*, 5 (1904), 338–57) which included a discussion of *Lex Orandi*. The letters are reproduced by kind permission of Father André Venard.

The '*via media*': an unwritten chapter of *Lex Orandi*

Richmond, Yorkshire – Jan. 15, 1905

My dear Abbé Venard –

I am immensely obliged to you for your excellent piece of criticism which, it is no paradox to say, has enabled me to understand myself better and to see my relationship to those other three from whom I have learned so much, and with whom I deem it a great honour to be thus associated by you. As regards my own book *Lex Orandi* it was a great satisfaction to me to see how exactly you have comprehended my less obvious implications; and amongst these, my designed ambiguity in regard to the point which divides M. Loisy from Père L.[1] and from M. Blondel, namely the determination of history (and, *mutatis mutandis*, science or philosophy) by dogma. At that time my mind was groping after a sort of *via media* in the matter; but I had not as yet been able to formulate my thought. Since then, I have hinted at this *via media* here and there in my publications, but have not ventured to develop it. I might provisionally put my conclusion thus: we cannot argue from any *single* historical implication of dogma to the historical truth of that implication; but, taking the *total* historical implication of Catholic dogma *in globo* (i.e. the

149

religious or ecclesiastical reading of history, etc.) we may infer that facts were approximately and equivalently thus; that this 'religious reading' of history is related to the truth, as a dramatist's reading of history might be; that in the interests of religion (as of drama), thro' the instinctive, unconscious, *justifiable* bias of the religious (as of the dramatic) spirit and purpose, facts are warped and distorted in such a way as to render inference *from particulars* unsafe, and yet to leave the religious (or dramatic) reading true *fundamentaliter, cum fundamento in re*. I would defend this conclusion by a somewhat difficult and yet, I think, very necessary and defensible distinction between 'prophetic' truth and 'historic' (or scientific, or philosophical) truth. 'Prophetic' truth is analogous with poetic, artistic, dramatic truth in that the religious and moral values of its utterances, like the aesthetic values of artistic utterances, are to a certain extent independent of the fact-values or historical values. It can, for certain purposes, utter itself equally well in the language of facts or of fiction, or of a mixture of fact and fiction i.e. in more or less idealised facts. Though Shakespeare's 'King John' is founded on fact we should not use it as a historical authority; yet its dramatic truth may be greater, just because its historical truth is less; and I would say the same of the Christian 'dramatisation' of history that is implied in our dogmatic system. To go to the root of the matter: Prophetic truth (and artistic truth in some way) is reached, not by reason working on sensible experience, but by the sympathy of man's spirit with the Divine spirit immanent in man's spirit; it is a divination guided by a spiritual sentiment. As God is the root and immanent cause of all that is and is going to be, or is in process of becoming, this sympathetic divination of prophecy reaches the truth of what *is* in the divine or eternal order of reality; and the truth of what *ought to be* but *is* not, or is only in process of becoming, in the order of finite reality. In other words its concern is with the *ideal* rather than with the actual.[2] According to the greater or less imperfection of its historical information, and according [*sic*] the precise degree of its sympathy with the Divine Spirit, the prophetic spirit will be more or less successful in determining how the course of history must (*a priori*) have shaped itself in the past and must shape itself in the future, or how, in the present, the unknown may be interpreted by the known. We do see daily how the pious and devout (somewhat recklessly and unscrupulously) interpret history (e.g. the life of our Lady) *a priori* in accordance with the exigencies of their devotion; the interpretation has little value; but it may sometimes be right. There is a conceivable non-historical divination of historical facts – just as animal instinct can exercise a chemical discrimination between poisonous and wholesome food. The collective prophetic or religious spirit of the Christian Church has, no doubt, a claim to be listened to with respect in its general reading of history

150

in accordance with the exigencies of the spiritual life. The dramatist will not, or may not, deliberately infer that *because*, in the dramatic interest, things *ought* to have happened more sensationally than they did happen, *therefore* they *must* have so happened – for he knows that the world is not ruled by God in the interests of drama; but the religious man knows that the world is ruled in the interests of religion; and hence he rightly infers that things *did* happen as (*a priori*) they *ought* to have happened. His 'ought-judgement' is probably wrong or inadequate owing to his ignorance of facts and conditions, and perhaps to his imperfect sympathy with the Divine. But even if historically wrong it may be *truer* than history; truer to the inward reality, to the ultimate meaning of things, to what is in process of becoming. Because the world is ruled in the interest of religion, religious truth cannot be indifferent to history, as can poetic truth; there *must be* a prophetic or religious reading of history; and this is part and parcel, though it is not the whole, of Catholic dogma. But plainly this prophetic reading of history is subject to the correction of historical methods – which correction, nevertheless, affects, not the religious truth-value, but only the fact-value; it merely shows that in this particular point the ideal construction of history is discordant with the real, that what *ought-to-be is* not, yet; or that its conditions were mistakingly assumed to exist – a mistake of no *religious* importance, in many cases. We have no right to expect anything like a perfect accord between the religious and the scientific readings of history; but only an *in globo* similitude – as between the dramatic and the historic presentment of the same episode; or between the artistic and the photographic presentment of the same landscape. On the contrary, the religious spirit desires to see God's will *already* done upon earth as it is in heaven; and this very ardent desire of the prophetic spirit inclines it to a premature completion and narrowing-up of God's designs; and thus acts as a principle of historic falsification. Thus there is a sort of opposition or tension between prophetic and historic truth; each is corrective of the other, the prophetic reading being truer to the deeper reality of things; the historical, to the actual course and nexus of phenomena.

This is, in brief, the *via media* I propose; and I think moreover it is what M. Loisy *implies*, even if he does not explicitly mean it. I feel sure from the great acumen of your article that you will grasp my idea more clearly than I have been able to express it. For myself, I have little or no liberty of writing about these matters *freely* and under my own name; but if you saw your way to giving publicity to these thoughts either in the *Bulletin* or in the *Annales de Ph. Ch.*[3] or elsewhere I think it might stimulate better brains than my own to elaborate some clearer and better solution of the difficulty. You could say, if you liked, that you had good reason to believe that you were representing my views; or that it was the substance of a correspondence with an English theologian etc. etc. Needless to say that *Lex Orandi* is a very guarded utterance of my full opinion. I have here given you the substance of the supplementary chapter that I would have written had I any hope of making myself intelligible to my censors. Once more thanking you for the keen pleasure and real help that I have derived from your admirable criticism, believe me with all respect and esteem,

Yours very faithfully

George Tyrrell

More on the '*via media*'

Richmond, Yorkshire   29 III 1905

My dear Abbé Venard

I hasten to thank you at once for your very valuable and interesting letter, as it is often hard to bring my attention back to a point if I procrastinate. As you say; the difficulty lies in the *application* of my theory to these two great facts of Catholic and Christian tradition. My immediate object was to repudiate what Batiffol has since called my 'radical symbolism' and to show not merely that I regarded Christianity as a religion incarnate in fact, but even that one could and *should* pass from dogma to history as far as the 'substantial' facts of Christianity were concerned. To resume my illustration: There is a 'substance' of fact common to the dramatist and the historian, though, in some respects, and on most occasions the historian will be better able to determine the limits between substance and treatment (or form). Yet one can well conceive that the substance of a fact should be enshrined for us in a poetic legend and yet lost altogether to history. That Christ *existed* is obviously a fact given to us by faith; it is the core of the substance of Christianity. Equally obviously, as Blondel admits, the 'Visit of the Magi' lies outside the substance of Christian fact. It *may* be fact, or it may be 'dramatisation'. Hitherto it has been accepted that the Virgin Birth and the *physical* Resurrection are as substantial, if not as central, as the very existence of Christ. It is hard to think otherwise, even though we are shown that they did not enter into the Christianity of St Paul as given us in the N.T. To me it seems that the question: 'What is the *substance* of Christianity? What is the precise basis of fact idealised by faith?' is a question of theology in a broad sense. However, if the Church has not spoken clearly on these points of the Birth and Resurrection, when has she ever spoken clearly? If she is wrong there, when can she ever be trusted? – that is I suppose what most of us feel.

Your criticism of P. de Grandmaison is exactly after my mind. No error could be *universally* and *steadily* fruitful of life. As to Bouddhism and other religions, the most conservative theologians allow them some rays of the 'Lux Vera' and their experience renders testimony to many truths common to all. Again, I state explicitly in the Preface to '*Lex Orandi*' that this criterion is supplementary, and not exclusive nor sufficient. It is a method of confirmation and verification, rather than of discovery. I do not mean that an individual or even a council should sit down *tout à coup* and sift the Creed by applying the *Lex Orandi*; but I only point out the process by which the Creed shapes itself and critices [*sic*] itself in the slow process of centuries. I had no intention of supplying an artificial method of forcing development (the theologians, alas, have done that) but to point out Nature's method i.e. God's method. Hence it is enough for me to say: '"*Omnis plantatio* etc."; [4] if the physical character of the Resurrection is of its spiritual substance, that belief will never die.' Blondel sees that it is so; and therefore he can be at rest. To me it is not so cogently clear. Still too, I can be at rest because I believe that religion can take care of itself as surely as Nature can; tho' our theologies and natural-philosophies may call for periodical revolutionary reconstructions.

I hope in a few days to be able to send you the brochures you speak of. I need not say that I confide entirely in your discretion. I should not like (e.g.) Blondel to see them. The '*Church of the Future*' [*sic*] is of course lamentably deficient and would need to be supplemented by much that I have thought and written since. I also venture to send you an article 'Semper Eadem' which raises but does not answer what seems to me a very acute dilemma. I trust later to be able to suggest a solution, but I have at present little or no freedom of utterance.

Ever, Dear Abbé Venard
Yours faithfully
G. Tyrrell

P.S. I am not quite sure that Abbé Loisy would agree with me when I say that to argue from the totality of Christian dogma to the existence of an historical kernel of the tradition (*quoad substantiam*) is to argue *historically*. However weak and vague, it is none the less a reason of which the historian *as such* should take account. The very existence of the Bouddha has been questioned by critics; but the existence of a religion which centres round him and is professedly built upon him is surely an *historical* argument or presumption in favour of his historical reality. And so, of the Resurrection: the dogma speaks to science as well as to Faith, albeit obscurely.

Notes

1. Tyrrell and Arnold 'between two worlds'

1 P. Honan, *Matthew Arnold: A Life* (London, 1981), p. 73.
2 'Stanzas from the Grande Chartreuse', line 84.
3 *Ibid.*, lines 85–6.
4 H. Denzinger, *Enchiridion Symbolorum*, thirtieth edition, translated by R. J. Deferrari (London, 1957), 1780.
5 *Ibid.*, 2105.
6 This has been well done by A. R. Vidler in *The Modernist Movement in the Roman Church* (Cambridge, 1934), which still retains its usefulness. Émile Poulat has provided a scholarly and comprehensive account of the French aspects of the crisis in *Histoire, Dogme et Critique dans la Crise Moderniste*, second edition (Paris, 1979). T. M. Loome, *Liberal Catholicism, Reform Catholicism, Modernism*, Tübinger Theologische Studien 14 (Mainz, 1979) is an indispensable bibliographical compendium.
7 In her edition of Tyrrell's *Autobiography*, and in the *Life* (London, 1912).
8 C. C. Abbott (ed.), *Further Letters of Gerard Manley Hopkins*, second edition (London, 1956), p. 161.
9 This correspondence survives almost complete in the British Museum (Add. MSS 44, 927–31). Extracts have been published in AL2; SL; B. Holland (ed.), *Baron Friedrich von Hügel, Selected Letters* (London, 1928); M. D. Petre, *Von Hügel and Tyrrell* (London, 1937).
10 Edited and translated into French by A. Louis-David, *Lettres de George Tyrrell à Henri Bremond* (Paris, 1971). The originals are in the Bibliothèque Nationale, Paris. Bremond's letters to Tyrrell have not survived.
11 Certain letters and some of Maude Petre's diaries are in the British Museum (Add. MSS 52, 367; 52, 372–9).
12 M. J. Weaver (ed.), *Letters from a 'Modernist'* (London, 1981). The originals are in St Andrews University Library. Ward's letters to Tyrrell have not survived.
13 *The Weekly Register*, 100 (16 December 1900), 797–800; reprinted EFI pp. 158–71.
14 In my use of this notion I owe a particular debt to the careful work of J. Coulson, especially *Newman and the Common Tradition* (Oxford, 1970). For a comprehensive theological account of tradition, see Y. Congar, *Tradition and Traditions*, translated by M. Naseby and T. Rainborough (London, 1966).

2. The history of an opinion

1 'The Limitations of Newman', *The Monthly Register*, 1 (1902), 264.

2 Letter to von Hügel, 5 December 1902.

3 See M. D. Petre, *The Soul's Orbit* (London, 1904), the salvaged remains of Tyrrell's projected commentary on the *The Spiritual Exercises* of St Ignatius: 'From the first "annotation", as it is called, to the very end, the book of the Spiritual Exercises is pervaded by the principle that, on the whole, what we think depends on what we feel far more than our feeling depends on our thought' (pp. 11–12).

4 Letter to Bremond, 15 July 1900 (BN Fonds Bremond).

5 *Henri Bremond et Maurice Blondel: Correspondance*, ed. A. Blanchet (2 vols., Paris, 1970–1), vol. I, p. 128.

6 *L'Inquiétude Religieuse*, first series (Paris, 1919), p. 2.

7 Letter to F. Brunetière, 4 August 1901 (BN N.a.f. 25033). I am indebted to É. Goichot for this and other references to Matthew Arnold in the writings of Bremond. See É. Goichot, 'Henri Bremond, historien du sentiment religieux', unpublished thesis, University of Paris, 1977.

8 Note of 23 December 1907.

9 A letter of Bremond to Loisy, written on 11 November 1926, and published in A. Loisy, *George Tyrrell et Henri Bremond* (Paris, 1936), pp. 44–5, shows Bremond's understanding of Tyrrell: 'Au fond, je crois, *un mysticisme fondamental*, moins conscient, et qui n'avait rien de ce que nous appelons dévotion. Très pénétré, avec cela, et c'est assez dans l'ordre, de sacramentalisme...*Le besoin* de rites, *d'une Église*, romaine ou non. Avec cela, – et pas malgré – *une tendance très forte au panthéisme*, mais combattue, comme tentation.' I have italicised the remarks that bring out the similarity with Arnold. Bremond concludes a brilliantly incisive characterisation by saying, in English, 'He was wild.'

10 A. Loisy, *Mémoires pour servir à l'Histoire Religieuse de Notre Temps* (3 vols., Paris, 1930–1), vol. III, p. 267. The book was *Jean-Adam Möhler et l'École Catholique de Tubingue (1815–1840)* (Paris, 1913), by Edmond Vermeil, subtitled, 'Étude sur la théologie romantique en Wurtemburg et les origines germaniques du modernisme'. Vermeil chooses his words carefully and does not argue that Newman, Tyrrell or Loisy were directly dependent upon Möhler and the theologians of Tübingen. However, he argues for the existence of 'une tradition intellectuelle' of which the roots lay in German romanticism and the development was not yet exhausted.

In his introduction to Blondel's *Letter on Apologetics, and History and Dogma* (London, 1964), p. 48, Alexander Dru criticises Vermeil's thesis as an overstatement, but accepts the link in the cases of Blondel, Laberthonnière and Bremond, whom he sees as 'neither Modernists nor Veterists' but 'carrying on (unbeknown, at first, to themselves) the tradition of Tübingen'. In Bremond's letter to Loisy of June 1913 (BN Fonds Loisy, N.a.f. 15650), he wrote of himself and Tyrrell, 'Nous étions ensemble à Fribourg lorsque, guidé par J. Sauer, je découvrais les principes catholiques du XIX siècle commençant. Il y a là, en effet, un groupe très important aigu et doucement novateur, bref modernisant.' He mentions Möhler, Staudenmaier and

Hirscher and 'un autre' (Drey? Kuhn?) and comments to Loisy 'Le mouvement allait bien dans le même sens que vous, mais sans trop le savoir.'

11 Letter to Loisy, June 1913, BN Fonds Loisy, N.a.f. 15650.

12 Letter to Bremond, 22 December 1899.

13 *The Hibbert Journal*, 6 (1908), 924.

14 P. Gardner, *Modernism in the English Church* (London, 1926), p. 50.

15 P. Gardner, *The Religious Experience of St Paul* (London, 1911), p. vii.

16 Vidler, *The Modernist Movement*, pp. 159–62. There was a hint that Vidler associated Tyrrell and Arnold in a book published the previous year: W. L. Knox and A. R. Vidler, *The Development of Modern Catholicism* (London, 1933), p. 176. The authors quote from *The Programme of Modernism*, a reply to '*Pascendi*' translated by Tyrrell. Knox and Vidler comment on the concept of God as a power immanent within both the universe and the life of man and say, 'Modernism tended to this view under the influence of purely scientific thought, just as Matthew Arnold had done.'

17 J. A. Laubacher, *Dogma and the Development of Dogma in the Writings of George Tyrrell* (Louvain, 1939), p. 36.

18 J. Ratté, *Three Modernists* (London, 1968), pp. 32–3.

19 *Ibid.*, p. 251, n. 2. The most likely friend would be C. E. Osborne, and the source a misreading of his memoir in *The Hibbert Journal*, 8 (1910), 255, where Osborne likens Tyrrell to Arnold because both were attracted to the Roman Catholic Church as 'the Church of the people'.

20 D. J. DeLaura (ed.), *Victorian Prose* (New York, 1973), p. 313.

21 B. M. G. Reardon, *Roman Catholic Modernism* (London, 1970), p. 43.

22 Louis-David (ed.), *Lettres*, p. 124. Mme David is commenting on a remark in a letter to Bremond written on 14 April 1902: 'Qu'est-ce que Arnold? nous ne le savons pas davantage.' Tyrrell alludes to an article by Bremond on *Thomas Arnold* in *L'Enfant et la Vie* (Paris, 1902) and may well be thinking of the father rather than the son.

23 'Revelation as Experience', edited by T. M. Loome, *The Heythrop Journal*, 12 (1971), 148–9.

24 W. Robbins, *The Ethical Idealism of Matthew Arnold* (London, 1959), pp. 209–10.

25 This is correct. In the introduction to *The Faith of the Millions* Tyrrell wrote, 'The dominant note of that Thomistic and Augustinian theology to which the reigning Pontiff has recalled us, is the immanence of the supernatural in the natural' (p. xx). At the end of his life he decisively rejected 'pure immanentism' because it 'limits spirit and confines it within its self-made mechanisms as the motor power' (SL p. 241). For Tyrrell the supernatural could never be opposed, or reduced, to the natural. (See also CF p. 165, EFI p. 95.)

26 G. Daly, *Transcendence and Immanence* (Oxford, 1980), p. 147.

27 Tyrrell criticised Arnold's phrase in 'Religion and Ethics', *The Month*, 101 (1903), 141. He offered an alternative definition of religion in Arnoldian style as 'Divine love, making for righteousness or morality'.

28 J. Coulson, *Religion and Imagination* (Oxford, 1981), p. 104.

29 D. G. Schultenover, *George Tyrrell* (Shepherdstown, USA, 1981), pp. 189–90.

3. 'Definite evidence'

1 Vidler, *The Modernist Movement*, p. 160.
2 Also FM2 pp. 217, 253. Tyrrell's introduction of the qualifying epithet 'personal' is suggestive of his lasting disquiet at the impersonality of the Arnoldian concept. He is arguing here for the existence of a shadowy analogue to the Christian God in the perception of even the most primitive tribes – hence his concern with personality. Compare *The Month*, 92, p. 355 (FM2 p. 261) where Tyrrell follows Lang in describing the concept of a Supreme Being known to all savages as – *amongst other personal epithets* – 'a power making for goodness'. Lang played with the Arnoldian phrase in his book (e.g. pp. 177, 188) but did not quote it entire as Tyrrell does.
3 Letter of 11 January 1899. Mme Louis-David (*Lettres*, p. 48) surmises that Tyrrell had read the recently published *Life and Letters of B. Jowett* by E. Abbott and L. Campbell (London, 1897).
4 He was doomed to disappointment. The first semi-biographical study of Arnold, by G. Saintsbury in the Modern English Writers series, appeared only in 1899. Arnold had stipulated that he wanted no biography written. His letters were edited in 1895 by G. W. E. Russell.
5 AL2 p. 73 gives the date wrongly as 20 September. See Louis-David, *Lettres*, p. 55, n. 5. The shape of Tyrrell's argument in this letter foreshadows 'Revelation as Experience', written ten years later. This letter is perceptively discussed in Laubacher, *Dogma*, pp. 46–52.
6 Amédée de Margerie, *Saint Francis de Sales* (London, 1900).
7 Arnold does not mention St Francis de Sales in *Culture and Anarchy* but in *Literature and Dogma* he twice mentions Francis as an exemplar of 'righteousness', a man who 'threw [himself] on the method and secret of Jesus with extraordinary force' (S VI (LD) pp. 115, 350).
8 R. H. Hutton, *Aspects of Religious and Scientific Thought* (London, 1899), p. 329. In July 1900 Tyrrell wrote to Bremond recommending R. H. Hutton's work. The two essays on Arnold in this volume are perceptive, respectful, but hostile. Hutton also discusses Arnold in *Essays on Some of the Modern Guides to English Thought in Matters of Faith* (London, 1887) and *Criticisms on Contemporary Thought and Thinkers* (London, 1894), vol. I.
9 For futher discussion of the *Civilizing of the Matafanus* as a Christological allegory see pp. 93–5.
10 On Arnold's 'Reformed Catholicism', see A. O. J. Cockshut, *The Unbelievers* (London, 1964), p. 72.
11 In a letter written on 14 April 1902, Tyrrell complained to Bremond about 'an ignorance of matters of common education' in the Church.
12 *Paradiso*, XXXIII, line 135 (Cary's translation).
13 Drawn from William James, *The Will to Believe* (London, 1897). See SL p. 22.
14 'Semper Eadem', *The Month*, 103 (1904), 1–17. Reprinted, in TSC pp. 106–32. 'Semper Eadem (II)' follows, TSC pp. 133–54. For accounts of Tyrrell's behaviour over the articles see AL2 pp. 210–23; Maisie Ward, *Insurrection versus Resurrection* (London, 1937), pp. 165–70.
15 In the last of the *University Sermons*, Newman discusses the way in which

revelation is received, and 'the idea' thus communicated is developed, but he does not make clear exactly how he is using the term 'revelation'. What he says about 'the Catholic idea' (Tyrrell uses the phrase 'the deposit of faith') is compatible with Tyrrell's conception of 'liberal theology', which assumes revelation to be in some sense perennial, but Newman would have been horrified at this interpretation. N. Lash argues that although Newman 'believed that "new" revelation, subsequent to the events to which the scriptures bear witness, was impossible... much of the argument in the *Essay* [*On Development*] is difficult to reconcile with any coherent defence... of the claim that "revelation closed with the death of the last apostle"' (*Newman on Development* (London, 1975), p. 100). This follows O. Chadwick, *From Bossuet to Newman* (Cambridge, 1957), p. 160. P. Misner discusses Chadwick's contention in 'Newman's concept of revelation and the development of doctrine', *The Heythrop Journal*, 11 (1970), 32–47. He finds inadequacies in both Newman's and Tyrrell's concepts of revelation.

16 Letter to Kitty Clutton, 27 September 1906.
17 In discussing Tyrrell's concept of revelation I am particularly indebted to J. A. Laubacher (*op. cit.*) and to F. M. O'Connor, 'The concept of revelation in the writings of George Tyrrell', unpublished thesis, Institut Catholique, Paris, 1963.
18 *Demain*, 1, 1 (27 October 1905), p. 6, 'L'Affaire Loisy et la situation religieuse en Angleterre'; 1, 5 (24 November 1905), p. 8, 'Lettre d'Angleterre'. Williams somewhat extravagantly claimed that the English were better prepared for the impact of Biblical criticism than other European nations because of the work of Matthew Arnold. Tyrrell would have appreciated Williams's saying of Arnold: 'Il voulait montrer qu'il y a une profonde vérité naturelle dans le christianisme, une beauté unique et une compréhension que lui permettra de survivre à tous les effets désagrégeants de la critique', and his criticism of Arnold's superficiality in handling the ideas behind such words as 'dogma', 'Church', 'Kingdom of Heaven', etc.
19 Letter to Bremond, 28 December 1905.
20 The triadic shape of Tyrrell's anthropology comes not from Arnold but from von Hügel. Compare F. von Hügel, *The Mystical Element of Religion* (London, 1908), chapter 2, 'The three elements of religion'. Tyrrell was closely involved in the production of the Baron's great work.
21 My stress; 'the whole' was a major concern of Tyrrell's at this period.
22 Translated by H. C. Corrance, introduction by G. Tyrrell (London, 1907).
23 *The Heythrop Journal*, 12 (1971), 148.
24 Vidler, *The Modernist Movement*, p. 161.
25 Letter dated 8 January 1904, Weaver (ed.), *Letters from a 'Modernist'*, p. 160.
26 H. Egerton, *Father Tyrrell's Modernism* (London, 1909). Hakluyt Egerton was a pseudonym of Arthur Boutwood.
27 Letter to William Gibson, 7 December 1906, SL p. 103.
28 Letter to E.D., 1908–9, SL pp. 221–2.
29 Letter to von Hügel, 19 April 1909.
30 In J. Crehan's memoir of *Father Thurston* (London, 1952), p. 69.

4. Fundamental convergence: epistemology and metaphysics

1 B. Willey, 'Arnold and religion', in K. Allott (ed.), *Matthew Arnold*, Writers and their Background Series (London, 1975), p. 239.

2 Quoted in B. Willey, *Nineteenth-Century Studies* (Penguin edition, Harmondsworth, 1964), p. 276.

3 P. Gardner in review of *Through Scylla and Charybdis*, *The Hibbert Journal*, 6 (1908), 924.

4 A. Fawkes, 'Modernism: a retrospect and a prospect', *The Hibbert Journal*, 8 (1909–10), 75. (Fawkes misquotes Arnold.) In February 1908, Tyrrell wrote, 'An immense revolution is inevitable; the old is dead, the new not yet born' (SL p. 54).

5 Cf. 'To a Friend', line 12.

6 In this both were manifestly indebted to Coleridge. Coleridge's famous remark in *Aids to Reflection* (Bohn edition, London, 1884, p. 134): 'Christianity is not a Theory, or a Speculation; but a *Life*; – not a *Philosophy* of Life, but a Life and a living Process...TRY IT' is echoed by Arnold's assertion, 'That there *is* an enduring Power, not ourselves, which makes for righteousness, is verifiable...by experience; and that Jesus *is* the offspring of this Power is verifiable from experience also...It *is* so! try, and you will find it to be so!' (S VI (LD) p. 375). Tyrrell says little of Coleridge until he quotes *Confessions of an Enquiring Spirit* at great length in TSC pp. 66–71, and applies what is there said about the *proven* efficacy of Scripture to the whole Catholic tradition. However, in learning from Newman he had learnt from Coleridge, as John Coulson showed in *Newman and the Common Tradition*. See also J. Goetz, 'Analogy and symbol: a study in the theology of George Tyrrell', unpublished thesis, Cambridge University, 1969, appendix 3 (p. 418), 'Coleridge, Newman and Tyrrell'.

7 Letter of 15 October 1908, BN Fonds Houtin, N.a.f. 15743 (Houtin's translation). This letter convinced Houtin that Tyrrell was no longer a Christian.

8 This is Arnold's own brief summary of his 'fundamental thesis' in *Literature and Dogma*. It is interesting to compare the following words of T. H. Huxley, who wrote to Kingsley in 1860: 'The absolute justice of the system of things is as clear to me as any scientific fact. The gravitation of sin to sorrow is as certain as that of the earth to the sun, and more so – for experimental proof of the fact is within reach of us all' (L. Huxley, *Life and Letters of Thomas Henry Huxley*, second edition (3 vols., London, 1903), vol. I, p. 317). This remark is quoted by Cockshut, *The Unbelievers*, pp. 96–7. Cockshut points out that in later life Huxley was less sure about this 'fact'.

9 *Bibliothèque Universelle et Revue Suisse*, 49 (1874), 342–59.

10 In 'A Comment on Christmas' (S X p. 227), a late essay written in 1885, Arnold explicitly showed himself aware of the value of *testimony* and also spoke of 'instinctive anticipations' which precede experience. Secrétan (p. 347) comes to the conclusion that 'Le fond de ses idées est d'un kantien beaucoup plus que d'un empirique.'

11 Tyrrell echoed Arnold's exact words in a letter of 24 December 1907. Given the 'root error' of 1870, he wrote to Augustin Leger, there was bound to

be an abuse of Papal power: 'It would be a miracle if things were otherwise, and miracles don't happen' (AL2 p. 340).

12 Letter to A. L. Lilley, 17 June 1904, SAUL MS 30783.

13 *Ibid.* Compare Tyrrell's remark to Loisy, Letter of 20 October 1907, BN Fonds Loisy, N.a.f. 15662, 'The crudest positivist sets out with a philosophy of science and criteriology...The true critic begins by determining the right *method* (a philosophical effort) and then accepts the results honestly and impartially.'

14 Newman's epistemology is well described in S. Prickett, *Romanticism and Religion* (Cambridge, 1976), pp. 174–210, and Coulson, *Religion and Imagination*, pp. 46–83.

15 D. J. DeLaura has studied Arnold's relation to Newman with great care and concludes: 'The man is treated with considerable deference, and his words are quoted, usually somewhat out of context, when Newman's literary and intellectual authority seems helpful to Arnold's argument; but Newman is impatiently thrust aside as soon as his more "arbitrary" and "impossible" – and central – views are glimpsed' (D. J. DeLaura, *Hebrew and Hellene in Victorian England* (Austin, Texas, 1969), p. 88.

16 Letter of 11 December 1903, Weaver (ed.), *Letters from a 'Modernist'*, p. 88.

17 For example, he wrote to Houtin: 'D'après mon idée, les atomes, les électrons et l'éther étaient des entités purement hypothétiques, commodes pour l'explication de certains groupements et de certains enchaînements de phénomènes. Je ne savais pas qu'ils eussent jamais été atteints et prouvés' (Letter of 15 October 1908, BN Fonds Houtin, N.a.f. 15743). Note however, that when it came to Biblical criticism, Tyrrell was almost naive in accepting apparently 'scientific' results.

18 There are useful accounts of Tyrrell's writing on conscience in J. J. Stam, *George Tyrrell (1861–1909)* (Utrecht, 1938) and F. J. O'Connor 'The concept of revelation in the writings of George Tyrrell', unpublished thesis, Institut Catholique, Paris, 1963.

19 Compare LO p. xxxi: 'Viewed from the standpoint taken in these pages, tested by the criterion of life, of spiritual fruitfulness, the truths of this Christianity cannot be expected to present the same precision and clearness of outline as when deduced from defined premisses and built up into a coherent intellectual system. We can but see men as trees walking; blurred contours; mountain shapes looming through mist. Yet the verification is not valueless.'

20 Letter to Bremond, 18 September 1902.

21 Tyrrell's hold on the personal nature of the Spirit fluctuated. On 8 April 1903 he wrote to von Hügel, 'By the Christian spirit I mean that spirit which spoke from the beginning in the prophets and men of faith, and found its [*sic*] most docile organ in Christ, and which still speaks in the corporate life of the Church...The Spirit of Christ rather than Christ Himself is the creator of the Church' (AL2 p. 187). In his thesis, O'Connor finds Tyrrell's notion of the Spirit 'somewhat impersonal' (p. 380).

22 Letter to Kitty Clutton, 2 October 1907.

23 Letter to Loisy, 27 January 1903, BN Fonds Loisy, N.a.f. 15662. This was written after Loisy's *L'Évangile et L'Église* had been condemned by Cardinal Richard.

24 Letter to Loisy, 12 July 1903, BN Fonds Loisy, N.a.f. 15662.

25 See F. Neiman, 'The *Zeitgeist* of Matthew Arnold', *PMLA*, 72 (1957), 977–96.

26 H. F. Lowry (ed.), *Letters to Clough* (Oxford, 1932), p. 95.

27 E. Alexander, *Matthew Arnold and John Stuart Mill* (London, 1965), p. 73.

28 Fred A. Dudley, 'Matthew Arnold and science', *PMLA*, 57 (1942), 275–94.

29 *Ibid.*, p. 280.

30 Arnold does not use the terms 'higher' and 'lower', though 'Perfection' for him is a kind of Platonic ideal. David Newsome, in his essay 'Was Matthew Arnold a Platonist?' (appendix to *Two Classes of Men* (London, 1974), pp. 126–31) rightly emphasises that if Arnold was in any sense a Platonist it was as an exponent of the *Republic* rather than the metaphysical dialogues, but he seems to underestimate the sense in which Arnold's cultural ideal was not simply a balance of jostling forces, but a transcendent unity. In conduct, religion, art, in culture as a whole, and in science, we find the elements through which we can pass to 'perfection'.

31 Letter to T. H. Huxley, 17 October 1880, quoted in W. H. G. Armytage, 'Matthew Arnold and T. H. Huxley: some new letters 1870–1880', *RES*, n.s. 4 (1953), 352.

32 Tyrrell made exactly the same point in LC, 'Instead of dismissing it as a complete mistake, we ought to distinguish between the religious and the scientific values of the condemnation of Galileo . . . What the religious instinct implicitly affirmed was only that fundamental religious truth which seemed to be implicitly denied by Galileo's affirmation' (pp. 60–1). He further discussed the case of Galileo in a letter to von Hügel and concluded that the Church 'condemns heliocentrism because it implies a denial of the inspiration of Scripture' (Letter of 10 February 1907, SL p. 59).

33 John Root, 'English Catholic Modernism and science', *The Heythrop Journal*, 18 (1977), 271–88, gives an excellent survey of Tyrrell's position, and shows his consistent opposition to premature syntheses or illegitimate hegemony. Tyrrell was of course deeply influenced by von Hügel in this area.

34 On 4 December 1907, Tyrrell sent to Houtin a copy of his 'Letter to the Roman Catholic Bishop of Southwark'. On the back he wrote, 'Personally I believe Newman was an incurable ecclesiast, fighting for ecclesiasticism with modern weapons' (BN Fonds Houtin, N.a.f. 15743).

35 On 27 January 1904, Tyrrell wrote to Loisy, who was under great pressure from the Vatican, 'It seems to me that you must hold fast to your distinction between the religious and the scientific aspects and approaches of the same questions, allowing the Church's jurisdiction over the former; firmly denying it over the latter' (BN Fonds Loisy, N.a.f. 15662). As an epistemological distinction Tyrrell held to this as strongly as Loisy, but he wanted to allow the possibility that in some sense history *could* be determined by dogma. In this he sought a *via media* between Loisy, who was opposed to such a position, and Blondel, who accepted that history could be shaped by dogma. This is made clear in the letter to Venard of 15 January 1905, presented in the appendix.

36 He wrote to Ward on 21 February 1902, 'Is there then some new orientation which will make it possible to be almost indifferent not merely to what criticism has done, but to anything it could conceivably do? I suppose, at present, we should have to say: "No, Christianity would fall with the denial

of certain facts of the positive order." Yet, for hypothesis' sake, I have endeavoured to find a way' (Weaver (ed.), *Letters from a 'Modernist'*, p. 75). See also RFL pp. 36, 50.

37 Tyrrell discussed this by letter with von Hügel, 27 January 1904 (von Hügel quoted this letter in 'Father Tyrrell: Some memorials of the last twelve years of his life' in the *Hibbert Journal*, 8 (1910), 241); and with Lilley (Letter of 30 January 1904, SAUL MS 30772); and no doubt with others.

38 M. H. Abrams, *The Mirror and the Lamp, Romantic Theory and the Critical Tradition* (Norton edition, New York, 1958), p. 335.

39 Compare Coleridge's note to R. Southey, *Life of Wesley*, third edition (2 vols., London, 1846), vol. II, pp. 71–2, 'But in the great majority of our gentry, and of our classically educated clergy, there is a fearful combination of the *sensuous* and the *unreal*. Whatever is subjective, the true and only proper *noumenon*, or *intelligible*, is unintelligible to them. *But* all *substance ipso nomine* is necessarily subjective; and what these men call reality, is object unsouled of all subject.' Arnold obviously read this edition of Southey as he quotes from it in SPP (S VI p. 18). See Super's note, p. 427.

40 The close links between CA and SPP as criticism offered by 'a man of letters' rather than a theologian are brought out by J. A. Smallbone, '*St Paul and Protestantism*: its place in the development of Matthew Arnold's thought', unpublished thesis, London University, 1950, pp. 52, 158. Arnold wrote to M. Fontanès in 1872, 'En parlant de St Paul, je n'ai pas parlé en théologien, mais en homme de lettres mécontent de la très mauvaise critique littéraire qu'on appliquait à un grand esprit; si j'avais parlé en théologien, on ne m'eût pas écouté' (*Letters* II p. 88).

41 William Blackburn, in 'Matthew Arnold and the Oriel Noetics' (*PQ*, 25 (1946), 70–8) finds that 'from the point of view of the history of his ideas, Arnold's *St Paul and Protestantism, Literature and Dogma, God and the Bible* are one and indivisible' for 'all these works are based on a single notion: the distinction between symbolic and explicative language' (p. 72).

42 Arnold's concern with this 'common substratum' brought about some very insecurely based philological argument. Jowett remarked that Arnold's 'argument of the meaning of words from their etymology is fallacious, and a most Philistine sort of fallacy' (E. Abbott and L. Campbell, *The Life and Letters of Benjamin Jowett* (2 vols., London 1897), vol. II, p. 80).

43 Unpublished thesis, 1969.

44 Goetz, 'Analogy and symbol', p. 36.

45 *Ibid.*, pp. 166–7.

46 As early as 1889 Tyrrell talked of the 'prophetic' nature of much Biblical narrative and of 'many of the principal miracles of our Blessed Lord'. See 'The Contents of a Pre-Adamite Skull', *The Month*, 67 (1889), 70–1. In ER he said of Christ, 'Every deed and event of His mortal life was prophetic; was as it were a sacrament or symbol of the mysteries of the Kingdom of God; was crowded with inexhaustible meaning touching the things of the eternal and invisible world' (p. 31).

47 Letter of 15 January 1905. See appendix.

48 *Ibid.*

49 In this Tyrrell is followed magnificently by S. Langer, *Philosophy in a New*

Key, third edition (Harvard, 1957), a philosopher much indebted to Ernst Cassirer whose *Philosophy of Symbolic Forms* (E.T., 3 vols., Yale, 1955) should be a seminal work for theologians, but has not yet been adequately exploited. He provides a philosophical framework in which Christian doctrine can be understood as 'symbolic form' without loss of cognitive content. This was what Tyrrell was feeling for at the end of his life, and in this he is differentiated from Arnold, though in a looser sense there are hints of the same quest in Arnold – especially in his growing appreciation of the Catholic Church.

50 Letter to Venard, 15 January 1905. See appendix.
51 Wordsworth wrote in 'Tintern Abbey':

> ...Therefore am I still
> A lover of the meadows and the woods,
> And mountains; and of all that we behold
> From this green earth; of all the mighty world
> Of eye, and ear, – both what they half create,
> And what perceive.   (lines 102–7)

Tyrrell typically, says '*more* than half creates'.

52 To this we might well apply the famous remark of Tyrrell, 'The Christ that Harnack sees, looking back through nineteen centuries of Catholic darkness, is only the reflection of a Liberal Protestant face' (CCR p. 44).
53 Perhaps the most repeated quotation from Scripture in Tyrrell's works is John 6. 63: 'It is the spirit that quickeneth; the flesh profiteth nothing.' Such an appeal has obvious hermeneutic dangers.

5. The life of the spirit: ecclesiology and culture

1 Letter of 20 July 1899, quoted in chapter 3, pp. 21–2. See AL2 p. 73.
2 Tyrrell saw himself as having proceeded quite oppositely to Newman: 'Newman's Catholicism was the outcome of his theism, practical and speculative' (AL1 p. 112). We should also note the signal contrast between the motive of Newman in writing the *Apologia* and Tyrrell in writing the *Autobiography*. Newman wrote the *Apologia* to establish his integrity; Tyrrell wrote his *Autobiography* to disabuse Maude Petre of flattering notions about himself.
3 By Bremond, at his funeral. See AL2 p. 444.
4 Letter to William Gibson, 7 December 1906; SL p. 103.
5 DeLaura, *Hebrew and Hellene*, pp. xii–xiii.
6 Raymond Williams, *Culture and Society 1780–1950* (Penguin edition, Harmondsworth, 1961), p. 120.
7 Tyrrell's ecclesiology has been studied by C. J. Healey, 'The invisible Church and the visible Church in the writings of George Tyrrell' (unpublished thesis, Gregorian University, Rome, 1970), who made a particular study of the Mystical Body in the early writings; Charles J. Mehok, 'The ecclesiology of George Tyrrell' (unpublished thesis, Catholic University of America, Washington DC, 1970), who somewhat uncritically emphasises the acceptance of many of Tyrrell's ecclesiological insights at Vatican II; Ellen Leonard, 'The question of Catholicism in the Modernist period: the contribution of George

Tyrrell' (unpublished thesis, University of St Michael's College, Toronto, 1978), who concentrates more on the challenge to Catholic self-understanding by Protestant critics. The historical development of the doctrine of the Mystical Body is comprehensively described by E. Mersch, *Le Corps Mystique du Christ*, second edition (Louvain, 1963).

8 My stress. The words are carefully chosen. In another passage (pp. 363–4), he deals with the question of the person who finds the Church *morally* unacceptable because of scandals and corruption.

9 Letter to Ward, 16 March 1900, Weaver (ed.), *Letters from a 'Modernist'*, p. 39.

10 Letter to von Hügel, 10 May 1899.

11 My stress.

12 In an early article, 'Aquinas Resuscitatus' (*American Catholic Quarterly Review*, 16 (October 1891), 673–90), Tyrrell had argued that even within the clergy, only those who are to teach theology need study scholastic theology in depth, so that they can apply the principles creatively. For others, a knowledge of conclusions, gained from manuals, is adequate.

13 Here Tyrrell's debt to Newman is apparent. See especially Newman's *Rambler* article, *On Consulting the Faithful in Matters of Doctrine*, edited by John Coulson (London, 1961); also S. D. Femiano, *Infallibility of the Laity*, *The Legacy of Newman* (New York, 1967).

14 Letter to Tyrrell, 8 October 1899.

15 Where 'revelation' means '*revelatio revelata*', Tyrrell uses 'the deposit' and 'revelation' interchangeably.

16 When this essay was reprinted in *The Faith of the Millions* Tyrrell dropped all reference to 'the deposit' in the two quotations we have given. He then restored the references to 'the deposit' for *Through Scylla and Charybdis*, thus providing a neat indication of two shifts in his thinking.

17 Compare 'The Mind of the Church' (*The Month*, 96 (1900), 132), 'The full and adequate receptacle of the entire deposit of faith was not the mind of each individual bishop; or any local synod of bishops; but the mind of the Universal Church, which was discerned, formulated, and declared in ecumenical council.' The metaphor of the 'Mind' links with the metaphor of the 'Body'.

18 Tyrrell acknowledges the change in a letter to Wilfrid Ward of 2 October 1900, where he says that his view of the deposit in the first version of 'The Mind of the Church' did not allow for that development by which the Church grows in 'the power of mental vision' – understanding better the primitive expression with greater maturity (Weaver (ed.), *Letters from a 'Modernist'*, pp. 54–5). Tyrrell was later less sanguine about the progress of the Church in understanding and stressed the normative value of primitive expression ('the form of sound words').

19 In this discussion of Tyrrell's changing view of the 'deposit' I have drawn heavily on Laubacher's excellent *Dogma and the Development of Dogma in the Writings of George Tyrrell* (Louvain, 1939).

20 See J. M. Cameron, *The Night Battle* (London, 1962), pp. 219–43 on 'Newman and Empiricism'.

21 The effect of the Joint-Pastoral on Tyrrell has been closely studied by Mary

Jo Weaver in 'George Tyrrell and the Joint-Pastoral Letter', *The Downside Review*, 99 (1981), 18–39. See also W. J. Schoenl, 'George Tyrrell and the English liberal Catholic crisis, 1900–1901', *The Downside Review*, 92 (1974), 171–84. The letter was published in *The Tablet*, 5 January 1901, pp. 8–12, 12 January 1901, pp. 50–2; reprinted in Weaver (ed.), *Letters from a 'Modernist'*, pp. 131–57.

22 *The Tablet*, 5 January 1901, p. 9; Weaver (ed.), *Letters from a 'Modernist'*, p. 135.

23 *Ibid.*, p. 9; p. 136.

24 *Ibid.*, p. 10; p. 137. In view of the strong division between the *Ecclesia docens* and the *Ecclesia discens*, it is ironical to read: 'God in His wisdom has constituted all organic life upon earth complex, with interdependent parts... and no form of beauty worthy of contemplation, no integrity of life worthy of admiration, can ever be attained, without the contribution of each and every part to the perfection and beauty of the whole' (pp. 12, 146–7). This is applied only to the *religious devotions* of the laity!

25 'The recent Anglo-Roman Pastoral', *The Nineteenth Century*, 49 (1901), 736–54.

26 Letter to von Hügel, 20 February 1901.

27 *The Pilot*, 2 March 1901, p. 282; AL2 p. 154.

28 *The Weekly Register*, 3 May 1901, 'Lord Halifax Demurs'; quoted by Weaver, *Downside Review*, 99, pp. 33–4.

29 The Gallican position sought to defend the independence of the national Church, especially in France, from the authority of the Pope. The four Gallican Articles of 1682 denied the authority of the Pope over temporal matters, affirmed the authority of general councils over the Pope, insisted that the ancient liberties of the Gallican Church were inviolable, and asserted that, pending the consent of the Church (i.e. by a general council), the judgment of the Pope was not irreformable. The articles were condemned in 1690 and the general Gallican position was untenable after the First Vatican Council. See articles in F. L. Cross and E. A. Livingstone (eds.), *The Oxford Dictionary of the Christian Church*, second edition (London, 1974).

30 Tyrrell had been deeply shaken by the apparently sceptical conclusions of contemporary Biblical and historical scholarship and was alarmed at the prospect of further intellectual erosion of the historical basis for Christianity. He therefore tried to put the Faith above such criticism: '"*Spiritus est qui vivificat, caro non prodest quidquam.*" ['It is the spirit that quickeneth; the flesh profiteth nothing.'] If therefore in any point of philosophy, history or science, the traditional Christian belief should prove, as it has so often proved, mistaken, it matters as little as the discovery that Dives and Lazarus never existed; it is not *ad rem*' (CF p. 90).

31 However, compare SL pp. 89–91, where in a letter of 22 February 1904, Tyrrell makes it clear that he believes the 'official *Ecclesia docens*' to have moral power to impose the general mind on recalcitrant individuals.

32 This is the basis of Tyrrell's important and moving paper 'Beati Excommunicati' of May 1904 (BM Add. MSS 52, 369) where he argues that one may be excommunicated by the visible Church (as many saints have been) but still in communion with the invisible Church.

Notes

33 P. J. Keating writes of Arnold, 'His analysis of English society relies for its justification almost entirely upon his own insight and reasoning power, and allows no influence of political party or religious doctrine' (*Matthew Arnold*, ed. Allott, p. 213). What he does rely on is his membership of a 'clerisy' whose function is to maintain and promote a tradition vital to the nation's integrity. See Ben Knights, *The Idea of the Clerisy in the Nineteenth Century* (Cambridge, 1978).

34 Laubacher is of the opinion that Tyrrell made this shift precisely to redeem his position from the appearance of Liberal Protestantism (p. 154).

35 Compare Coleridge's oft-quoted remark, that 'It is among the miseries of the present age that it recognises no medium between *Literal* and *Metaphorical*' (*The Statesman's Manual* (London, 1816), p. 36).

36 This was the title he took for the final section of the book (part 3, pp. 139–46). James C. Livingston's *The Ethics of Belief* (Tallahassee, Florida, 1974), discusses the debate on the ethics of subscription that took place in and around the Church of England over the previous forty years. Tyrrell was alluding to this debate.

37 The influence of von Hügel is manifest here, even though Tyrrell does not hold to the triadic expression of *The Mystical Element* and stresses the element of conflict. Both slight changes are a move in Arnold's direction. Although Arnold works with the triad: conduct, art, science (weighted overwhelmingly towards conduct), in his later works he often reiterates a fourfold scheme: conduct, intellect and knowledge, beauty, social life and manners are the 'lines' along which human life is to be developed into a harmonious whole (S IX p. 27, cf. S VIII pp. 287, 372, etc.). Arnold often thinks in terms of two, three or four elements that should together form a harmonious whole, but in fact struggle for hegemony. The tradition of such thinking, especially in triadic form, leads back to Coleridge, who wrote, for example, in *The Statesman's Manual*: 'There exists in the human being, at least in man fully developed, no mean symbol of Tri-unity, in Reason, Religion, and the Will. For each of the three, though a distinct agency, implies and demands the other two, and loses its own nature at the moment that from distinction it passes into division or separation. The perfect frame of a man is the perfect frame of a state: and in the light of this idea we must read Plato's *Republic*' (p. vii). Newman and von Hügel applied this to the Church; Arnold to society at large. Tyrrell benefited from both applications.

38 Tyrrell recognises the power of ancient ritual and symbolism in maintaining a living tradition. It helps 'to gather up the Whole into the consciousness of each several part' (TSC p. 42). This important insight is woven into his understanding of apocalyptic imagery and Catholic continuity in CCR.

39 'From Heaven or of Men' (TSC pp. 355–86) is important on this theme and confirms the Arnoldian tone of his thoughts.

40 The description of liberal Catholicism conforms perfectly to the Arnoldian ideal; 'It implies nothing more or less than the Catholicism of a man of liberal education; of a broad outlook over the world of the past and present – such an education as delivers a man from parochialism and provincialism of every sort; enables him to enter into the heart and mind of other races, times, religions, and civilisations than his own...and, while deepening his loyalty

166

and devotion to it, preserves him from bigotry, one-sidedness and fanaticism' (TSC p. 79). Tyrrell considered himself the product of just such an education.

41 The picture is really too sketchy to let us know to what extent such a religion of the future would in Tyrrell's mind have been specifically Christian. It would to him have been the *fulfilment* of historical Christianity.

42 In *The Idea of the Symbol* (Cambridge, 1980) Sr Jadwiga Swiatecka criticises Tyrrell's incoherent use of the term 'symbol' in *Christianity at the Crossroads*. It is true that he had not yet given renewed attention to the relation of symbol and referent; this might have come with time.

43 Compare what Arnold says to be the task of the believer in culture: 'It is his business...to get the present believers in action, and lovers of political talking and doing, to make a return upon their own minds, scrutinise their stock notions and habits much more, value their present talking and doing much less; in order that, by learning to think more clearly, they may come at last to act less confusedly' (S V (CA) p. 226).

44 Matthew Arnold's debt to his father is carefully discussed in Eugene L. Williamson's *The Liberalism of Thomas Arnold* (Alabama, 1964), pp. 95–102, 147–51, 205–10; his debt to Newman in DeLaura's *Hebrew and Hellene*, pp. 152–61. See also note 62 below.

45 Thomas Arnold, *Principles of Church Reform*, with an introductory essay by M. J. Jackson and J. Rogan, (London, 1962), p. 163. Dr Arnold was much indebted to Coleridge who propounded the ideal of a 'National Church' in his *On the Constitution of the Church and State*.

46 Thomas Arnold, *Fragments on Church and State* (London, 1845), pp. 98–9.

47 A. P. Stanley, *Life and Correspondence of Thomas Arnold, D.D.* (Ward Lock edition, London, no date), p. 262 (Letter 117).

48 R. W. Church, *The Oxford Movement* (London, 1900), p. 94.

49 Thomas Arnold, *Principles of Church Reform*, pp. 107–8.

50 *The Miscellaneous Works of Thomas Arnold, D.D.*, edited by A. P. Stanley, (London, 1845), p. 473.

51 Thomas Arnold, *Fragments on Church and State*, p. 21.

52 *Ibid.*, p. 22, note.

53 Letter of 1844, Balliol MSS. Quoted by Honan, *Matthew Arnold: A Life*, p. 73.

54 *Life of Thomas Arnold*, p. 86.

55 The following words of Thomas Arnold on 'culture' and Scriptural interpretation are interesting for the way in which they foreshadow Matthew's approach: 'It is by the study of the great principles of all goodness and all wisdom contained in the Christian Scriptures, that we are fashioned after our own imperfect measure to goodness and wisdom also. But for this study to be profitable in the highest possible degree, we see in practice that large experience, that a spirit rising above the influence of its age, and a pure love of excellence, combined with a clear and manly understanding, are all necessary' (*Fragments on Church and State*, p. 13).

56 For example, J. C. Shairp made this criticism in *Culture and Religion in some of their Relations* (Edinburgh, 1870). David DeLaura (*Hebrew and Hellene*, p. 70) says that 'Arnold is setting up a frankly rival ideal to that of historic Christianity.'

57 T. S. Eliot, *Notes Towards the Definition of Culture* (London, 1962), p. 28.

58 My stress.

59 *Hebrew and Hellene*, p. 110. If Newman really had been the epitome of culture, he would not have held the 'impossible' religious notions for which Arnold criticised him.

60 The influence of von Hügel is manifest here, and behind von Hügel, Eucken. See F. von Hügel, 'The Religious Philosophy of Rudolf Eucken', *The Hibbert Journal*, 10 (1911–12), 660–77.

61 Lionel Trilling, *Matthew Arnold*, second edition (London, 1949), p. 251.

62 Not only by DeLaura (pp. 152–3), but also by John Dover Wilson who says of Newman's *Idea of a University* and *Culture and Anarchy* that 'their hearts beat as one' (Introduction to *Culture and Anarchy* (Cambridge, 1932), p. xiii) and Raymond Williams in *Culture and Society*, chapter 6.

63 John Dover Wilson, Introduction to *Culture and Anarchy*, p. xxxviii.

64 'Culture is indispensably necessary, and culture is *reading*' (S VI (LD) p. 162). In *Literature and Dogma* Arnold presupposes that the Bible will be a powerful agent for social change, and that wide and careful reading will enable one to read the Bible intelligently. The social influence that he associates with culture in *Culture and Anarchy* is thus distanced as he applies himself to the more particular problem of religious language.

65 For instance, he speaks of 'salvation' as 'a harmonious perfection only to be won by unreservedly cultivating many sides in us' (S V (CA) p. 243).

66 Letter to von Hügel, 28 September 1898.

67 See Blondel, *The Letter on Apologetics*, p. 226.

68 Card to von Hügel, 24 October 1899. Arnold made play with the word 'machinery' in *Culture and Anarchy*.

69 Letter to Bremond, 22 December 1899.

70 Letter to Ward, 7 September 1901, Weaver (ed.), *Letters from a 'Modernist'*, p. 70.

71 Cockshut, *The Unbelievers*, p. 72.

72 *Hebrew and Hellene*, p. 28, referring to *The Note-Books of Matthew Arnold*, edited by H. F. Lowry, K. Young, and W. H. Dunn (Oxford, 1952), p. 23.

73 Letter to Kitty Clutton, 21 October 1907.

6. Christology: the parting of the ways

1 M. D. Petre, *Modernism: Its Failure and Its Fruits* (London, 1918), p. 84ff.

2 Letter to von Hügel, 19 April 1909.

3 See the letter that Tyrrell wrote about Dolling in C. E. Osborne, *The Life of Father Dolling* (London, 1903), pp. 19–22.

4 Letter of von Hügel to Tyrrell, 4 December 1899, printed in *Selected Letters* of Baron von Hügel, pp. 77–82.

5 Tyrrell wrote to von Hügel on 12 November 1900, saying what a help Blondel's notion of the Incarnation as a 'visibilising' of what goes on invisibly in every conscience had been to him; but this was an example of his finding in Blondel the thought that had been his before.

6 Letter of von Hügel to Tyrrell, 4 December 1899; *Selected Letters* of von Hügel, p. 78.

7 Daly, *Transcendence and Immanence*, p. 153.

8 Letter to A. R. Waller, 11 October 1900.

9 When Tyrrell had recently read E. Récéjac, *Essay on the Bases of the Mystic Knowledge*, translated by Sara Upton (London, 1899), he wrote to von Hügel about 'an oft-dreamt-of-never-to-be-realised treatise on materialism in religion' and explained that 'Récéjac rearoused the idea with his theories of symbolism' (Letter of 17 June 1901). Arnold had complained that 'our religion has materialised itself in the fact, in the supposed fact' (S IX p. 161). This was precisely Tyrrell's complaint against neo-scholasticist orthodoxy.

10 Some of the problems associated with these two approaches to Christology, and with the assumption that today we can only do Christology 'from below' are discussed in a paper by N. L. A. Lash, 'Up and down in Christology', in S. Sykes and D. Holmes (eds.), *New Studies in Theology I* (London, 1980), pp. 31–46, to which I am indebted.

11 For a detailed account of this controversy, see Poulat, *Histoire, Dogme et Critique*, pp. 513–620; also R. Marlé (ed.), *Au Coeur de la Crise Moderniste* (Paris, 1960).

12 Letter to von Hügel, 8 April 1903.

13 Letter to von Hügel, 21 April 1903.

14 M. Nédoncelle, *Baron Friedrich von Hügel* (London, 1937), p. 101.

15 Letter to M. D. Petre, 21 June, 1903.

16 Letter to von Hügel, 8 April 1903.

17 Review of R. J. Campbell, *The New Theology* in *The Hibbert Journal*, 5 (1907), 920.

18 Letter to Houtin, 13 December 1907.

19 Letter to Loisy, 16 March 1909.

20 See 'Jesus or Christ?', *The Hibbert Journal*, Supplement (London, 1909), 5–16.

21 Tyrrell is clearly dependent on Le Roy here: 'Imaginez un assemblage quelconque de syllabes dénué de toute signification positive; soit A cet assemblage; "Dieu est personnel" n'a pas, dans notre hypothèse, d'autre sens que "Dieu est A"; est-ce là une idée?' (É. Le Roy, *Dogme et Critique*, sixth edition (Paris, 1907), p. 17). The general point about differing uses of the term 'personality' is made by Le Roy in this passage, by Loisy in *Autour d'un Petit Livre* (Paris, 1903), p. 152 and by Tyrrell in TSC pp. 339–40.

22 Von Hügel dissociated himself from the 'immanentismes' of Loisy and Tyrrell in a letter to Professor René Guiran (*sic*) of 11 July 1921, printed in the *Selected Letters*, pp. 333–7. See p. 334.

23 Marlé, *Au Coeur*, p. 82.

24 Loisy, *Mémoires*, vol. II, p. 582.

25 Letter of M. Blondel to A. Valensin, 18 July 1907, in M. Blondel and A. Valensin, *Correspondance 1899–1947* (3 vols., Paris, 1957–65), vol. I, pp. 339–40. Blondel's complex, and for his time unorthodox, use of the term 'supernatural' is discussed by Illtyd Trethowan in the introduction to the *Letter on Apologetics*, pp. 98–105. Trethowan acknowledges his debt to H. Bouillard, *Blondel et le Christianisme* (Paris, 1961). For Bouillard the heart of *L'Action* and the *Letter on Apologetics* lies in the thesis that the supernatural is both indispensable and inaccessible to men (p. 67). He stresses the important distinction made by Blondel between the 'indeterminate supernatural', which

is the necessary condition of all human action, and the 'Christian supernatural', which is specifically made known by revelation, and is a 'further determination' of the first. See, for example, Bouillard p. 102, quoted by Trethowan p. 101.

26 W. R. Inge, review of *Christianity at the Crossroads* in *The Hibbert Journal*, 8 (1910), 434–8.

27 W. Barry, *Memories and Opinions* (London, 1926), p. 266.

28 Crehan, *Father Thurston*, p. 69.

29 Letter to von Hügel, 14 February 1900.

30 Letter of 12 November 1867 to Mr Henry Dunn, quoted in C. B. Tinker and H. F. Lowry, *The Poetry of Matthew Arnold: A Commentary* (London, 1940), pp. 271–2.

31 Here he is in debate not with the Puritans but with F. C. Baur and the Tübingen school who asserted that the Fourth Gospel was a Hellenic development of the teaching of Jesus.

32 Cockshut, *The Unbelievers*, p. 64.

33 *Letters* I pp. 201, 243.

34 Tyrrell appreciated Le Roy's stress on the practical as opposed to the intellectual meaning of dogma. He also took up his stress on the negative function of dogma, proscribing error, rather than defining truth. In 1907 he wrote, 'I feel sure that Le Roy is right; and what we need is a new conception of the very nature of dogma' (AL2 p. 409).

35 See Blondel's critique of 'historicism' in *The Letter on History and Dogma*, especially pp. 231–41. It is normally assumed that Blondel had Loisy specifically in mind as the 'historicist', but this assumption has been criticised by R. J. Resch in 'History and dogma and individual psychology', *The Journal of Religion*, 59 (1979), 35–55.

36 Adam Fox, *Dean Inge* (London, 1960), p. 264; quoted by Swiatecka, p. 132. Fox oversimplifies drastically when he says that (both Loisy and) Tyrrell 'assumed that the historic Jesus was a peasant of exciting but deluded Messianic views' (p. 171). Such a comment entirely overlooks Tyrrell's commitment to the notion of 'prophetic' truth, by which he attempted to overcome what Inge objected to in Roman Catholic Modernism: 'the irreconcilable dualism between the will-world and the world of phenomena' ('Roman Catholic Modernism', *Outspoken Essays* I (London, 1919), p. 159). Inge never realised how committed Tyrrell was to overcoming – but never prematurely or cheaply – such a dualism.

7. God, and 'the Power that makes for Righteousness'

1 The issue of God's *personal being* is at the centre of this chapter. C. C. J. Webb pointed out in *God and Personality* (London, 1918), pp. 61–8, a theological shift of importance. Until the eighteenth century, 'person' was always used of God in a Trinitarian context, to speak of plurality within the unity of the divine nature ('personality *in* God'). Since that time the term has been central to the discussion about the possibility of personal relations with God ('the personality *of* God'). It is in this second area that the debate between Arnold and Tyrrell lies. There are further possibilities for confusion in the use of the term 'personality' to mean not 'personal nature' but 'peculiar characteristics'.

('What sort of personality does God have?') Tyrrell raises questions in this area; Arnold does not (or only, as in the case of the 'three Lord Shaftesburys' illustration, ironically). See also, W. R. Inge, *Personal Idealism and Mysticism* (London, 1907), pp. 33–4, 93–4.

2 Mrs Humphry Ward, *A Writer's Recollections* (London, 1918), p. 44. The italicisation is perhaps Mrs Ward's.

3 *Ibid.*, p. 45.

4 A. Whitridge (ed.), *Unpublished Letters of Matthew Arnold* (New Haven, 1923), pp. 18–19.

5 'To a Friend', line 12.

6 See, for example, the frequent use of the word 'whole' in the Preface to the *Poems* of 1853 (S I pp. 1–15). Arnold contrasts the Greeks with the moderns: 'They regarded the whole; we regard the parts' (p. 5).

7 'To a Friend', line 1.

8 'Resignation', line 278.

9 'In Harmony with Nature', lines 12–14. Compare S III (EC1) p. 176.

10 'The New Sirens', lines 187–94.

11 Lowry (ed.), *Letters to Clough*, p. 106.

12 *Ibid.*, p. 87.

13 Kenneth Allott guesses from its position in the 1867 volume of poems that it was written in Summer 1863 (K. Allott (ed.), *The Poems of Matthew Arnold*, Longmans Annotated English Poets Series, second edition, edited by M. Allott (London, 1979), p. 530).

14 'The Divinity', lines 3–5.

15 *Ibid.*, lines 9–11.

16 Robbins, *Ethical Idealism of Matthew Arnold*, p. 99.

17 A full study of Arnold's doctrine of God would involve an examination of his debt to Spinoza, Goethe, the Cambridge Platonists and others, all of which would carry us too far afield. Robbins gives a rather clotted account; Trilling is much more vigorous. See also, the unpublished thesis by C. K. Kenosian, 'The position of Matthew Arnold in the religious dilemma of his time', Boston University Graduate School, 1960.

18 For instance, Joubert is quoted as saying, 'It is not hard to know God, provided one will not force oneself to define him' (S III p. 197). One is reminded of Tyrrell's scorn for theologians 'who can define a mystery, but have never felt one' (ER p. 119).

19 He thought that this was the proper thing for the literary critic to do, since he was concerned not with the doctrines but the 'spirit' of the work. Arnold found that such a stance increasingly drove him to a critical evaluation of the theologians' estimate of what doctrine was, and on to complete religious reconstruction.

20 Compare S III (EC1) p. 181: 'Spinoza has made his distinction between adequate and inadequate ideas a current notion for educated Europe.'

21 E. P. de Senancour, *Obermann*, critical edition by G. Michaut (2 vols., Paris, 1912–13), vol. I, p. 195. The whole of letter 44 is particularly important for Arnold.

22 J. B. Orrick, 'Matthew Arnold and Goethe', *Publications of the English Goethe Society*, n.s. 4 (1928). Orrick says that Arnold misunderstood Goethe because

he came to him via Carlyle. See also J. Simpson, 'Arnold and Goethe', in Allott (ed.), *Matthew Arnold*, pp. 286–318.

23 In discussing this phrase, Robbins rightly speaks of Arnold 'passing through metaphor into metaphysics without admitting it' (p. 165). The concept comes from Spinoza; the phrase 'stream of tendency' from Wordsworth (S VI pp. 423–4, note). Arnold clearly expected his contemporaries to know what he meant: Martineau called him 'high among moralists' for calling attention to the way that 'in "the stream of tendency" the defiling contents gradually subside and leave the waters purer as they flow' (*Essays, Reviews and Addresses* (4 vols., London, 1890–1), vol. IV, pp. 273–4).

24 My stress. Note that Arnold is here dismissing 'personality' not as unjustifiable anthropomorphism, but as a technical term of theology.

25 We noted in chapter 4 that Arnold never considers the ambiguities and difficulties of 'verification'.

26 This has been well explored by John Holloway in *The Victorian Sage* (London, 1953), pp. 202–43, who says of Arnold, 'Like other moralists, he regards his important function as that merely of bringing familiar knowledge alive' (p. 204). Holloway explores the stylistic means by which Arnold does this, but unfortunately does not consider the religious works.

27 The extent of the controversy surrounding *Literature and Dogma* is brought out by F. Gudas in his unpublished thesis, 'The debate on Matthew Arnold's religious writings', University of Chicago, 1952. See especially chapter 5, 'The attack on *Literature and Dogma*' (pp. 109–98). Gudas brings out the way in which the issue of God's personal being was at the centre of the debate.

28 J. M. Livingston has drawn my attention to the final chapter of K. Thomas, *Religion and the Decline of Magic* (London, 1971), in which he considers the decline of belief not only in magic but in all forms of divine intervention, drawing on the insights of social anthropologists. Arnold considered witchcraft and the modern world-view in 'A Psychological Parallel' (S VIII (LE) pp. 111–47).

29 Eugene L. Williamson Jr has written well on 'Significant points of comparison between the Biblical criticism of Thomas and Matthew Arnold', *PMLA*, 76 (1961), 539–43. The key difference, which he does not bring out, between father and son, is the concern in Matthew for a clear *point d'appui* in interpretation.

30 We have not space to review and discuss the extensive critical literature on Matthew Arnold's doctrine of God. In his thesis Gudas concentrates on periodical literature. Of the books, F. H. Bradley's critique in *Ethical Studies* (first published 1876, second edition (Oxford, 1927), pp. 315–19) is classic. He criticises Arnold's use of 'the Eternal' for God as 'literary claptrap' because it means nothing more than 'whatever a generation sees happen, and believes both has happened and will happen – just as the habit of washing ourselves might be termed "the Eternal not ourselves that makes for cleanliness"'. Bradley criticises Arnold's lack of attention to the meaning of verification, and the fact that when Arnold offers a maxim like 'Be virtuous and as a rule you will be happy' instead of God, he gives us nothing to *worship*. In *Studies in Philosophy and Literature* (London, 1879), pp. 70–118, W. Knight has a useful discussion of 'personality' as applied to God, which finds Arnold to

be on the horns of a false dilemma between personality and infinity. J. Tulloch refers in *Modern Theories in Philosophy and Religion* (Edinburgh, 1884), pp. 277–315, to the Dutch school of theologians known as 'De Modernen', who were attempting, like Arnold, 'to rescue religion from metaphysics, and to plant it on the tangible and felt basis of moral experience' (p. 278). He says well, 'God is not a power outside [men] which they seek to verify after Mr Arnold's manner, but a power within them which their whole life confesses' (pp. 305–6). R. H. Hutton was relentlessly critical of Arnold's religious views. See *Essays* (1887), pp. 106–10 and *Criticisms* (1894), vol. I, pp. 214–20. James Martineau's paper on 'Ideal Substitutes for God' in *Essays, Reviews and Addresses*, vol. IV, pp. 269–91, is particularly perceptive. Trilling (pp. 351–9), Dudley (pp. 285–6) and Robbins (pp. 94–117) also provide useful discussions. R. B. Braithwaite, *An Empiricist's View of the Nature of Religious Belief* (Cambridge, 1955) outlines a modern position which is indebted to 'that great but neglected Christian thinker, Matthew Arnold' (p. 28).

31 London, 1909. The book was by Arthur Boutwood.

32 Loome (ed.), 'Revelation as Experience'.

33 Egerton, *Father Tyrrell's Modernism*, p. 181.

34 Egerton, like Arnold, looks for a *verifiable* base to build upon. He does not understand the theory of truth with which Tyrrell is largely working. So he complains, 'Revelation [Tyrrell] tells us is "experience", not "statement", and each line of his argument starts with a description of revelational experience. These descriptions are noteworthy, if only for one thing, – they do not discover anything that is certainly a mark of the Divine Presence. This is important, because, if experience be not revelational, and we nevertheless have received a Revelation, that Revelation must have come to us as "statement", and the very foundation of Father Tyrrell's Modernism must be false' (p. 186). Egerton does not see that Tyrrell would argue the revelation *as a whole*, supernatural experience expressed in natural language, to be self-authenticating (recognised) as well as, in the long term, pragmatically verified.

35 In 1908 he wrote, 'My private revelation is naturally a simple affair. It gives me the image of a sort of indwelling Christ-God – my conscience, my judge, my other and better self, with whom I converse silently much as I converse with my own mind, and with whom I am often at variance, never at peace. This being, I know, is a construction of my understanding and imagination inspired by and explanatory of the Power within me that makes for righteousness, and of whose real nature I have no idea' (SL p. 35).

36 Paul Misner discusses Tyrrell's concept of revelation in 'Newman's concept of revelation and the development of doctrine', *The Heythrop Journal*, 11 (1970), 32–47. Had he known 'Revelation as Experience' he might well not have written, 'Tyrrell was of course right in seeing that there was more to revelation than just intellectual concepts, but wrong in refusing to acknowledge any intellectual content at all in the original revelation-impression' (p. 41). If there were *no* 'intellectual content' the revelation would not be to the whole man, and there would be nothing to express intellectually in the Creeds, and Tyrrell always argued that the Creeds were cognitively significant. His point was that revelation, like meeting, is not an intellectual process. It does not

consist of *statements*. Compare Daly, *Transcendence and Immanence*, pp. 157–8, for a better account.

37 See Wilfrid Ward's excellent article 'Two mottoes of Cardinal Newman' in *Problems and Persons*, pp. 260–82, which makes plain Tyrrell's intellectual lineage. Tyrrell calls for 'a spirit to answer the Spirit' (TSC p. 304).

38 J. H. Newman, *Certain Difficulties Felt by Anglicans in Catholic Teaching Considered* (London, 1876), pp. 248–9.

39 Arnold's complaint is taken up with respect to modern ('that is to say post-seventeenth century') Catholic theology by N. L. A. Lash in *Theology on Dover Beach* (London, 1979), pp. 30–1.

40 Cf. K. Rahner, *Foundations of Christian Faith* (London, 1978), p. 18: 'In knowledge not only is something known, but the subject's knowing is always co-known.' This, for Rahner, is the locus of experienced, pre-conceptual transcendence. In his article, Misner brings out the similarities between Tyrrell and Rahner on revelation – overstating, as we have seen, Tyrrell's reaction against the intellectual aspect of revelation.

41 In March 1903 Tyrrell contributed a critique of a paper by McTaggart to the Synthetic Society (*Papers Read Before the Synthetic Society* (London, 1909), pp. 404–7). He restated his belief in analogy: 'We can only speak of the infinite in terms of the finite – *i.e.* analogously, and not adequately. Not even "being" is said in the same sense of God and man; not even spirit, person, nature, will, knowledge, power' (p. 406). Tyrrell was stretching the terms of analogy further and further as he put more emphasis on the preconceptual experience of God. However, he remained committed to the use of analogy in understanding God. See his paper 'Analogy and Agnosticism' (30 April 1903, pp. 421–4).

42 Laubacher, *Dogma*, p. 46. OW p. 228 clearly anticipates what is said of 'real causes' in 'Revelation as Experience'. Cf. EFI pp. 11–12.

43 Daly, *Transcendence and Immanence*, p. 153; discussed in chapter 6, pp. 92–3. 'Immanentism' is a slippery word, quite as slippery as 'Modernism'. The method of immanence, where God is sought within the structure of human experience as experienced should not be confused with the 'immanentism' to which Daly refers: the accusation that in adopting such a method Tyrrell and others like him were denying, or selling short, the transcendence of God. See *The Programme of Modernism*, introduced by A. L. Lilley, (London, 1908), pp. 117–35. (The translation from the Italian is by Tyrrell.)

44 D. F. Wells, 'George Tyrrell: precursor of process theology', *Scottish Journal of Theology*, 26 (1973), 71–84.

45 Tyrrell began reading Bergson on von Hügel's recommendation in 1900. He began with *Essai sur les Données Immediates de la Conscience* and progressed to *Matière et Mémoire* in 1901. He wrote to von Hügel, 'Had it not been for Bergson I don't think I should have had the courage to formulate what I have really felt in regard to the problem of knowledge, and to banish the representative and picture theories altogether, so that the problem of the correspondence of thought to reality becomes non-existent' (Letter of 22 September 1901). After reading *L'Évolution Créatrice* he wrote to Bremond 'I do believe he has made great discoveries of method and has eviscerated scholasticism *forever*' (Letter of 16 September 1907). Schultenover (p. 133)

finds Bergson second only to Blondel in his influence on Tyrrell's philosophy of religion.

46 Tyrrell wrote to Kitty Clutton when her brother was dying of cancer: 'A God who *can* heal and *won't*; who measures out doses of agony; who does not suffer in all suffering; who is not Himself a victim of necessity is intolerable' (Letter of 9 September 1908).

47 M. Hurley, 'George Tyrrell: some post-Vatican II impressions', *The Heythrop Journal*, 10 (1969), 244.

48 The whole letter is extremely important as a statement of Tyrrell's beliefs about God.

8. Conclusions

1 Coulson, *Newman and the Common Tradition*, p. 55.
2 *Ibid.*, p. 11.
3 J. Coulson, 'The adjectives for God' in Ian Gregor and Walter Stein (eds.), *The Prose for God* (London, 1973), p. 42.
4 E. Lawless to Norah Shelley, 25 July 1909, SAUL MS 30756 B.
5 'Dover Beach', lines 22–3.
6 Letter to Maude Petre, 25 January 1906.
7 Gerard Manley Hopkins, 'God's Grandeur', lines 11–12.
8 See E. Duffy, 'George Tyrrell and Liberal Protestantism', *King's Theological Review*, 2 (1979), 13–21.
9 P. Ricoeur, *Freud and Philosophy: An Essay on Interpretation*, translated by Denis Savage (New Haven, Conn., 1970), pp. 28–36.
10 *Ibid.*, p. 33.
11 Martineau, *Essays*, vol. IV, p. 271.
12 *Ibid.*, p. 272.
13 Prickett, *Romanticism and Religion*, p. 219.
14 See John S. Eells, *The Touchstones of Matthew Arnold* (New York, 1955).
15 See Inge's review of *Christianity at the Crossroads*, *The Hibbert Journal*, 8 (1910), 434–8; H. Rashdall, *Conscience and Christ* (London, 1916), pp. 67–8.

Appendix

1 Père Laberthonnière.
2 Tyrrell added in the margin: 'The "ideal" itself being, however, the revelation of a higher order of activity.'
3 *Annales de Philosophie Chrétienne*.
4 '*Omnis plantatio quam non plantavit Pater meus caelestis, eradicabitur*', Matt. 15. 13.

Select bibliography

Unpublished sources

(A) *Letters, papers and manuscripts*

Bibliothèque Nationale, Paris

Fonds Bremond   Bremond's papers are at present being catalogued, but I was allowed to see Tyrrell's letters to Bremond, and a number of notebooks and papers.

Fonds Houtin   Letters of Tyrrell to Houtin, plus the draft of a biography of Tyrrell (N.a.f. 15743).

Fonds Laberthonnière   At present being catalogued. I was allowed to see Tyrrell's letters to Laberthonnière.

Fonds Loisy   Letters of Bremond to Loisy (N.a.f. 15650). Letters of Tyrrell to Loisy (N.a.f. 15662).

British Library, British Museum, London

Add. MSS 44,927–31   Tyrrell–von Hügel correspondence
- Vol. I: 20 September 1897–20 December 1901
- Vol. II: 3 January 1902–29 December 1904
- Vol. III: 10 January 1905–23 December 1906
- Vol. IV: 2 January–25 December 1907
- Vol. V: 21 February 1908–?24 May 1909

Add. MSS 52,367   Letters of Tyrrell to Maude Petre

Add. MSS 43680–1   Letters of Tyrrell to A. R. Waller

St Andrews University Library

Lilley Papers   Letters of Tyrrell to A. L. Lilley

MS 37018/9-18   Letters of Tyrrell to C. E. Osborne

Wilfrid Ward Papers   Letters of Tyrrell to Wilfrid Ward (published London, 1981 as *Letters from a 'Modernist'*, edited by M. J. Weaver)

Private archives

Papers of Kitty Clutton, including letters from Tyrrell, Oxford

Letters of Tyrrell to M.-A. Raffalovich, Oxford

(B) *Unpublished theses*

Goetz, J., 'Analogy and symbol: a study in the theology of George Tyrrell', Cambridge University, 1969

Goichot, É., 'Henri Bremond, historien du sentiment religieux', University of Paris, 1977

Gudas, F., 'The debate on Matthew Arnold's religious writings', University of Chicago, 1952

Healey, C. J., 'The invisible Church and the visible Church in the writings of George Tyrrell', Gregorian University, Rome, 1970

Kenosian, C. K., 'The position of Matthew Arnold in the religious dilemma of his time', Boston University, 1960

Leonard, E., 'The question of Catholicism in the Modernist period: the contribution of George Tyrrell', University of St Michael's College, Toronto, 1978

Mehok, C. J., 'The ecclesiology of George Tyrrell', Catholic University of America, Washington DC, 1970

O'Connor, F. M., 'The concept of revelation in the writings of George Tyrrell', Institut Catholique, Paris, 1963

O'Mahoney, S. C., 'Tyrrell and Newman', Bristol University, 1970

Schapker, H. B., 'Theologies in conflict: a study and interpretation of the impasse between the Encyclical "*Pascendi*" and the religious anthropology of George Tyrrell', Fordham University, 1972

Smallbone, J. A., '*St Paul and Protestantism*: its place in the development of Matthew Arnold's thought', London University, 1950

Published sources

(A) *Books*

Abbott, E. and Campbell, L., *The Life and Letters of Benjamin Jowett* (2 vols., London, 1897)

Abrams, M. H., *The Mirror and the Lamp, Romantic Theory and the Critical Tradition* (Norton edition, New York, 1958)

Alexander, E., *Matthew Arnold and John Stuart Mill* (London, 1965)

Allott, K. (ed.), *Matthew Arnold*, Writers and their Background Series (London, 1975)

  (ed.), *The Poems of Matthew Arnold*, Longmans Annotated English Poets Series, second edition, edited by M. Allott (London, 1979)

Arnold, T., *Fragments on Church and State* (London, 1845)

  The Miscellaneous Works of Thomas Arnold D.D., edited by A. P. Stanley (London, 1845)

  Principles of Church Reform, edited with an introductory essay by M. J. Jackson and J. Rogan (London, 1962)

Barmann, L. F., *Baron Friedrich von Hügel and the Modernist Crisis in England* (Cambridge, 1972)

Barry, W., *Memories and Opinions* (London, 1926)

Blanchet, A., *Henri Bremond 1865–1904* (Paris, 1975)

  (ed.), *Henri Bremond et Maurice Blondel: Correspondance* (2 vols., Paris, 1970–1)

Blondel, M., *The Letter on Apologetics, and History and Dogma*, presented and translated by A. Dru and I. Trethowan (London, 1964)

Blondel, M. and Valensin, A., *Correspondance (1899–1947)* (3 vols., Paris, 1957–65)

Bonnerot, L., *Matthew Arnold, Poète: Essai de Biographie Psychologique* (Paris, 1947)

Bouillard, H., *Blondel et le Christianisme* (Paris, 1961)

Boutwood, A. (pseud.: Hakluyt Egerton), *Father Tyrrell's Modernism* (London, 1909)

Bradley, F. H., *Ethical Studies*, second edition (Oxford, 1927)

Braithwaite, R. B., *An Empiricist's View of the Nature of Religious Belief* (Cambridge, 1955)

Bremond, H., *L'Enfant et la Vie* (Paris, 1902)
  L'Inquiétude Religieuse (2 vols., Paris, 1919, 1909)
  The Mystery of Newman (London, 1907)
  (pseud.: Sylvain Leblanc), *Un Clerc Qui n'a pas Trahi*, edited by É. Poulat (Rome, 1972)

Bush, D., *Matthew Arnold: A Survey of his Poetry and Prose*, Masters of World Literature Series (London, 1971)

Cameron, J. M., *The Night Battle* (London, 1962)

Campbell, R. J., *The New Theology* (London, 1907)

Cassirer, E., *The Philosophy of Symbolic Forms* (3 vols., New Haven, 1955)

Church, R. W., *The Oxford Movement: Twelve Years, 1833–1845* (London, 1900)

Cockshut, A. O. J., *The Unbelievers* (London, 1964)

Coleridge, E. H., *Life and Correspondence of John Duke, Lord Coleridge* (2 vols., London, 1904)

Coleridge, S. T., *Aids to Reflection and the Confessions of an Enquiring Spirit* (Bohn edition, London, 1884)
  On the Constitution of the Church and State According to the Idea of Each, edited by J. Barrell (Everyman edition, London, 1972)
  The Statesman's Manual (London, 1816)

Coulson, J., *Newman and the Common Tradition* (Oxford, 1970)
  Religion and Imagination (Oxford, 1981)

Crehan, J., *Father Thurston* (London, 1952)

Daly, G., *Transcendence and Immanence, A Study in Catholic Modernism and Integralism* (Oxford, 1980)

DeLaura, D. J., *Hebrew and Hellene in Victorian England* (Austin, Texas, 1969)
  (ed.), *Victorian Prose: a Guide to Research* (New York, 1973)

Eells, J. S. Jr, *The Touchstones of Matthew Arnold* (New York, 1955)

Eliot, T. S., *The Idea of Christian Society* (London, 1939)
  Notes Towards the Definition of Culture (London, 1962)
  Selected Essays, third enlarged edition (London, 1951)
  The Use of Poetry and the Use of Criticism (London, 1933)

Essays and Reviews (London, 1860)

Faupel, B., *Die Religionsphilosophie George Tyrrells* (Freiburg, 1976)

Fitch, Sir J., *Thomas and Matthew Arnold and their Influence on English Education*, Great Educators Series (London, 1897)

Gadamer, H.-G., *Truth and Method* (London, 1975)

Gardner, P., *Modernism in the English Church* (London, 1926)
  The Religious Experience of St Paul (London, 1911)

Gregor, I. and Stein, W. (eds.), *The Prose for God* (London, 1973)

Harnack, A., *What is Christianity?* (London, 1901)

Holloway, C. J., *The Victorian Sage* (London, 1953)

Honan, P., *Matthew Arnold: A Life* (London, 1981)

Hügel, F. von, *Essays and Addresses on the Philosophy of Religion, First Series* (London, 1921)

    Essays and Addresses on the Philosophy of Religion, Second Series (London, 1926)

    The Mystical Element of Religion as Studied in Saint Catherine of Genoa and Her Friends, second edition (2 vols., London, 1923)

    Selected Letters (1896–1924), edited by B. Holland (London, 1928)

Hutton, R. H., *Aspects of Religious and Scientific Thought* (London, 1899)

    Criticisms on Contemporary Thought and Thinkers, Selected from the Spectator (2 vols., London, 1894)

    Essays on Some of the Modern Guides of English Thought in Matters of Faith (London, 1887)

Inge, W. R., *Personal Idealism and Mysticism* (London, 1907)

James, D. G., *Matthew Arnold and the Decline of English Romanticism* (Oxford, 1961)

James, W., *The Varieties of Religious Experience* (Fontana edition, London, 1960)

    The Will to Believe, and Other Essays in Popular Philosophy (Dover edition, New York, 1956)

Knight, W., *Studies in Philosophy and Literature* (London, 1879)

Knights, B., *The Idea of the Clerisy in the Nineteenth Century* (Cambridge, 1978)

Knox, W. L. and Vidler, A. R., *The Development of Modern Catholicism* (London, 1933)

Krook, D., *Three Traditions of Moral Thought* (Cambridge, 1959)

Lang, A., *The Making of Religion* (London, 1898)

Langer, S. K., *Philosophy in a New Key*, third edition (Cambridge, Mass., 1957)

Lash, N. L. A., *Change in Focus* (London, 1973)

    Theology on Dover Beach (London, 1979)

Laubacher, J. A., *Dogma and the Development of Dogma in the Writings of George Tyrrell* (Louvain, 1939)

Le Roy, É., *Dogme et Critique*, sixth edition (Paris, 1907)

Lilley, A. L., *Modernism: a Record and Review* (London, 1908)

    (translation attrib.; in fact by G. Tyrrell), *The Programme of Modernism* (London, 1908)

Livingston, J. C., *The Ethics of Belief* (Tallahassee, Florida, 1974)

Loisy, A., *Autour d'un Petit Livre* (Paris, 1903)

    L'Évangile et L'Église (Paris, 1902)

    George Tyrrell et Henri Bremond (Paris, 1936)

    Mémoires pour servir à l'Histoire Religieuse de Notre Temps (3 vols., Paris, 1930–1)

Loome, T. M., *Liberal Catholicism, Reform Catholicism, Modernism*, Tübinger Theologische Studien 14 (Mainz, 1979)

Louis-David, A. (ed.), *Lettres de George Tyrrell à Henri Bremond* (Paris, 1971)

Lowry, H. F. (ed.), *The Letters of Matthew Arnold to Arthur Hugh Clough* (Oxford, 1932)

Lowry, H. F., Young, K. and Dunn, W. H. (eds.), *The Note-Books of Matthew Arnold* (Oxford, 1952)

Select bibliography

Marlé, R. (ed.), *Au Coeur de la Crise Moderniste* (Paris, 1960)

Martineau, J., *Essays, Reviews and Addresses* (4 vols., London, 1890–1)

May, J. L., *Father Tyrrell and the Modernist Movement* (London, 1932)

Miller, J. H., *The Disappearance of God: Five Nineteenth Century Writers* (Cambridge, Mass., 1963)

Nédoncelle, M., *Baron Friedrich von Hugel* (London, 1937)

Newman, J. H., *Apologia Pro Vita Sua*, edited by M. J. Svaglic (Oxford, 1967)

  An Essay in Aid of a Grammar of Assent (London, 1870)

  An Essay on the Development of Christian Doctrine, edited by J. M. Cameron (1845 text, republished by Penguin Books, Harmondsworth, 1974)

  The Idea of a University, edited by C. F. Harrold (New York, 1947)

  On Consulting the Faithful in Matters of Doctrine, edited by J. Coulson (London, 1961)

  University Sermons (1826–43), with an introduction by D. M. MacKinnon and J. D. Holmes (London, 1970)

  The Via Media of the Anglican Church (2 vols., London, 1877)

Newsome, D., *Two Classes of Men* (London, 1974)

Osborne, C. E., *The Life of Father Dolling* (London, 1903)

Papers Read Before the Synthetic Society 1896–1908 (London, 1909)

Petre, M. D., *Modernism: Its Failure and Its Fruits* (London, 1918)

  My Way of Faith (London, 1937)

  Von Hügel and Tyrrell (London, 1937)

Poulat, É., *Histoire, Dogme et Critique dans la Crise Moderniste*, second edition (Paris, 1979)

Prickett, S., *Romanticism and Religion* (Cambridge, 1976)

Quick, O. C., *Liberalism, Modernism and Tradition* (London, 1922)

Rahner, K., *Foundations of Christian Faith* (London, 1978)

Rashdall, H., *Conscience and Christ* (London, 1916)

Ratté, J., *Three Modernists: Alfred Loisy, George Tyrrell, William L. Sullivan* (London, 1968)

Reardon, B. M. G., *Liberalism and Tradition: Aspects of Catholic Thought in Nineteenth-Century France* (Cambridge, 1975)

  (ed.), *Liberal Protestantism* (London, 1968)

  (ed.), *Roman Catholic Modernism* (London, 1970)

Récéjac, E., *Essay on the Bases of the Mystic Knowledge* (London, 1899)

Ricoeur, P., *Freud and Philosophy: An Essay on Interpretation*, translated by Denis Savage (New Haven, Conn., 1970)

Rivière, J., *Le Modernisme dans l'Église* (Paris, 1929)

Robbins, W., *The Ethical Idealism of Matthew Arnold* (London, 1959)

Sabatier, A., *Esquisse d'une Philosophie de la Religion d'après La Psychologie et l'Histoire* (Paris, 1897)

  Les Religions d'Autorité et La Religion de l'Esprit (Paris, 1904)

  The Vitality of Christian Dogmas and their Power of Evolution (London, 1898)

Sanders, C. R., *Coleridge and the Broad Church Movement* (Durham, North Carolina, 1942)

Schleiermacher, F., *On Religion, Speeches to its Cultured Despisers* (Harper Torchbooks edition, New York, 1958)

Schultenover, D. G., *George Tyrrell, In Search of Catholicism* (Shepherdstown, USA, 1981)

Schweitzer, A., *The Quest of the Historical Jesus* (London, 1910)
Senancour, E. P. de, *Obermann*, critical edition by G. Michaut (2 vols., Paris, 1912–13)
Shairp, J. C., *Culture and Religion in some of their Relations* (Edinburgh, 1870)
Smith, N. C. (ed.), *Wordsworth's Literary Criticism* (London, 1905)
Southey, R., *Life of Wesley*, third edition, with notes by S. T. Coleridge (2 vols., London, 1846)
Spinoza, B. de, *The Chief Works of Benedict de Spinoza*, translated by R. H. M. Elwes (2 vols., London, 1883–4)
Stam, J. J., *George Tyrrell (1861–1909)* (Utrecht, 1938)
Stanley, A. P., *The Life and Correspondence of Thomas Arnold, D.D.* (Ward Lock edition, London, no date)
Super, R. H., *The Time-Spirit of Matthew Arnold* (Ann Arbor, 1970)
Swiatecka, M. J., *The Idea of the Symbol* (Cambridge, 1980)
Thomas, K., *Religion and the Decline of Magic* (London, 1971)
Tinker, C. B. and Lowry, H. F., *The Poetry of Matthew Arnold: A Commentary* (London, 1940)
Trilling, L., *Matthew Arnold*, second edition (London, 1949)
Tulloch, J., *Modern Theories in Philosophy and Religion* (Edinburgh, 1884)
Vermeil, E., *Jean-Adam Möhler et l'École Catholique de Tubingue (1815–1840)* (Paris, 1913)
Vidler, A. R., *The Modernist Movement in the Roman Church* (Cambridge, 1934)
   A Variety of Catholic Modernists (Cambridge, 1970)
Ward, Mrs H., *Robert Elsmere*, thirteenth edition (London, 1888)
   A Writer's Recollections (London, 1918)
Ward, M., *The Wilfrid Wards and the Transition: Volume 1, The Nineteenth Century* (London, 1934); *Volume 2, Insurrection versus Resurrection* (London, 1937)
Ward, W., *Problems and Persons* (London, 1903)
   W. G. Ward and the Oxford Movement (London, 1889)
   Witnesses to the Unseen and other Essays (London, 1893)
Weaver, M. J. (ed.), *Letters from a 'Modernist'* (London, 1981)
Webb, C. C. J., *God and Personality* (London, 1918)
Weiss, J., *Jesus' Proclamation of the Kingdom of God*, translated, edited and with an introduction by R. H. Hiers and D. L. Holland, Lives of Jesus Series (Fortress Press, Philadelphia, 1971)
White, A. D., *A History of the Warfare of Science with Theology in Christendom* (one volume reprint, London, 1955)
Whitridge, A. (ed.), *Unpublished Letters of Matthew Arnold* (New Haven, 1923)
Willey, B., *Nineteenth-Century Studies* (Penguin edition, Harmondsworth, 1964)
Williams, R., *Culture and Society 1780–1950* (Penguin edition, Harmondsworth, 1961)
Williamson, E. L. Jr, *The Liberalism of Thomas Arnold* (Alabama, 1964)
Wilson, J. D. (ed.), *Culture and Anarchy* (Cambridge, 1932)

(B) *Articles*
Archbishops of the Province of Westminster, 'The Church and Liberal Catholicism', *The Tablet*, 5 January 1901, pp. 8–12; 12 January 1901, pp. 50–2

Armytage, W. H. G., 'Matthew Arnold and T. H. Huxley: some new letters 1870–1880', *RES*, n.s. 4 (1953), 346–53

Ballard, R., 'George Tyrrell and the apocalyptic vision of Christ', *Theology*, 78 (1975), 459–67

Blackburn, W., 'The background of Arnold's *Literature and Dogma*', *Modern Philology*, 43 (1945), 130–9

'Matthew Arnold and the Oriel Noetics', *PQ*, 25 (1946), 70–8

Chapman, R., 'The thought of George Tyrrell' in *Essays and Poems Presented to Lord David Cecil*, edited by W. W. Robson (London, 1970), pp. 140–68

Crehan, J., 'More Tyrrell letters – 1', *The Month*, n.s. 40 (1968), 178–85

'Tyrrell in his workshop', *The Month*, 2nd n.s. 3 (1971), 111–15, 119

Dudley, F. A., 'Matthew Arnold and science', *PMLA*, 57 (1942), 275–94

Duffy, E., 'George Tyrrell and Liberal Protestantism', *King's Theological Review*, 2 (1979), 13–21

Fawkes, A., 'Modernism: a retrospect and a prospect', *The Hibbert Journal*, 8 (1909–10), 67–82

Gardner, P., Review of TSC, *The Hibbert Journal*, 6 (1908), 923–6

Hügel, F. von, 'Father Tyrrell: Some memorials of the last twelve years of his life', *The Hibbert Journal*, 8 (1909–10), 233–52

'The religious philosophy of Rudolph Eucken', *The Hibbert Journal*, 10 (1911–12), 660–77

Hurley, M., 'George Tyrrell: some post-Vatican II impressions', *The Heythrop Journal*, 10 (1969), 243–55

Inge, W. R., Review of CCR, *The Hibbert Journal*, 8 (1909–10), 434–8

'The meaning of Modernism', *Quarterly Review*, 210 (1909), 571–603; reprinted as 'Roman Catholic Modernism' in *Outspoken Essays*, first series (London, 1919), pp. 137–71

Lash, N. L. A., 'Modernism, aggorniamento and the night battle', in A. Hastings (ed.), *Bishops and Writers* (Wheathampstead, 1977), pp. 51–79

'Up and down in Christology', in S. Sykes and D. Holmes (eds.), *New Studies in Theology 1* (London, 1980), pp. 31–46

Loome, T., 'A bibliography of the published writings of George Tyrrell (1861–1909)', *The Heythrop Journal*, 10 (1969), 280–314

'A bibliography of the printed works of George Tyrrell: supplement', *The Heythrop Journal*, 11 (1970), 161–9

(ed.), '"Revelation as Experience": an unpublished lecture of George Tyrrell', *The Heythrop Journal*, 12 (1971), 117–49

Misner, P., 'Newman's concept of revelation and the development of doctrine', *The Heythrop Journal*, 11 (1970), 32–47

Neiman, F., 'The *Zeitgeist* of Matthew Arnold', *PMLA*, 72 (1957), 977–96

Orrick, J. B., 'Matthew Arnold and Goethe', *Publications of the English Goethe Society*, n.s. 4 (1928)

Osborne, C. E., 'George Tyrrell: a friend's impressions', *The Hibbert Journal*, 8 (1909–10), 253–63

Reardon, B. M. G., 'Liberal Protestantism and Roman Catholic Modernism', *The Modern Churchman*, n.s. 13 (1969–70), 72–86

Root, J. D., 'English Catholic Modernism and science: the case of George Tyrrell', *The Heythrop Journal*, 18 (1977), 271–88

Schoenl, W. J., 'George Tyrrell and the English liberal Catholic crisis, 1900–1901', *The Downside Review*, 92 (1974), 171–84

Secrétan, C., Review of LD, *Bibliothèque Universelle et Revue Suisse*, 49 (1874), 342–59

Stephenson, A. M. G., 'Liberal Anglicanism in the nineteenth century', *The Modern Churchman*, n.s. 13 (1969–70), 87–102

Weaver, M. J., 'George Tyrrell and the Joint Pastoral Letter', *The Downside Review*, 99 (1981), 18–39

Wells, D. F., 'George Tyrrell: precursor of process theology', *Scottish Journal of Theology*, 26 (1973), 71–84

Williams, W. J., 'L'affaire Loisy et la situation religieuse en Angleterre', *Demain*, 1, 1 (27 October 1905), 6–8

'Lettre d'Angleterre', *Demain*, 1, 5 (24 November 1905), 8–9

Williamson, E. L. Jr, 'Significant points of comparison between the Biblical criticism of Thomas and Matthew Arnold', *PMLA*, 76 (1961), 539–43

Index

Abrams, M. H., 53
Aeterni Patris, 6
Alexander, E., 48
analogy, 24–5, 27–8, 30, 33, 55, 81, 91, 93, 121, 126, 131–2, 150, 174
Anglicanism, 6, 10, 17, 88, 139
apocalyptic, 10, 35, 54, 74, 98, 103–4, 110, 114, 137, 146–7, 166
Aquinas, St Thomas, 2, 5, 6, 8, 11, 13–14, 51, 59, 88
Aristotle, 33, 117
Arnold, Mary, 117
Arnold, Matthew: *Aberglaube*, 54, 59, 76, 109–10, 122, 133, 145; 'The Better Part', 119; Catholicism, 24–6, 60–2, 72, 76, 78, 85–7, 163; the Church, 74–9; civilisation, 25, 60, 80, 82, 93–4; 'A Comment on Christmas', 108, 112, 159; conduct, 16, 27, 32, 36, 43–6, 58, 62, 81–2, 110–12, 138, 147, 161, 166; conscience, 43–4, 58, 109, 127, 147; criticism, 29, 36, 42, 49–50, 76, 80, 111; culture, 23, 26, 42, 49, 53, 57, 60, 62–3, 71–2, 78–82, 120, 126, 145–7, 161, 167–8; *Culture and Anarchy*, 11, 22–3, 47, 54, 78–82, 88, 107, 120, 148, 157, 162, 167–8; 'The Divinity', 118–20; 'Dover Beach', 142; dogma, 17, 26, 50, 54, 72, 85–7, 121, 126, 171; *Essays in Criticism* (first series), 10–11, 22–3, 44, 49, 78, 85–6, 107, 119, 142, 171; *Essays in Criticism* (second series), 41, 112; on God, 17, 32, 35, 54, 116–27, 170–3; *God and the Bible*, 11, 38–42, 108–10, 122–6, 162; 'In Harmony with Nature', 118; Jesus Christ, 16, 36, 58–9, 81, 87, 89–90, 106–15; *Literature and Dogma*, 4, 11, 15–17, 24, 26, 31–3, 39–41, 43, 45, 47, 49, 53–4, 58, 88, 109–12, 120–3, 126, 130, 140, 145, 148, 157, 159, 162, 168, 172; *Last Essays on Church and Religion*, 11, 25, 44, 47, 62, 76–8, 86–7, 109, 112, 126; metaphysics, 16, 36, 39, 50, 111–12, 123–7; miracles, 16, 28, 41, 86, 111–13, 123–4, 126; *Mixed Essays*, 82, 87; 'The New Sirens', 118; Obermann, 120; 'Obermann Once More', 106; perfection, 22, 47–8, 79–82, 119, 161, 168; revelation, 16–17, 26, 62, 128; 'Rugby Chapel', 81; *St Paul and Protestantism*, 11, 16, 31, 44, 47, 54, 58, 107–9, 111–12, 121, 162; science, 48–9; 'Selections from Theodore Parker's Unpublished Sermons', 119–20; 'Stanzas from the Grande Chartreuse',

Index

Thurston, H., 43
Times, The, 10
Time-Spirit, *see Zeitgeist*
Tractarians, 75–6
tradition, 3, 12–13, 18, 29, 48, 55, 74, 78–9, 82–3, 88, 101, 103, 115, 147, 152–5, 166; English liberal or literary tradition, 4, 7, 11–12, 14–16, 18–22, 141–2, 147
transcendence, 29, 35–6, 46, 48, 53, 73, 83–4, 88, 90, 102–5, 110–11, 116–17, 129–134, 136–8, 144, 146, 174
Trilling, L., 82
Troeltsch, E., 9
Tyrrell, George: 'Among the Korahites', 45–6; Arnold (Matthew), criticism of, 16–18, 20, 24–30, 32–5, 37, 58, 88, 106, 110–11, 114–16, 138–9, 157; on authority, 63, 65–6, 72–3, 87, 94, 132–3, 165; 'Authority and Evolution', 67; *The Autobiography of George Tyrrell*, 2, 4, 13, 45, 52, 55, 61, 163; biographical summary, 1–2, 4–10; Catholicism, 2, 5, 16, 22, 26, 38, 46–7, 60–1, 71–4, 82, 136–7; 'A Change of Tactics', 6; *Christianity at the Crossroads*, 2, 10, 35, 43, 51, 57–9, 74, 93, 103–5, 110, 114–15, 137–8, 144–6, 163, 166–7; *The Church and the Future*, 9, 28–30, 57, 69–71, 98–9, 131, 133, 153, 156, 165; *The Civilizing of the Matafanus*, 8, 24–6, 46, 93–5; conscience, 21–2, 34–5, 42, 44–6, 63, 70, 72, 91–2, 99, 103, 126, 129–30, 135–6, 138, 140, 144, 147, 168; 'The Contents of a Pre-Adamite Skull', 45, 162; 'deposit of faith', 8, 30–1, 33, 51, 66–71, 158, 164; doctrine, dogma, 10, 16, 28, 33, 55, 64, 72, 83–5, 91–3, 113–14, 126, 130, 140, 146–7, 149–53, 161, 170; ecclesiology, 63–74, 87–8, 90–2, 95, 104–5, 147, 163–5; *Essays on Faith and Immortality*, 58, 72, 83–4, 99, 104, 131, 135–7, 156, 174; ethics, 18, 24, 26–7, 30, 32, 43–6, 58, 71–2, 81, 100–1, 130, 132, 136, 139, 144, 146–7, 166; experience, 16, 18, 21, 29, 31, 33–6, 39–44, 46, 48, 59, 62, 71, 74, 96, 101, 103, 113, 127–8, 131, 135, 137–8, 140, 144, 147, 173; *External Religion*, 7, 21, 45, 65–6, 68, 84, 91–2, 105, 131, 162; *The Faith of the Millions* (first series), 8, 24, 43, 52, 55, 58, 67, 85, 131, 142, 156, 164; *The Faith of the Millions* (second series), 8, 25, 157; on God, 27, 30, 34–5, 83, 90, 93, 103, 127–39, 148, 170–1, 175; *Hard Sayings*, 7, 63–6, 83, 129–30; Jesus Christ, Christology, 16, 21–2, 35–7, 43, 45, 59, 63, 66, 69–71, 74, 90–106, 113–15, 126, 129, 137–8, 143, 147–8, 152, 160, 170, 173; *Lex Credendi*, 9, 31–2, 34, 53, 57, 72, 100, 144, 161; *Lex Orandi*, 9, 29–30, 32, 34, 42–3, 50, 53, 56, 71–2, 83, 95–7, 104, 143, 149, 152–3, 160; *The Life of George Tyrrell from 1884 to 1909* (M. D. Petre), 8–9, 13–14, 69, 138, 142, 154, 157, 160, 163, 170; *Medievalism*, 10, 46, 84–5; 'The Mind of the Church', 24, 67, 164; miracles, 16, 28, 43, 94, 133, 160; 'A More Excellent Way', 82–3; *A Much-Abused Letter*, 9, 34, 57–8; mystery, 18, 34, 55, 57, 61, 71–2, 85, 87, 92, 100, 105, 117, 130–1, 136, 162, 171; *The Mystery of Newman*, introduction to, 33; *Nova et Vetera*, 6–7, 52–3, 63, 83, 90–1, 93, 129–30, 134, 144; *Oil and Wine*, 9,

191

92–3, 131, 134, 144, 174; 'A Perverted Devotion', 8, 58, 65;
'pragmatism', 27, 29–30, 35, 42, 71, 95–8, 100, 128, 133, 147, 153, 170;
'prophetic truth', 31, 55–7, 71, 92, 114, 149–52, 162, 170; 'The Relation
of Theology to Devotion', 23–4, 66–7; 'Religion and Ethics', 27–8, 156;
Religion as a Factor of Life, 8–9, 27, 34, 45, 58, 72, 81, 95–6, 99–100,
131–2, 162; revelation, 8, 10, 16, 26, 30–1, 33, 51, 55, 57, 59, 66–7, 71,
94, 114, 127–8, 130, 137, 140, 158, 164, 173–4; 'Revelation as
Experience', 34, 127–8, 157, 173; 'The Rights and Limits of Theology',
17, 56; sacraments, sacramental world-view, 29, 52–3, 63–4, 66, 69, 72,
74, 88, 90, 92, 103, 105, 133, 137, 162; *Selected Letters*, 10, 30, 44, 47, 110,
114, 130, 138–9, 142–3, 158–9, 161, 165; 'Semper Eadem', 30, 153;
Spirit/spirit, 30–1, 46–7, 56–9, 64–5, 68–70, 72, 74, 81, 97–101, 104, 117,
131, 133–8, 144, 148, 150–1, 160, 163, 165, 174; supernatural, 17, 32, 52,
91, 96, 128, 156; theology, 29, 33, 36, 39, 51, 55, 57, 59, 66, 74, 99, 101,
114, 122, 128, 139–40, 152, 171; *Through Scylla and Charybdis*, 9, 16,
30–1, 34, 38, 51, 55–6, 71–3, 84, 127, 157, 164, 166–7, 169, 174;
Will/will, 21, 27, 29–30, 32, 34–5, 43, 45–6, 56, 71–2, 81, 96, 99–102,
117, 128–135, 138, 144, 147, 151, 170, 174
Tyrrell, William, 5

Vatican II, 3, 163
Venard, L., 56, 71, 149–53
Vermeil, E., 15, 155
Vidler, A. R., 16–18, 20, 33, 154, 156

Ward, Mrs Humphry, 21, 117
Ward, Wilfrid, 6–7, 30–1, 43–4, 62, 65, 84, 154, 161, 164
Ward, W. G., 6–7, 22, 44
Weekly Register, The, 69
Weiss, J., 10, 14, 59, 74, 90, 95, 102–3, 115, 146–7
Wells, D., 134
Williams, W. J., 30–1, 158
Wilson, J. D., 82, 168
Wordsworth, William, 57, 141, 145, 163, 172
Wrede, W., 115

Zeitgeist, 41, 46–52, 132